lonely planet

SOUTH PACIFIC

Craig McLachlan, Chantae Reden, Neema Githere, Rebecca Stirnemann, Anirban Mahaptra, Tiare Tuuhia, Jessica Lockhart, Kate Webster, Brett Atkinson

Anirban Mahapatra

www.anirbanmahapatra.com

Anirban is a multimedia journalist, conservation filmmaker and photographer with a knack for exploring the world's cultures and cuisines.

Tiare Tuuhia

Tiare is Swiss-born and Australian-raised with Polynesian roots. Her favourite experience is watching the breathtaking traditional dance performances during the Heiva i Tahiti (p165). She lives in Tahiti, and loves exploring the islands with her family.

Jessica Lockhart

@WynneLockhart

Originally from Canada, Jessica Lockhart is Lonely Planet's Destination Editor for Oceania. An avid backcountry hiker and paddler, her outdoor adventures have taken her throughout the South Pacific region. She is based in Christchurch, New Zealand.

Kate Webster

@travellerkate

Kate is a world traveller, ocean lover and conservation warrior who is determined to make every moment count for herself and the world around her.

Brett Atkinson

@travelwriternz

From his home in Auckland, Brett has island-hopped much of his South Pacific backyard. Highlights include swimming with whales on Niue (p208), ascending Mt Yasur on Tanna island, and enjoying a *tumunu* bush-beer session on remote 'Atiu in the Cook Islands.

Contents

CLAUDIO SIEBER/GETTY IMAGES

Crocodile Festival (p205), Papua New Guinea

ESSAYS

VISUAL GUIDES

COLOURFUL **CULTURES**

On a map, all the little dots that make up the islands of the South Pacific look the same, their many-vowelled names tripping over the tongue. But on the ground, there's a diversity befitting any such earthly expanse, myriad languages, customs, histories and landscapes that make each island group unique. It's not just homogenous beaches and reefs – expect to find societies and experiences as rich as coconut cream.

Left Island Night in the Cook Islands (p117) **Below** Kava (p60) **Right** Samoa Cultural Village in Apia (p221)

→ MELANESIA & POLYNESIA

The islands of the western South Pacific (Melanesia) were populated well before those of the central and eastern South Pacific (Polynesia).

PEACEFOO/SHUTTERSTOCK

THE POLYNESIAN TRIANGLE

Polynesia is huge: at its northern tip is Hawai'i; Aotearoa New Zealand is at the southern tip; Rapa Nui (Easter Island) is in the east.

FROM LEFT: ROBERTHARDING/ALAMY.

↑ KAVA IN COMMON

Consumed throughout the Pacific, *kava* is a muddy narcotic drink made from ground kava roots that will slow you down to 'island time'.

Best Cultural Experiences

- **Enjoy an Island Night in the Cook Islands** (p117)
- **Visit the Ekasup Cultural Village in Vanuatu** (p75)
- **Go to church on Sunday in Tonga** (144)
- **Attend a traditional Fijian kava ceremony** (p60)
- **Head to the Samoa Cultural Village in Apia** (p221)

BEACH TIME

Life moves slowly under the southern sun, more so if you've found your idyllic beach. Any of these countries could feature on that 'Travel to Paradise' poster that makes you want to quit your job and sit on a beach forever, but the South Pacific is far from an endless string of white-sand, palm-backed beaches with turquoise seas. Beach landscapes here are just as diverse as the people and cultures.

Left One of the Yasawa islands (p56) **Below** Île des Pins (p96) **Right** Aitutaki Lagoon (p118)

→ BEACHES ARE NOT ALL THE SAME

After some relaxing swimming, snorkelling and time in the sun? Hang out on a sheltered beach within a protected lagoon.

CHAMELEONSEYE/GETTY IMAGES

COME PREPARED FOR THE SUN

Don't forget to bring reef-safe sunscreen and slap it on regularly, especially if you've just arrived from a cold Kiwi or Aussie winter.

FROM LEFT: STEVEALLENPHOTO/GETTY IMAGES,

↑ SOME ARE BETTER THAN OTHERS

Not every island in the South Pacific is laced with accessible, swimworthy beaches; do your homework before choosing where to go.

Best Beaches

- **Visit amazing uninhabited islets in Aitutaki Lagoon, Cook Islands** (p118)
- **Escape to the offshore Yasawa islands, Fiji** (p56)
- **Marvel at glorious Île des Pins, New Caledonia** (p96)
- **Remote white-sand Ofu Beach in American Samoa is legendary** (p233)
- **Enjoy stunning stretches of sand in Ha'apai, Tonga** (p141)

PULSATING PACIFIC **FESTIVALS**

For a direct line into island life, time your visit with a major cultural festival. If there's one thing that the peoples of the South Pacific have in common, it's that they take their festivals seriously and love to party.

Festivals are a window into the soul of the islands, with mesmerising music, dance and costumes telling stories and traditions with movement, rhythm and communal celebration.

TOMFRY/SHUTTERSTOCK

Left Goroka Mask Festival (p203) **Below** Teuila Festival (p230) **Right** Food prepared in an *umu* (p221)

→ PARTY TIME: FIRE UP THE UMU

A big community celebration usually calls for a feast prepared in a traditional earthen oven; try the local delicacies.

CAN'T MAKE IT AT FESTIVAL TIME?

Dance and feast shows can be like mini-festivals; performers seem to enjoy themselves just as much as tourists being entertained.

FROM LEFT: MARC DOZIER/GETTY IMAGES, CHESTER VOYAGE/ALAMY

↑ GET IN EARLY

You're not going to be the only one attending these festivals; plan ahead and get in early with flight and accommodation bookings.

Best Festivals

- **Attend the colourful Heiva Festival of French Polynesia** (p165)
- **Enjoy the enthralling Goroko Mask Festival in Papua New Guinea** (p203)
- **Marvel at Naghol, Land Diving Festival, in Vanuatu (p76)**
- **Yam festivals mark the harvest in New Caledonia** (p106)
- **The Teuila Festival celebrates all things Samoan** (p230)

MAGICAL **MARKETS**

If you love mooching around at markets, checking out the local fruit and veg, carvings and jewellery, people watching and chatting with locals, there's nowhere better than the town market. Playing an integral part in local life in the islands, these vary from large city markets that may open daily and have live entertainment right down to small local markets only open on Saturday mornings.

PETER UNGER/GETTY IMAGES

Left Honiara's Central Market (p186)
Below Punanga Nui Market (p123)
Right Market, Tanna Island (p80)

→ CASH IS KING

Take cash when heading to local markets; there won't be many places where you can use a credit card.

BARGAINING

In most countries, bargaining is not the norm for fresh produce (locals won't be bargaining), but it can be common for handicrafts and souvenirs.

FROM LEFT: SAEED KHAN/AFP VIA GETTY IMAGES, CHAMFI FONSFYF/GETTY IMAGES

↑ ROADSIDE STALLS

On some islands you'll find roadside stalls selling everything from fruit and vegetables to fish, possibly even fresh, full tuna that's as long as you are tall.

Best Local Markets

- **Get fruit, veges and croissants at Noumea's Port Moselle Market** (p94)
- **Bustling Fugalei Market has it all in Apia, Samoa** (p219)
- **Punanga Nui Market in Rarotonga is a must on Saturday mornings** (p123)
- **Try Indo-Fijian curry and local fare at Municipal Suva Market, Fiji** (p49)
- **Breakfast at vibrant Marché de Pape'ete** (p154)

Cover up from the sun, take plenty of liquids and hydrate regularly. It's often best to hike in the cool of the early morning. Sturdy footwear is a must, especially over volcanic rock.

RAWMN/SHUTTERSTOCK

ADVENTURING ON FOOT

There's more to the Pacific than just watery pursuits and not all islands are low-lying atolls. On higher, bigger islands there are terrific opportunities to walk through magnificent forest interiors, climb mountainous peaks and even visit live volcanoes. Expect to encounter colourful tropical flora and fauna. Some walks cross land under customary ownership; you may be required to pay a fee or use a local guide.

Best Hikes

- **Hike the Highlands in the Solomon Islands** (p182)
- **Make the cross-island trek on Rarotonga, Cook Islands** (pictured, p121)
- **Walk the historic Kokoda Track in Papua New Guinea** (p201)
- **Enjoy lots of hikes in the National Park of American Samoa** (p233)

SNORKELLING & DIVING

If eyeballing a kaleidoscope of technicolour tropical fish and coral is your goal, you're heading to the right place. The South Pacific is as much of a Garden of Eden below the waterline as on land. As if that weren't enough, waters are warm year-round and each island has its own personality.

DAMOCEAN/GETTY IMAGES

★ SNORKELLING WITHIN THE REEF

You don't need to go far to have fun; stay in shallow waters within the reef. Bring your own snorkelling gear if you've got it.

JASON EDWARDS/GETTY IMAGES

Best Under Water

- ▶ **Diving in the Tuamotu archipelago, French Polynesia** (p158)
- ▶ **Explore the soft coral capital of the South Pacific, Fiji** (p52)
- ▶ **Enjoy the reefs in New Caledonia's World Heritage–listed lagoon** (p105)
- ▶ **Snorkelling in the Giant Clam Sanctuary, Savaia, Samoa** (p224)

← DIVING IN THE DEEP

Divers can expect awesome walls, close encounters with sharks and manta rays, iconic wrecks and gorgeous coral reefs replete with multihued fish.

Above Reefs off New Caledonia (p105) **Left** Rainbow Reef (p53)

Insects thrive in the warmth of the tropics; use insect repellant.

Saltwater crocodiles are present in Papua New Guinea, Vanuatu and the Solomon Islands.

THE WILD **SIDE**

On the land, Papua New Guinea is rich in wildlife, but like the Pacific's human colonisers, most species moved across the ocean from west to east. As we move eastwards, wildlife on land becomes much more spartan. Birdlife is abundant throughout the Pacific and, of course, there are wondrous opportunities to meet wildlife in the water, from whales, dolphins and turtles to dugongs.

Best Wildlife Experiences

- **Watching whales in Ha'apai, Tonga** (pictured, p140)
- **Spotting dugongs in the waters around Vanuatu** (p79)
- **Seeing turtles in reef passages around Rarotonga** (p123)
- **Spot whales up close and personal in Niue** (p208)

MICHAEL ZEIGLER/GETTY IMAGES

FUN IN & ON THE WATER

There are so many fun activities to be had out on the warm tropical waters in the South Pacific. Think surfing, kayaking, windsurfing, kitesurfing, sailing, standup paddleboarding (SUP) and the list goes on. For the less active, enjoy a glass-bottomed boat tour or a sunset cruise. And of course, there's simply lolling about in the water a few metres off the beach.

MARTIN VLNAS/SHUTTERSTOCK

★ YOUR RESORT POOL

Lazing around the pool at your resort, reading a book and cooling off every now and then, may be more than enough to fulfil your desires.

CHAMELEONSEYE/GETTY IMAGES

Best Activities

- **Surf on a world-class wave in Fiji** (p50)
- **Explore Muri Lagoon in the Cook Islands using a SUP or kayak** (p120)
- **Descend the ladder into To Sua Ocean Trench, Samoa** (p223)
- **Try kiteboarding in New Caledonia** (p105)

← FRESHWATER FUN

Some larger islands such as 'Upolu in Samoa (p222) offer incredible freshwater swimming holes such as cave pools and the base of waterfalls.

Above To Sua (p223) **Left** Muri Lagoon (p120)

While it's the slow season for tourists, islanders living overseas head home to visit family over Christmas and New Year; flights will be full.

↓ Roviana Lagoon Festival

The Roviana Lagoon Festival in early December features elaborate floats, both on water and on land.

▶ Munda, Solomon Islands (p189)

↑ Christmas

Deeply religious South Pacific countries celebrate Christmas with unbridled enthusiasm; remember, it's summer in the southern hemisphere.

Demand for accommodation peaks over Christmas and New Year. View tours and overnight adventures in advance at lonelyplanet.com.

DECEMBER

December average daytime max: 31°C
Days of rainfall: 12

JANUARY

South Pacific in SUMMER

FROM LEFT: NIGEL MARSH/GETTY IMAGES, THAWORNNURAK/ GETTY IMAGES, CHRISPECORARO/GETTY IMAGES. BACKGROUND: MLENNY/GETTY IMAGES

← Chinese New Year

Islands with sizable Chinese communities celebrate Chinese New Year with gusto; expect dancing, fireworks and loads of food.

Pacific Islanders know that summer is the season of abundance; fishing is great and most fruits come into season.

From mid-January to April there'll be real bargains as airlines aim for bums on seats and resorts try to fill those empty rooms.

FEBRUARY

January average daytime max: 31°C
Days of rainfall: 14

February average daytime max: 31°C
Days of rainfall: 15

It's hot, humid and wet – and cyclone season in the South Pacific between November and April.

Packing Notes

Be adequately prepared with long sleeves, insect repellant (mosquitoes) and reef-safe sunscreen.

↙ Apia Arts and Crafts Festival

Held in March in the capital, this bustling event focuses on local artists and traditional handicrafts from all across the islands of Samoa.

▸ Apia, Samoa (p230)

← Hiri Moale Festival

PNG's Hiri Moale Festival in March commemorates the historical Hiri trade voyages with traditional canoe races and cultural presentations.

▸ Port Moresby, Papua New Guinea (p190)

Bargains are to be had on flights and accommodation in March and April, though the tourist season picks up in May.

MARCH

March average daytime max: 31°C
Days of rainfall: 16

APRIL

South Pacific in AUTUMN

↓ Te Mire Ura

Starting in April, Dancer of the Year in the Cook Islands includes junior, senior and masters events with incredibly enthusiastic competitions.

▶ Avarua (p117)

The weather is still hot and humid, but cyclone season finishes in April and the number of rainy days each month falls away.

↖ Naghol (Land Diving) Festival

The Naghol Festival (the origin of bungee jumping!) runs from April to July.

▶ Pentecost Island, Vanuatu (p76)

April average daytime max: 31°C
Days of rainfall: 10

MAY

May average daytime max: 30°C
Days of rainfall: 5

April and May offer some of the best diving conditions of the year; water clarity is at its peak after the rainy season and conditions are generally calm.

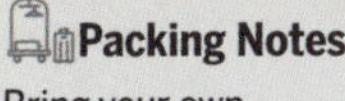

Packing Notes

Bring your own snorkelling gear if you've got it.

It's still warm, but humidity and rainfall drop away, making winter the ideal time to visit the South Pacific.

→ Heiva Festival

The Heiva Festival in French Polynesia is a colourful celebration of Polynesian culture, tradition and heritage.

▶ Pape'ete, Tahiti (p148)

→ Heilala Festival

Held in the first week of July, Tonga's Heilala Festival features music, dance and a whole lot of fun.

▶ Nuku'alofa, Tonga (138)

JUNE

June average daytime max: 29°C
Days of rainfall: 4

JULY

South Pacific in WINTER

It's full-on visitor season with ideal weather in the islands and Kiwis and Aussies escaping their cold winters.

FROM LEFT: GREGORY BOISSY/AFP VIA GETTY IMAGES, IGNACIO PALACIOS/GETTY IMAGES, THOMAS COCKREM/ALAMY, PHILIP GAME/ALAMY. BACKGROUND: ALEXIS ROSENFELD/GETTY IMAGES

↗ Te Maeva Nui

Top bill in the Cook Islands, Te Maeva Nui is a week of events to celebrate the 4 August anniversary of independence as a nation.

▶ Rarotonga, Cook Islands (p112)

↓ Shell Money Festival

The Shell Money Festival of mid-August includes cultural displays, demonstrations and entertainment.

▶ Langalanga Lagoon, Solomon Islands (p186)

July average daytime max: 28°C
Days of rainfall: 3

AUGUST

August average daytime max: 28°C
Days of rainfall: 4

Keen on spotting whales? The season runs June to October, but prime time is generally July to September.

Packing Notes

Winter doesn't mean cold in the tropical South Pacific; think warm and dry.

← Goroka Show

Held annually in September, the Goroka Show cultural event features traditional dances, music and costumes.

▸ Goroka, Papua New Guinea (p203)

↖ Hibiscus Festival

The mother of all Fijian festivals the Hibiscus Festival, is held in the first week of September.

▸ Suva, Fiji (p42)

← Teuila Festival

Samoa's biggest event, the Teuila Festival, held in early September, features a week of festivities of traditional dance and music.

▸ Apia, Samoa (p230)

SEPTEMBER

September average daytime max: 29°C
Days of rainfall: 5

OCTOBER

South Pacific in SPRING

FROM LEFT: MIKE ROBINSON/ALAMY, RON VAN DER STAPPEN/SHUTTERSTOCK, CHESTER VOYAGE/ALAMY, OLEKSII LISKONIH/GETTY IMAGES, HEMIS/ALAMY, CLIVE BROMHALL/GETTY IMAGES. BACKGROUND: NORINORI303/SHUTTERSTOCK

← Constitution Week

Constitution Week in October in Niue features all kinds of festivities celebrating self-government from New Zealand, achieved in 1974.

▸ Niue p208

← Vaka Eiva

Paddlers from across the Pacific converge for Vaka Eiva, a week of races, fun and friendship.

▸ Rarotonga, Cook Islands (p114)

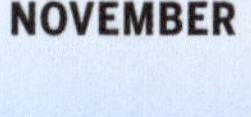

NOVEMBER

October average daytime max: 30°C
Days of rainfall: 6

November average daytime max: 31°C
Days of rainfall: 9

While September and October are still relatively dry, humidity and rainfall pick up in November and cyclone season begins.

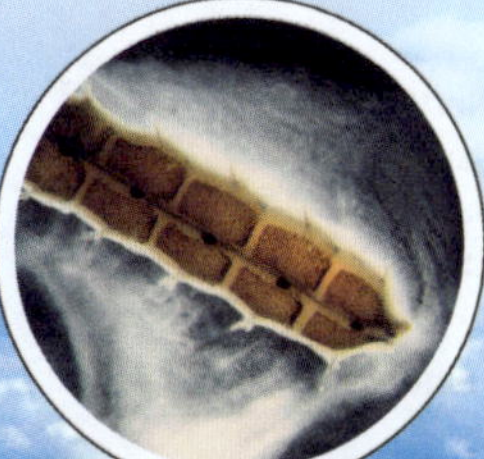

← Rise of the Palolo

It's time to celebrate procreating coral worms, a delicacy for Samoans in October or November, seven days after the full moon.

▸ Samoa (p230)

Packing Notes

Long sleeves and trousers help keep mosquitoes away, a good move once the summer rains set in.

FIJI, THE SAMOAS & TONGA
Trip Builder

TAKE YOUR PICK OF MUST-SEES AND HIDDEN GEMS

Make your way to Fiji for some fun in the Fijian sun, then make the most of Fiji Airways' extensive network of flights to visit islands of the central South Pacific such as Samoa, American Samoa and Tonga. It's easy to lose a lot of time in these laidback islands.

Trip Notes

How long? Give yourself as much time as you can to fully explore these amazing islands.

Flights Fly to Nadi, Fiji direct from North America, Asia, Australia or New Zealand on Fiji Airways; they also fly into both Samoa and Tonga. There are no direct flights between Samoa and Tonga.

Tips You can use ferries to travel to outer islands in Fiji, Samoa and Tonga, plus between Samoa and American Samoa.

FROM LEFT: PITA SIMPSON/GETTY IMAGES, BY WILDESTANIMAL/GETTY IMAGES, MARTIN VALIGURSKY/SHUTTERSTOCK, JOSH RIGO/GETTY IMAGES

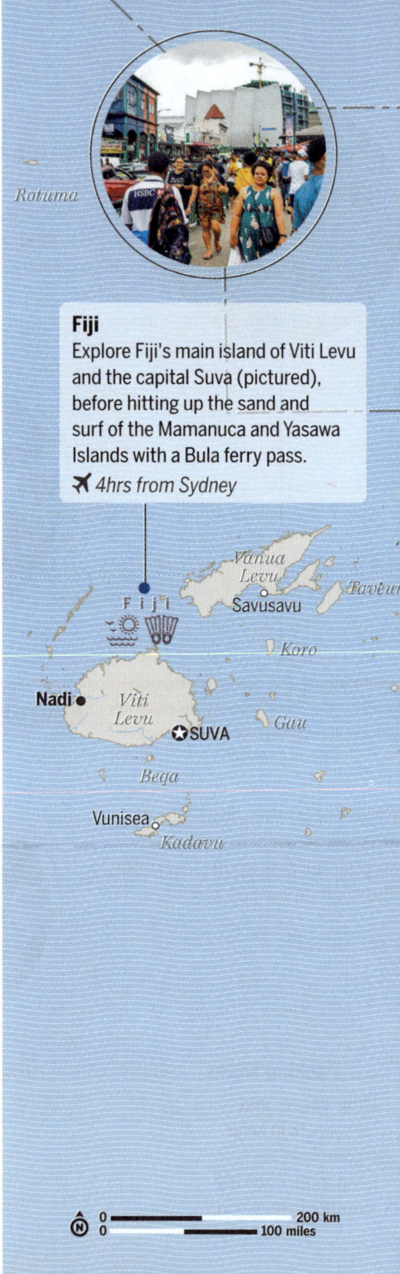

Samoa

Enjoy time in Apia's busy markets on the main island of ʻUpolu; take the ferry to Savaiʻi and stay in a beach *fale* (pictured).

2hrs from Fiji

American Samoa

Pago Pago is a short flight from Samoa. Hike in the National Park of American Samoa and visit legendary Ofu Beach (pictured) in the remote Manuʻa Islands.

25mins from Samoa

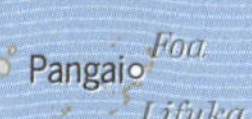

Tonga

Admire the heritage buildings of Nukuʻalofa, then fly or ferry to watch whales in the Haʻapai group (pictured) before relaxing in the idyllic Vavaʻu Islands.

1hr 30mins from Fiji

MELANESIAN ADVENTURE
Trip Builder

TAKE YOUR PICK OF MUST-SEES AND HIDDEN GEMS

Feeling adventurous? This trip takes in parts of the western South Pacific – Vanuatu, the Solomon Islands and Papua New Guinea. The latter two see far fewer international visitors than the other countries in this book, but offer an authentic off-the-beaten-track experience to be savoured.

Trip Notes

How long? One month, or as long as you can visit.

Flights Solomon Airlines flies from both Brisbane and Auckland into Vanuatu, then on to Honiara in the Solomon Islands; they also have direct flights from Brisbane to Honiara. Air Niugini flies between Honiara and Port Moresby in PNG.

Tips Take anti-malaria medication when heading out on this adventure; avoid getting bitten by mosquitoes.

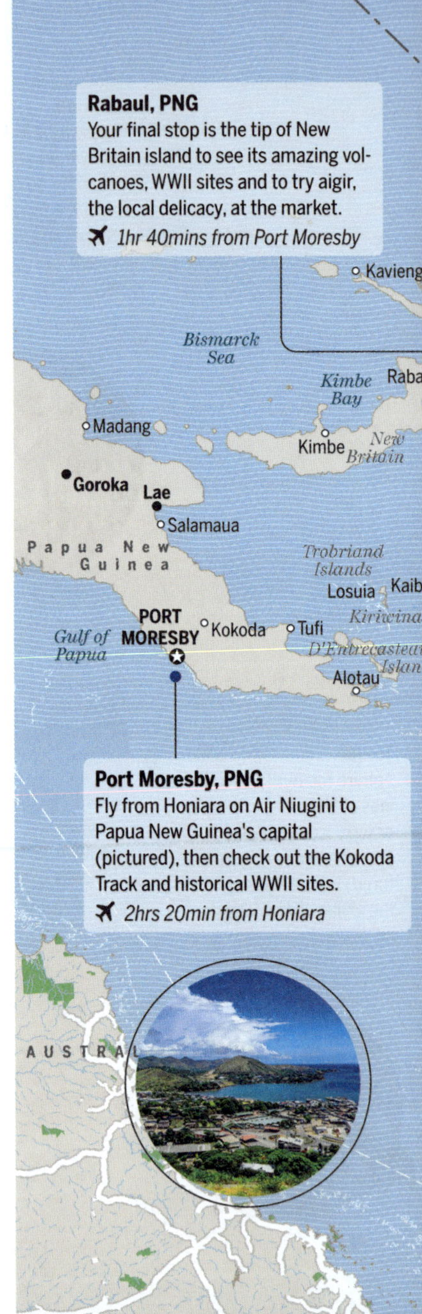

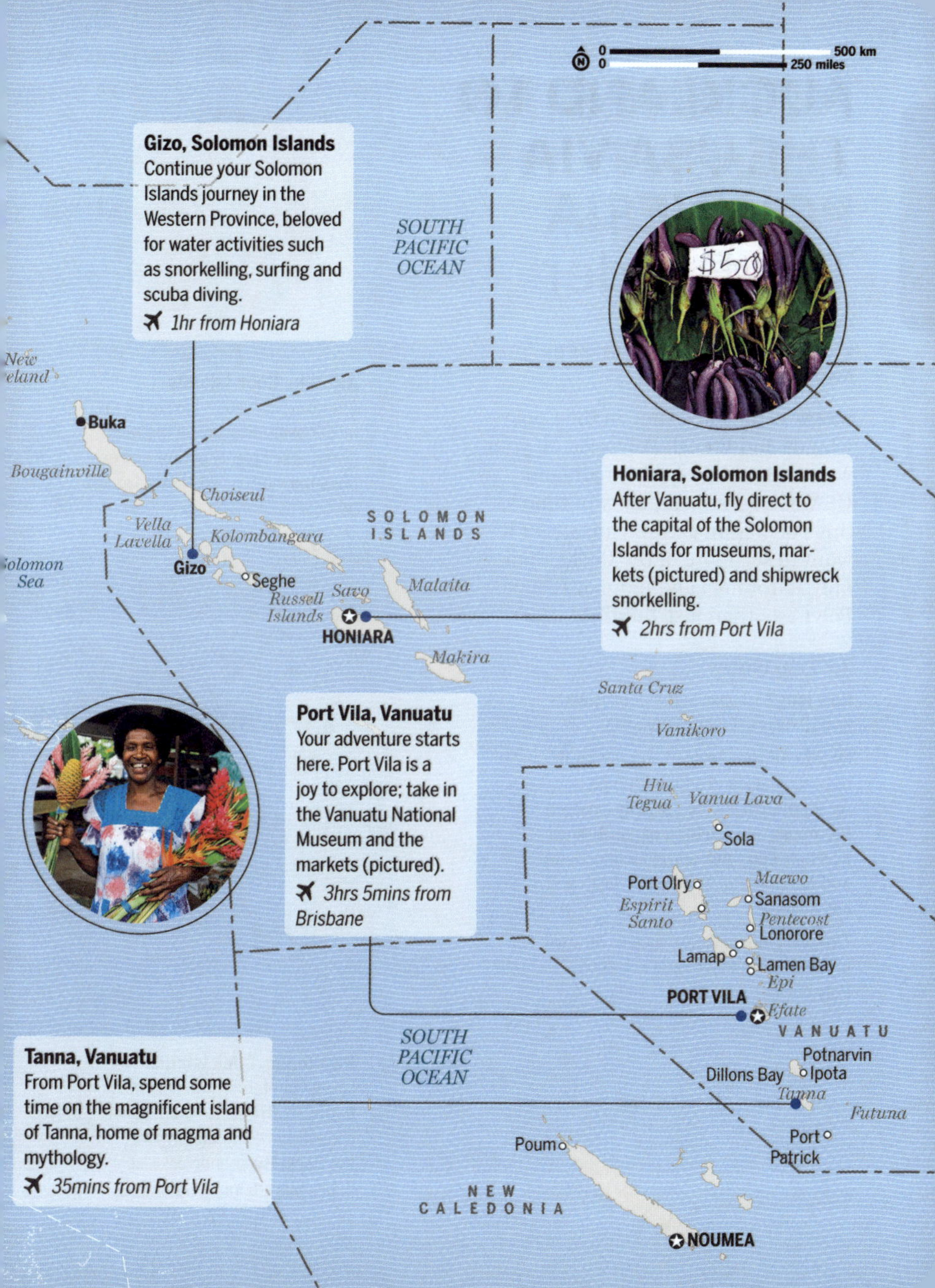
0 500 km
0 250 miles
Gizo, Solomon Islands
Continue your Solomon Islands journey in the Western Province, beloved for water activities such as snorkelling, surfing and scuba diving.
1hr from Honiara
SOUTH PACIFIC OCEAN
$50
Honiara, Solomon Islands
After Vanuatu, fly direct to the capital of the Solomon Islands for museums, markets (pictured) and shipwreck snorkelling.
2hrs from Port Vila
Buka
Bougainville
Choiseul
Vella Lavella
Kolombangara
SOLOMON ISLANDS
Gizo
Seghe
Russell Islands
Savo
Malaita
HONIARA
Makira
Santa Cruz
Vanikoro
Port Vila, Vanuatu
Your adventure starts here. Port Vila is a joy to explore; take in the Vanuatu National Museum and the markets (pictured).
3hrs 5mins from Brisbane
Hiu
Tegua
Vanua Lava
Sola
Port Olry
Espirit Santo
Maewo
Sanasom
Pentecost
Lonorore
Lamap
Lamen Bay
Epi
PORT VILA
Efate
VANUATU
SOUTH PACIFIC OCEAN
Tanna, Vanuatu
From Port Vila, spend some time on the magnificent island of Tanna, home of magma and mythology.
35mins from Port Vila
Potnarvin
Dillons Bay
Ipota
Tanna
Futuna
Poum
Port Patrick
NEW CALEDONIA
NOUMEA

AUCKLAND TO THE USA VIA POLYNESIA Trip Builder

TAKE YOUR PICK OF MUST-SEES AND HIDDEN GEMS

Want some time in the Cook Islands and French Polynesia on your way to Honolulu or the mainland USA? Give yourself plenty of time for this Polynesian extravaganza; you'll want to see more of the Cooks than only Rarotonga and more of French Polynesia than just Tahiti.

Trip Notes

How long? 10 days in the Cook Islands and 10 days in French Polynesia.

Flights Air New Zealand and Jetstar fly between Auckland and Rorotonga; Air Rarotonga and Air Tahiti fly between Rarotonga and Tahiti; Hawaiian Airlines flies between Tahiti and Honolulu; Delta and Air Tahiti Nui fly between Tahiti and Los Angeles.

Tips Visit outer islands such as Aitutaki in the Cooks and Mo'orea in French Polynesia.

FROM LEFT: PATRICK OBEREM/SHUTTERSTOCK, MARCONI COUTO/SHUTTERSTOCK, TYCHIAN/SHUTTERSTOCK

Aitutaki, Cook Islands
Aitutaki (pictured) is said to be the most beautiful lagoon in the world; give yourself plenty of time and explore the motu (islets) in the lagoon.
45mins from Rarotonga

Aitutaki

COOK ISLANDS

Rarotonga

Mangaia

Rarotonga, Cook Islands
Lovely Rarotonga is an ideal intro to the South Pacific. Your biggest conundrum – whether to take the clockwise or anticlockwise public bus around the island.
3hrs 45mins from Auckland

Mo'orea & Bora Bora, French Polynesia
Tahiti is one of the Society Islands, with a couple of other big names not far away in the same group – Mo'orea (pictured) and Bora Bora. Make the effort while you're here.
✈ *50mins Tahiti to Bora Bora*

Tuamotu Islands, French Polynesia
Head out east to the Tuamotu archipelago for some of the best diving in the world, including shark encounters and drift diving.
✈ *45mins from Tahiti*

Tehekega
Napuka
Ahe
Manihi
Teavaroa
Tenukupara
Tikehau
Arutua
Mataiva
Rangiroa
Tikei
The Tuamotus
Rangiroa
Apataki
Temao
Kaukura
Toau
Kauehi
Takume
Fangatau
Makatea
Rotoava
Raraka
Tupana
Taenga
Raroia
Bora Bora
Niau
Fakarava
Maupiti
Pouheva
Faaite
Kaitu
Reka Reka
Makemo
Tahanea
Maupiha'a
Ra'iatea
Huahine
Marutea Nord
Mo'orea
PAPE'ETE
Anaa
Hikueru
Amanu
Haraiki
Tupapati
Tahiti
Mehetí'a
Otepa
Society Islands
Marokau
Ravahere
Haorangi
Nengonengo
Paraoa
Manuhangi
Ahunui
SOUTH PACIFIC OCEAN

Pape'ete, Tahiti, French Polynesia
From Rarotonga, fly to the main city and capital of French Polynesia, Pape'ete; explore the island of Tahiti and don't miss breakfast at the Sunday morning market.
✈ *2hrs 40mins from Rarotonga*

The Australs
Moerai
Rimatara
Tubuai
Mataura
Raivavae
FRENCH POLYNESIA

N
0 500 km
0 250 miles

SOUTH PACIFIC BUILD YOUR TRIP

AUSTRALIA TO TOKYO VIA MELANESIA Trip Builder

TAKE YOUR PICK OF MUST-SEES AND HIDDEN GEMS

Want to check out Melanesia on your way to Japan? The islands make great stepping stones as part of an extended trip to other parts of the world. Once you reach Fiji, Fiji Airways flies direct to Japan, Honolulu, mainland USA and Canada.

Trip Notes

How long? One month – enough time to explore New Caledonia, Vanuatu and Fiji.

Flights Air Calin flies from both Sydney and Brisbane to New Caledonia; Air Calin flies between New Caledonia and Vanuatu; Fiji Airways flies between Vanuatu and Fiji; Fiji Airways flies between Fiji and Japan.

Tips Don't miss the outer islands in each country on this Melanesian meander.

FROM TOP: HOLGER LEUE/GETTY IMAGES, TORSTEN BLACKWOOD/AFP VIA GETTY IMAGES

0 400 km
0 200 miles

SOLOMON ISLANDS

Port Vila, Vanuatu

Fly from Noumea to Port Vila and explore the capital, visiting Vanuatu National Museum, Hebrida Market and enthralling Port Vila market.

1hr 35mins from Noumea

Mamanuca & Yasawa Islands, Fiji

With some time on your hands, explore the Mamanuca (pictured) and Yasawa islands with a hop-on hop-off Bula Pass for the ferry.

Fly out of Nadi when ready.

Vanua Levu
Savusavu
Nabouwalu
Somosomo
Ba
Dawasuma
Nadi
South Pacific Ocean
Suva
Nairai
Gau
Koro Sea
Vanua Vatu
Moala
Dravuni
Vunisea
Totoya
Erromango
Ipota
Port Patrick

Tanna, Vanuatu

Visit Mt Yasur on Tanna Island, one of Vanuatu's most popular tourist destinations and one of the world's most active volcanoes.

1hr from Port Vila

Nadi, Fiji

Fly from Port Vila to Nadi, Fiji. Take time on the main island of Viti Levu to hike and explore the capital of Suva.

2hrs 20mins from Port Vila

FIJI

Île des Pins, New Caledonia

Take time to visit gorgeous Île des Pins, either by air or by ferry. Spend a few days here for superb snorkelling and hiking before returning to Noumea.

30mins from Noumea

A CRUISE OUT OF SYDNEY OR BRISBANE
Trip Builder

TAKE YOUR PICK OF MUST-SEES AND HIDDEN GEMS

South Pacific cruise ships out of east coast Australia tend to stay relatively close at hand in the Melanesian islands if on seven- or nine-night cruises. Seven-night cruises head to New Caledonia, then Vanuatu before returning home. Nine-night cruises often add Fiji into the mix before heading home.

Trip Notes

Starting point Sydney or Brisbane, Australia.

How long? Seven or nine nights.

Inclusions Dining, entertainment, pools, onboard activities; offshore excursions usually cost extra.

Shore excursions While tours arranged by the cruise ship company can be pricey, there's always the option of exploring under your own steam.

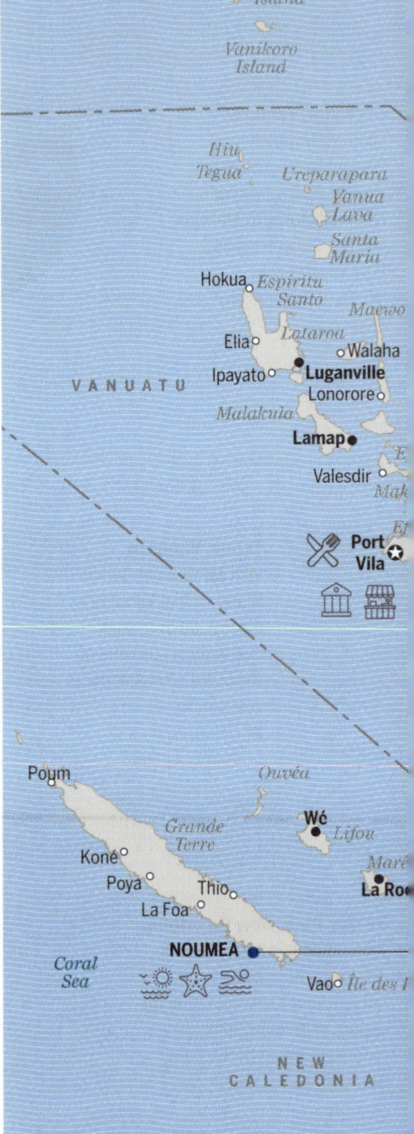

Vanuatu
Port Vila is the cruise ship port for Vanuatu; take some shore time to explore the capital either independently or on an excursion. Some ships also visit Mystery Island (pictured).

Ipota
Tanna
Port Patrick

New Caledonia
Noumea is all set up for cruise ship visits; many ships also drop into spectacular Île des Pins and/or Maré and Lifou Islands in the Loyalty Islands group.

Fiji
As it is further afield, longer cruises from Australia may include a visit to Fiji after New Caledonia and Vanuatu; they'll drop into Viti Levu and possibly one small island.

'THE MILK RUN' FOR YACHTIES

Trip Builder

TAKE YOUR PICK OF MUST-SEES AND HIDDEN GEMS

Yachties sailing across the Pacific as part of a circumnavigation try to cross from east to west, with easterly 'trade winds' pushing them along, between May and October. This avoids the South Pacific's cyclone season and the aim is to be tucked up safe and sound in New Zealand or Australia by mid-November.

Trip Notes

Starting point The western side of the Panama Canal

How long Anything up to six months.

Where to stop Islands with good, safe anchorages.

Tip There's usually a whole fleet of yachts each year following 'the milk run' across the Pacific. It's the easiest route, there's safety in numbers and if something goes wrong, hopefully there's help close at hand from fellow yachties.

CLOCKWISE FROM TOP LEFT: MARINA RILEY/SHUTTERSTOCK, ASIATRAVEL/SHUTTERSTOCK, REINHARD DIRSCHERL/GETTY IMAGES, SCSTOCK/SHUTTERSTOCK

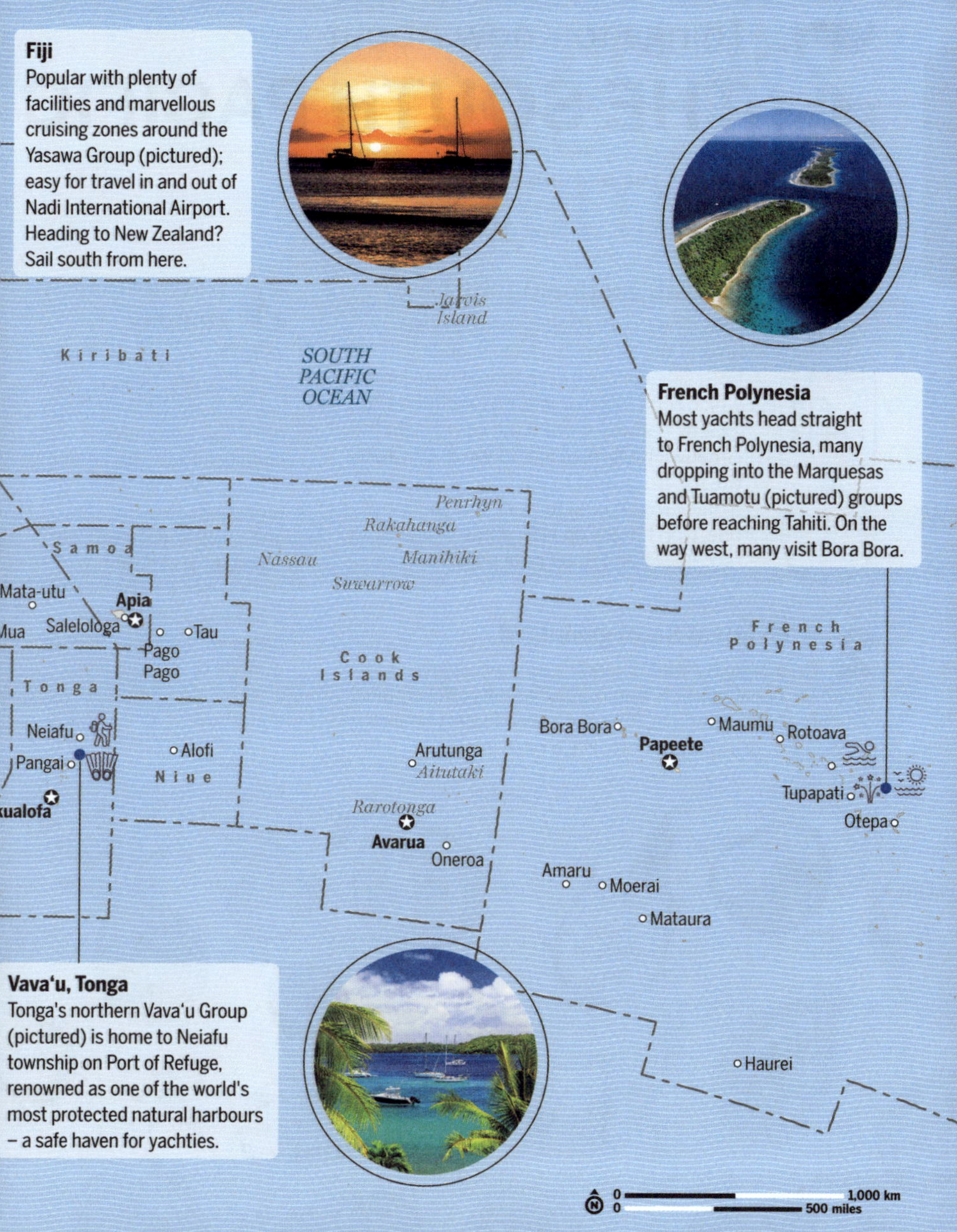
Fiji
Popular with plenty of facilities and marvellous cruising zones around the Yasawa Group (pictured); easy for travel in and out of Nadi International Airport. Heading to New Zealand? Sail south from here.
French Polynesia
Most yachts head straight to French Polynesia, many dropping into the Marquesas and Tuamotu (pictured) groups before reaching Tahiti. On the way west, many visit Bora Bora.
Vava'u, Tonga
Tonga's northern Vava'u Group (pictured) is home to Neiafu township on Port of Refuge, renowned as one of the world's most protected natural harbours – a safe haven for yachties.
Jarvis Island
Kiribati
SOUTH PACIFIC OCEAN
Penrhyn
Rakahanga
Nassau
Manihiki
Suwarrow
Samoa
Mata-utu
Apia
Salelologa
Tau
Pago Pago
Cook Islands
Tonga
Neiafu
Pangai
Alofi
Niue
Arutunga
Aitutaki
Rarotonga
Avarua
Oneroa
French Polynesia
Bora Bora
Papeete
Maumu
Rotoava
Tupapati
Otepa
Amaru
Moerai
Mataura
Haurei
0 1,000 km
0 500 miles

Things to Know About THE SOUTH PACIFIC

INSIDER TIPS TO HIT THE GROUND RUNNING

1 International Date Line

The South Pacific spans a huge area of the earth's surface, including both sides of the International Date Line, which runs more or less on longitude 180°, exactly halfway around the world from the Greenwich Merdian in London at 0°. Cross the IDL from west to east and you'll gain a day; cross it east to west and you'll lose one. Don't mess up with dates of flights, rental cars and hotel bookings!

2 A Tropical Smorgasboard

On a budget? You're heading into a fruit lover's paradise. Local markets and roadside stalls offer tropical delights such as papaya, mangoes, pineapple, bananas, coconuts, starfruit and more. Have cash in hand.

3 Have a Healthy Holiday

To really enjoy your idyllic South Pacific holiday, you'll want to stay healthy. Don't drink tap water unless specifically advised that it is safe, consider wearing reef shoes to avoid cuts and abrasions, use insect repellant and cover up in the evenings – the last thing you want to take home with you is a bout of malaria or dengue fever.

BELOW: GVARDGRAPH/GETTY IMAGES; RIGHT: CSA-PRINTSTOCK/GETTY IMAGES

4 Family Is Important

To meet locals, talking about family is a great ice-breaker; expect to be asked you're marital status, number of children, siblings and more.

5 Understanding the Pacific Ocean

This book may be about the South Pacific, but remember that the other part of the largest of the world's five oceans sits north of the equator – the North Pacific – and it also features countless far-flung islands.

As in the rest of the world, the seasons are opposite up there. While cyclone season in the South Pacific runs November to April, typhoon and hurricane season in the North Pacific is from June to October.

Of course, in both hemispheres, it's warmer the closer you get to the equator. While there's little wind around the equator in an area sailors know as 'the doldrums', in the lower latitudes of both hemispheres (10–30°), easterly trade winds prevail, while in latitudes over 30°, westerly winds are more common, stronger the further you get from the equator – this is due to the rotation of the earth.

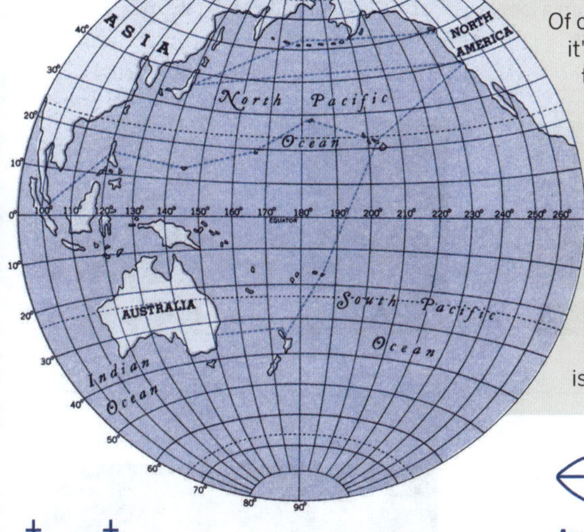

6 Take Me to Church

Christian missionaries converted South Pacific peoples with unbridled enthusiasm and many traditional religious beliefs have disappeared. Christianity is practiced with heartfelt devotion and many islands virtually close down on Sundays. A trip to a church can be an unforgettable experience; dress your best and let the locals welcome you. The hymnal harmonies may stay with you forever.

7 Local Lingo

There are a huge number of local languages and dialects across the South Pacific.

Here are some ways to say 'hello':

Bula – Fijian

Kia orana – Cook Island Māori

Tālofa – Samoan

Halo – Solomon Islands Pijin

La ora na – Tahitian

Malo e lelei – Tongan

Bozu – Drehu Kanak (New Caledonia)

Read, Listen, Watch & Follow

READ

Sea People (Christina Thompson; 2019) A mix of history, anthropology, and the science of navigation.

Breadfruit (Celestine Vaite; 2000) Novel of life in Tahiti from a local perspective.

Miss Ulysses from Puka-Puka (Florence Ngatokura Frisbie; 1948) The first book written by a Polynesian woman.

Sugar (Edward Narain; 2023) An ethnographic novel set in Suva, Fiji.

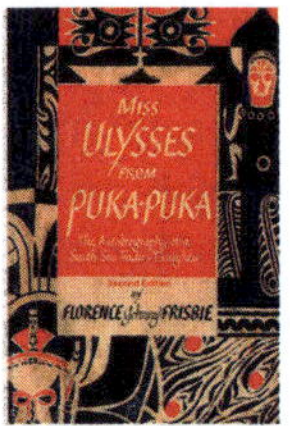

LISTEN

Polyunsaturated (Nesian Mystic; 2002) Pioneering Polynesian-influenced hip-hop from a mixed Pacific Island crew.

SOLΞ MIO (SOLΞ MIO; 2013) Award-winning operatic take on traditional and popular songs by a classically trained Samoan trio.

Tutuki Te Vaka (pictured, 2004) Original contemporary music – 'South Pacific Fusion'; contributed to *Moana* soundtrack.

South Pacific Islands (Putumayo; 2004) Collection of music from across the South Pacific, from Rapa Nui to Papua New Guinea.

JESSE GRANT/GETTY IMAGES FOR DISNEY

Kaito No Tetamanu (Tikahiri; 2011) Mixing rock, classical instruments and lyrics in Paumotu, the language of the Tuamotu archipelago (French Polynesia).

WATCH

The Orator (2011) Brilliant; entirely shot in Samoa, in Samoan, with a Samoan cast and story.

Tanna (pictured, 2015) Award-winning love story filmed in Vanuatu in local languages.

Leitis in Waiting (2018) Documentary about transgender rights in Tonga.

Moana (2016) Hugely successful animated Disney movie set in ancient Polynesia.

Vai (pictured, 2019) A feature film by by nine female Pacific filmmakers shot on seven islands.

ATLASPIX/ALAMY

ROBBY KLEIN/GETTY IMAGES

FOLLOW

Pacific Islands Report (pireport.org) Up-to-date Pacific-related news.

South Pacific Travel (podcasts.apple.com) Apple podcast on the South Pacific.

Oceania Currents (pireport.org/podcasts) Podcast on Pacific stories.

Pacific Waves (rnz.co.nz) RNZ podcast with a Pacific lens.

Pacific Tourism Organisation (southpacificislands.travel) Info and blog on the South Pacific.

FIJI
ISLANDS | ADVENTURE | CULTURE

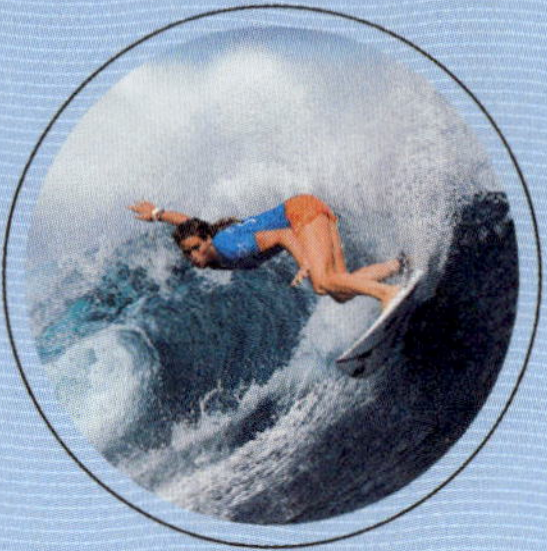

Snorkel with mantas in **Drawaqa Passage** (p58).
3hrs from Port Denarau

Hike to the summit of **Mt Tomanivi** (p55), Fiji's highest point.
2hrs from Rakiraki

Catch a wave in the **Mamanuca Islands** (pictured, p56).
1hr from Viti Levu

Hike the hills around **Nadi** (p54).
3½ hrs from Suva

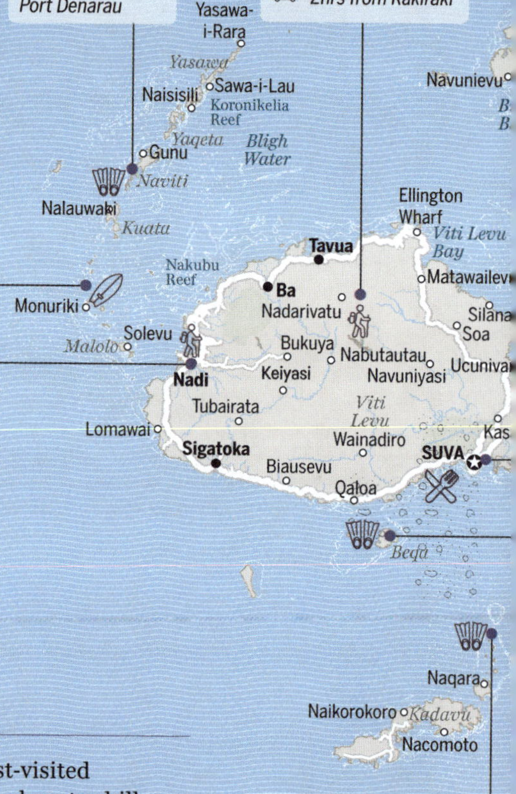
Yasawa-i-Rara
Yasawa
Naisisili
Sawa-i-Lau
Koronikelia Reef
Yaqeta
Bligh Water
Gunu
Naviti
Nalauwaki
Kuata
Navunievu
Ellington Wharf
Viti Levu Bay
Tavua
Nakubu Reef
Ba
Matawailevu
Monuriki
Nadarivatu
Silana
Soa
Solevu
Malolo
Bukuya
Nabutautau
Ucunivanua
Nadi
Keiyasi
Navuniyasi
Tubairata
Viti Levu
Lomawai
Wainadiro
Kas
Sigatoka
SUVA
Biausevu
Qaloa
Beqa
Naqara
Naikorokoro
Kadavu
Nacomoto

FIJI
Trip Builder

One of the South Pacific's most-visited countries for good reason, Fiji is equal parts chill and thrill. Take your pick from countless beachside resorts and dive centres. Or, get off the beaten path and embrace village life on an off-grid adventure in the highlands.

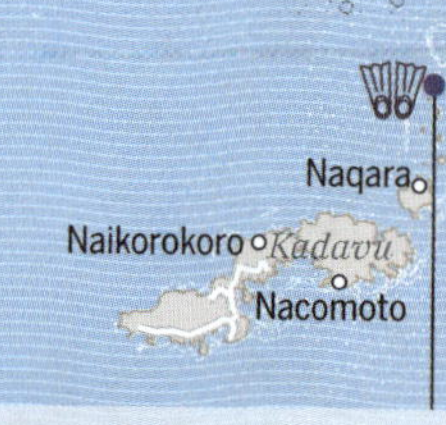

Embrace village life of Kadavu and explore the **Great Astrolabe Reef** (p65).
1hr from Suva

FROM LEFT: TOM SERVAIS/AFP VIA GETTY IMAGES, MARTIN PROCHAZKACZ/SHUTTERSTOCK, JOE BELANGER/SHUTTERSTOCK. PREVIOUS SPREAD: JOHN A. ANDERSON/SHUTTERSTOCK

South Pacific Ocean
Great Sea Reef
Nakelikoso
Wainigadru
Malau
vidamu
Seaqaqa
Labasa
Napuka
Rabi
Vanua Levu
Natewa Bay
Natuvu
Bagasu
Matei
Waivunia
Kocoma
Daria
Naweni
Tavenui
Kanacea
abouwalu
Dive among colourful soft corals off **Taveuni's Rainbow Reef** (pictured, p53).
1hr from Matei
Namena
Namena Marine Reserve
Nathamaki
Vanua Balavu
Mavana
Koro
Kade
nua Levu Barrier Reef
Wander around the quaint former capital city of **Levuka** (p65).
3hrs from Suva
Kanacea
Sawana
Mago
vokula
Ovalau
Koro Sea
Cicia
Tuvuca
Tuvuca
Nairai
Mabula
Shop and dine through **Suva** (p48).
3½hrs from Nadi
ird Sanctuary
Mangroves
Gau
Liku
Nayau
Lakeba
Tubou
Come eye to eye with bull sharks in **Beqa Lagoon** (pictured, p65).
30mins from Pacific Harbour
Vanua Vatu
Oneata
Waiqori
Moce
Namuka
Kabara
Udu
Natokalau
Matuku
Fulaga
Ogea Levu
0
100 km
0
50 miles
N

Practicalities

MTCURADO/GETTY IMAGES

ARRIVING

Nadi Airport Nearly all international flights arrive at Nadi Airport (pictured). Fly direct from Australia, New Zealand, United States, Japan, Singapore and many South Pacific nations. Taxis from the airport start at FJ$5-7. Transport can be arranged through your resort. It's a 30-minute flight (3.5-hour drive) to Suva (**Nausori International Airport**).

Denarau Marina Boats to the Mamanuca and Yasawa Islands depart from Denarau (25-minute drive).

Port of Suva & Port of Lautoka Cruise ships arrive here.

HOW MUCH FOR A

Local beer FJ$5

Fresh coconut FJ$3

Bowl of *kokoda* FJ$12

WHEN TO GO

JAN–MAR
Fewer travellers mean cheaper accommodation. Cyclone season.

APR–JUN
The start of the dry season; warm weather and clear skies.

JUL–SEP
Coolest time of the year; best for surfing and sailing.

OCT–DEC
Celebratory season with festivals and holidays. Chance of rain and cyclones.

GETTING AROUND

Car Hire & Taxi A rental car is the best way to cover long distances on larger islands. Car hire costs around FJ$90-150 per day. Taxis are easy to find in main towns. Plates starting with LT are metered. The meter starts at FJ$2 (6am-9pm) and adds FJ$1 per kilometre. Airport taxis start at FJ$5-7. Plates starting with LH have fixed distance rates.

Bus Air-conditioned buses lap Viti Levu and cost around FJ$20 from Suva to Nadi. Local buses run within towns (FJ$1-2 per trip). Minibuses are notorious for dangerous driving.

Boat & Plane Fiji Airways and Northern Air interlink the islands by plane, usually connecting through Suva or Nadi. Public ferries and private resort boats also run regularly between the islands.

TOP: SELLONLINEMARKETING/GETTY IMAGES

EATING & DRINKING

Eating in Fiji is a foodie's delight. Traditional cuisine (pictured) features fresh seafood, smoked meats, starchy root vegetables, produce from Fiji's fertile interior and creamy coconut milk. It all comes together during a *lovo*, a feast complete with singing and dancing. The islands' multicultural heritage means you're never far from a decadent Indian curry (enjoy it as a roti parcel for an on-the-go snack). Juicy tropical fruits (pictured) are sold by the pile – a treat on a hot day.

Best Fijian food Nadina Authentic Fijian Restaurant (p62)

Must-try Indian curries Ashiyana (p62)

CONNECT & FIND YOUR WAY

Wi-fi Mobile data is cheap. It's worth buying a SIM card at the airport or in town (Vodafone or Digicel). Resort wi-fi is often unreliable or expensive. Expect limited coverage on the outer islands and interior areas.

Navigation Online maps work well within major towns. They often underestimate the time needed to cover longer distances.

WHERE TO STAY

Whether you want cultural immersion, a palm-lined beach, a diver's retreat, a romantic getaway or a jungle escape, there's an island for that.

Island	Pro/Con
Viti Levu	Fiji's largest island, easy to get around. City living, village life, scuba diving, abundant food options. Lacks beaches.
Mamanuca & Yasawa Islands	White-sand beaches, world-class surfing, snorkelling and scuba diving. Everything from busy backpacker dorms to five-star luxury. Pricey.
Ovalau	Island for history buffs. Stay in the UNESCO World Heritage Site of Levuka. Village visits. Quiet.
Taveuni	A natural playground for those unfussed about beaches. Hiking, diving and an occasional wave.
Vanua Levu	Second-largest island. Stays are usually surrounded by nature. Access to incredible diving. Isolated.
Kadavu	Jump-off point for the Great Astrolabe Reef. Lacks choice of accommodation.

BEYOND THE ROOM RATE

Tally up mandatory meal plans, transport and activities for the true cost of your trip; some hotels lure travellers with a low room rate.

MONEY

Fiji uses the Fijian dollar (FJ$). Carry cash as small businesses outside major towns don't accept cards. ATMs typically charge FJ$10–15 for foreign card cash withdrawals. It's economical to take large sums out at once.

01 Sugar & Spice IN SUVA

FOOD | DRINK | CULTURE

Let your tastebuds lead you through Fiji's vibrant capital, where Pacific Islander cuisine blends with the rich flavours of Indian fare. Many restaurants showcase a delightful fusion of both and meals smell just as good as they taste.

BONCHAN/SHUTTERSTOCK

Kokoda

Kokoda (pictured) is Fiji's representative dish made with raw fish, bush lime, coconut milk, tomato, cucumber and chilli. Pair *kokoda* with an *ota* (wild fern) salad and you'll taste local flavours that are delicious without being too heavy.

Insights from Randall Kamea, chef and owner of Fiji Food Truck and Destination Dining @thefijifoodtruck

How to

Getting here/around: Suva's city centre is walkable. Taxis are easily found (around FJ$7 to cross the city).

When to go: This capital city is worth visiting all year round.

Rain or shine: Suva's unpredictable weather means you might need sun and rain protection on the same day.

Money matters: Most restaurants take credit cards; the market and stand-alone stalls only take cash. Hard bargaining is not expected for food items.

01 Start your morning at the **Suva Municipal Market** (pictured) to find tropical produce sold by the pile, sacks filled with spices, and locally grown kava. A chewy, warm *babakau* (fried bread) kickstarts the day.

02 Stroll across Suva's main stretch to **Ginger Kitchen** for a proper breakfast and coffee among **Thurston Gardens**. Spot fruit bats in the treetops and wander through the **Fiji Museum**.

03 Come lunchtime, walk along Suva's waterfront to enjoy traditional Fijian food at the **Bar-Belle**. Order a plate of *ota* (wild fern) and *nama* (sea grape) salad and seafood.

04 Head back to watch the sun sink over Suva Harbour while sipping cocktails at the **Grand Pacific Hotel** (pictured), a colonial-era architectural icon set on the waterfront.

05 No Suva stay is complete without a hearty Indian dinner. Muster a crowd and go to **Rajdhani** to share a fragrant feast of spiced potatoes, curries, biryanis and doughy naan.

Suva Harbour
Reservoir Rd
Viti Levu
Flagstaff Gardens
Gordon St
Bau St
Laucala Bay Rd
Grantham Rd
Ratu Sukuna Rd
Muanikau Rd
Fiji Museum
Vuya Rd
Queen Elizabeth Dr

N 0 — 2 km
0 — 1 mile

02 Catch a WAVE

OCEAN ADVENTURE | CULTURE | SURFING

Feel the sea's energy underneath your feet as you surf along the face of a perfect wave. Swells travelling from thousands of kilometres away clash with the islands' coral reefs, forming waves of sheer wonder. From world-class barrels to beginner-friendly whitewash to waves that have yet to make it onto the mainstream surf maps, Fiji is a destination for surfers.

How to

Getting here/around: You'll need a boat to reach most waves. Contact Brothers Surf Tours *(brother-surftours.com)*, Dream Surf Fiji (dreamsurffiji@gmail.com) or Momi Surf (momisurf.fiji@gmail.com).

When to go: Waves are consistent from April to November.

Surfboard scarcity: Good rental equipment is hard to find. Bring your own if this is a dedicated surf trip.

Money matters: Expect to pay around FJ$150 per person for a five-hour trip. Board hire is FJ$50.

0 10 km
0 5 miles
Nakubu Reef
Vomo
Tokoriki
Vunaqiliqili Reef
Covuli Reef
Monuriki
Beachcomber Island
Tivua Island
Lautoka
Lauwaki
Viseisei
Mana Island
Malamala Island
Malolo Island
Qalito
Koroiyaca
Solevu
Port Denarau
Malolo Barrier Reef
Malolo Lailai Island
Nadi
Sonaisali
Namotu Island
Yako
Cloudbreak
Momi Bay
Navula Reef
Nawau
South Pacific Ocean
Tau
Queens Rd
Viti Levu
Robinson Crusoe Island
Lomawai
Maro Rd
Vusama
Viti Levu Southwest Reefs
Sanasana

Mana in the Mamanucas

If one wave defines Fiji, it's **Cloudbreak** – a left-hander peeling over shallow reef, holding its shape from 3ft to 30ft. Pro surfer Hannah Bennett says, 'Cloudbreak holds a lot of *mana* (life force).' Watch the swell forecast and fly in for the barrel of your dreams. Nearby, **Wilkes Passage** delivers a powerful right-hander. The surf break of **Restaurants** serves up fast, hollow lefts.

Beginners can paddle into the mellow vibes of **Swimming Pools** and admire tiny island views of **Namotu** in between sets. If the current is light, **Namotu Left** has a friendly left. Most surf boats offering trips to the breaks depart from **Port Denarau**, **Momi Bay** or **Sonaisali**. Surfing with a local

Top right Cloudbreak
Bottom right Natadola Beach

Fiji Surf Tips

Participate in local customs. Offer a *sevusevu* (gift) and seek blessings from the landowners of Fiji's surf breaks. It's a wonderful experience to go to a village and drink kava with the chiefs to kick off your trip. Understand the local tide chart. Ease into your first few sessions to avoid burning out for the rest of your trip. Encourage the locals. Surfing in Fiji is in its infancy, and tourists influence the overall vibe in the lineup.

■ **Insights from Hannah Bennett,** a pro surfer and president of Fiji Surfing Association @_fiji_girl_

guide cuts out the guesswork of which waves to go for.

Coral Coast Curls Viti Levu's southwestern reefs are perfect for surfing safaris. Hotels here run boats to spots like **Fiji Pipe**, **Serua**, **J's and Shiftys**, all great for intermediates. Twenty kilometres offshore, **Frigates** delivers some of Fiji's longest, hollow lefts. **Sigatoka Rivermouth** welcomes local groms and adventurous visitors – though it's called 'sharky', incidents are rare. For beginners, **Natadola Beach** offers a bay of white sand and rentals at the **InterContinental Fiji**. Shoulders feeling sore? Unwind at one of the beachside massage *bures*.

ED SLOANE/WORLD SURF LEAGUE VIA GETTY IMAGES

NINA JANESIKOVA/SHUTTERSTOCK

03 Go on an Ocean ODYSSEY

SCUBA DIVING | WILDLIFE | ADVENTURE

Jacques Cousteau, a pioneer of scuba diving, believed Fiji to have the world's best soft coral. The waters around Taveuni and Vanua Levu teem with marine life. Peer into crevices of soft and hard corals to discover reef fish, crustaceans, octopuses and eels. In the deeper blue, you might just encounter sharks, whales, turtles and rays.

REINHARD DIRSCHERL/ULLSTEIN BILD VIA GETTY IMAGES

How to

Getting here/around: Stay in Savusavu on Vanua Levu (a 70-minute flight from Nadi; 45-minute flight or overnight ferry from Suva) or on Taveuni (1½-hour flight from Nadi, 1-hour flight or overnight ferry from Suva).

When to go: April through September offers clearest water visibility.

Smooth operator: A one-tank dive costs around FJ$220; two tanks cost around FJ$400 including gear. Ask for a custom package if you'll be diving for multiple days.

CRBELLETTE/GETTY IMAGES

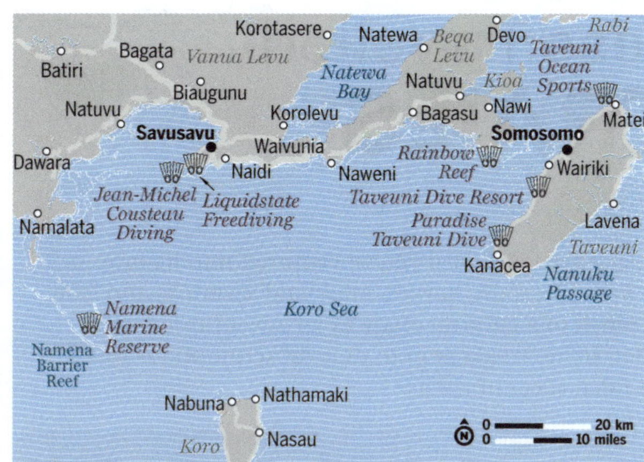

Far left Hawksbill Turtle, Namena Marine Reserve
Bottom Left Rainbow Reef

Radiant Reefscapes

Rainbow Reef The coral reefs in Fiji's waters are spectacular, but the Rainbow Reef in the Somosomo Strait, between Vanua Levu and Taveuni, is especially so. Changing tides bring a surge of nutrients, sustaining vibrant ecosystems of both soft and hard corals. Plan your trip around seeing the **Great White Wall**, carpeted in snowlike *Dendronephthya* corals. The **Purple Wall** is draped in lilac-hued soft corals, lacelike Gorgonian fans and long whip corals. **Cabbage Patch** is an expanse of yellow scroll corals resembling blooming cabbage heads. These reefs teem with life, offering the chance to dive with countless reef fish who take refuge in these kaleidoscopes of corals. The most convenient way to get to Rainbow Reef is with a dive operator from Taveuni. **Taveuni Dive Resort** *(taveunidiveresort.com)*, **Paradise Taveuni** *(paradiseinfiji.com)* and **Taveuni Ocean Sports** *(taveuniocean sports.com)* run regular trips.

Fiji's Largest Marine Reserve **Namena Marine Reserve**, off Namenalala, is an unspoiled reef where hard and soft corals thrive. From the deck of your dive boat, you might spot humpback, minke or pilot whales. Spinner dolphins perform acrobatics above the sea's surface, bottlenose dolphins occasionally swim alongside the bow. At Fiji's largest marine reserve, fin alongside reef fish and reef sharks. Look for hawksbill turtles – Namenalala is a nesting site. Scalloped hammerhead sharks school in deeper waters. Boat rides to the reef take around 40 minutes from Savusavu. **Jean-Michel Cousteau Diving** *(fijiresort.com)* offers scuba trips and **LiquidState Freediving** *(liquidstatefreediving.com)* runs freediving and snorkelling excursions.

Diving with the Big Ones

In winter (June to September), spot humpback whales and dive with manta rays at their feeding stations.

In summer (October to May), look for yellowfin tuna that feed on juvenile baitfish schools. Pilot whales feed on the tuna.

Fiji is known for its shark encounters, but they don't have to be bull or tiger sharks. At **Namena Marine Reserve**, chunky grey reef sharks patrol the deep ledges. Hammerheads occasionally cruise by.

There's nothing like seeing a rare silky shark on a bluewater freedive for those who want the thrill of a no-bottom, no-place-to-hide encounter.

Insights from Neelam Raff, a freediving instructor and co-owner of LiquidState Freediving @liquidstatefreediving.

04 Less Travelled TRAILS

HIKING | CULTURE | LANDSCAPES

You haven't truly experienced Fiji until you've ventured into its interior. Beyond the beaches, you'll find waterfalls, gorges, grassland savannas and leafy forests. Hiking in Fiji is as much of a cultural affair as an adventurous one. Villages at the trailhead often invite trekkers in to dine on scrumptious feasts and swap stories over kava-filled coconut shells.

ANDREW BAIN/GETTY IMAGES

How to

Getting here/around: Rent a 4WD or hire a driver for trails connected to Fiji's interior roads; the roads circling Viti Levu are reliably paved. Arrange multiday hikes through tour operators.

When to go: April to November brings the best chance of sunny skies.

Packing tips: Pack sun protection, a rain jacket, a portable water filter and hiking shoes with good grip. A *sulu* (sarong) is essential for village visits.

DON MAMMOSER/SHUTTERSTOCK

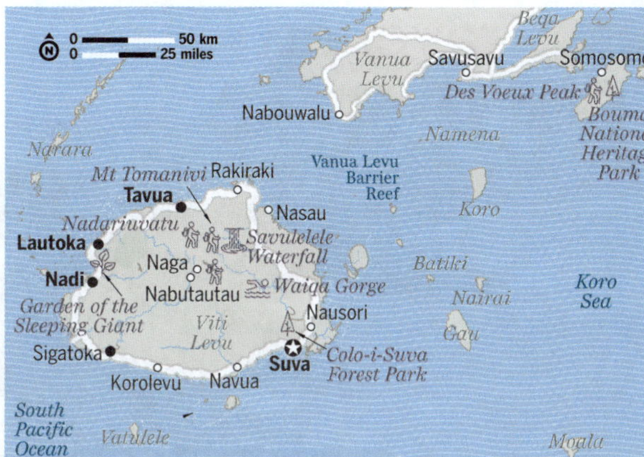

Far left Hiking, near Naga **Bottom Left** Bouma National Heritage Park

Into the Interior

Viti Levu's Highland Escape Cross Fiji's largest island on a three-day journey from **Naga** to **Nubutautau** hiking from rolling grasslands to misty rainforests, sleeping at the trail's villages. Evenings often end around a *tanoa* (wooden bowl), where kava is served. If there's energy to spare, tell tales from the trail or dance to Fijian melodies before tucking in for the night. Plan to hike around six hours per day. Treks arranged through **Talanoa Treks** *(talanoa-treks-fiji.com)*.

Stretch Your Legs If you're spending the day in Suva, soak in the refreshing pools at **Colo-i-Suva Forest Park**, only 20 minutes from the city centre by car (11km). If you're in Nadi, enjoy bright orchids, umbrella-sized monstera leaves, and views of the island's western end atop the **Garden of the Sleeping Giant** (20 minutes by car, 12km).

Trek to the Tallest Summit Climb 1324m above the clouds to **Mt Tomanivi** on Viti Levu (6hrs return). Sleep among the stars at **Navai** and get an early start to the top. Arrange your guided trip directly with the village by calling Esira (+679 9835430). Joji Tamani Adventures (tamani.jojib@gmail.com) plans multiday trips around the region.

Garden Island Goodness Fly or ferry to Taveuni, where tropical blooms make up for its dearth of beaches. Hike to 6km to **Des Voeux Peak** and **Lake Tagimoucia**, the only area where Fiji's rare Tagimoucia flower grows. A trio of cascades awaits at **Bouma National Heritage Park**. Bring your swimsuit.

Off-Map Adventures

I use a century-old map to unearth hidden trails on Viti Levu, where I live. Don't miss the short but slippery hike to thundering **Savulelele Waterfall**, accessible from Nabalesere village (1.5km each way). For a panoramic view of Viti Levu's main peaks, mountain bike or hike along the ridge of **Nadariuvatu**. Fiji's geological wonders are revealed on a hike-and-swim along **Waiqa Gorge**.

Visiting Fiji is not just about seeing its natural beauty and landscapes. Once you come and connect to a community, you'll always have that connection.

Insights from Joji Tamani, an adventure tour guide @jbtamani_vitian

05 Find Your ISLAND

FAMILY FUN | OCEAN ADVENTURES | ROMANCE

Limestone peaks and sparkling champagne beaches define the Mamanuca and Yasawa island groups, with the Mamanucas offering a more delicate charm. Sun-drenched and romantic, these islands are an ocean adventurer's playground, with enough activities to lure you from your lounge chair.

ASIATRAVEL/SHUTTERSTOCK

How to

Getting here/around: The *Yasawa Flyer II* ferry *(southseacruisesfiji.com)* stops at most islands along the chain. Tender boats retrieve you and your luggage from the ferry.

When to go: These islands are spectacular year-round, but you'll dodge most cyclones by coming from April to December.

Bula budget: Awesome Adventures Fiji *(awesomefiji.com)* offers reasonable packages that include transport, accommodation and meals. Dorm and private room options are available.

DON MAMMOSER/SHUTTERSTOCK

Spot for Sailors

Malolo is where Fijians say the sun goes to rest – as do sailors who anchor in its calm lagoon of **Malololailai** (little Malolo). Socialise with fellow salties over a cocktail and dinner at **Dick's Place Bar & Bistro**. Stretch your sea legs and hike to Malololailai's peak, **Mt Uluisilo**, where a WWII bunker offers panoramic views of the surrounding islands. The Fijian crested iguana, once thought extinct, hides in the island's leafy interior. Snorkeling near the **Musket Cove** reef pass reveals butterflyfish, angelfish, parrotfish, wrasse, trumpetfish and rays who buzz around a coral-fringed sandbank.

NIK WHEELER/CORBIS VIA GETTY IMAGES

Jaws & Awe

Kuata's coral reef is among Fiji's healthiest, protected as a marine reserve. Just a few fin kicks from shore, encounter hard and soft coral reefs

Best Mamanuca Day Trips

Sip a cocktail from the seaside infinity pool at **Malamala Beach Club**.

Take the kids to kayak, swim and snorkel around **South Sea Island**.

Cruise to a sandbank on **Sabre**, a sailing catamaran.

Hop onboard a 100ft sailboat, **Schooner Whale's Tale**, and feel the wind blow you to a tiny islet.

Far left Yasawa island **Left** Musket Cove **Above** Kayaking, Mamanuca islands

rife with fish, eels, cuttlefish and crustaceans, all vying for attention. Occasionally, a sea turtle glides through, taking centre stage. On the outer reefs, black-tip and white-tip reef sharks patrol the waters, caring little about the humans who swim around them. For thrill-seekers, **Barefoot Kuata Island Resort** offers guided dives to 20m depth to see up to 25 bull sharks – fast and agile, the Ferraris of the sea. Though somehow, through the quiet hiss of your scuba regulator, the scene is quite serene. If time is short, day trips to Kuata are available from **Port Denarau** *(barefootkuatafiji.com)*.

Gliding with Giants

Manta rays, or *vai* in Fijian, gather in **Drawaqa Passage** to feed on plankton. With a wingspan of up to 6m, a manta ray's presence can feel intimidating. Not to fear, these gentle giants are filter feeders with no venomous barbs. Swim alongside them with a guide and watch as they perform underwater acrobatics. They may glide near, but hands-off admiration is key. Currents

Meet the Mantas

Manta rays, the most intelligent fish, are inquisitive and identifiable by unique belly patterns. Manta Trust Fiji has documented 146 mantas around the Yasawa Islands, with 30 to 40 appearing during manta season (April–October).

They aggregate in the strong currents of Drawaqa Passage and feed on plankton. For a respectful encounter, avoid chasing or touching mantas. Stay 3m away (unless they come to you) and approach from the side – so their side-placed eyes can spot you.

If you capture a manta on video, send it to the Manta Trust Fiji website for data collection. If it's a new manta, you can name it.

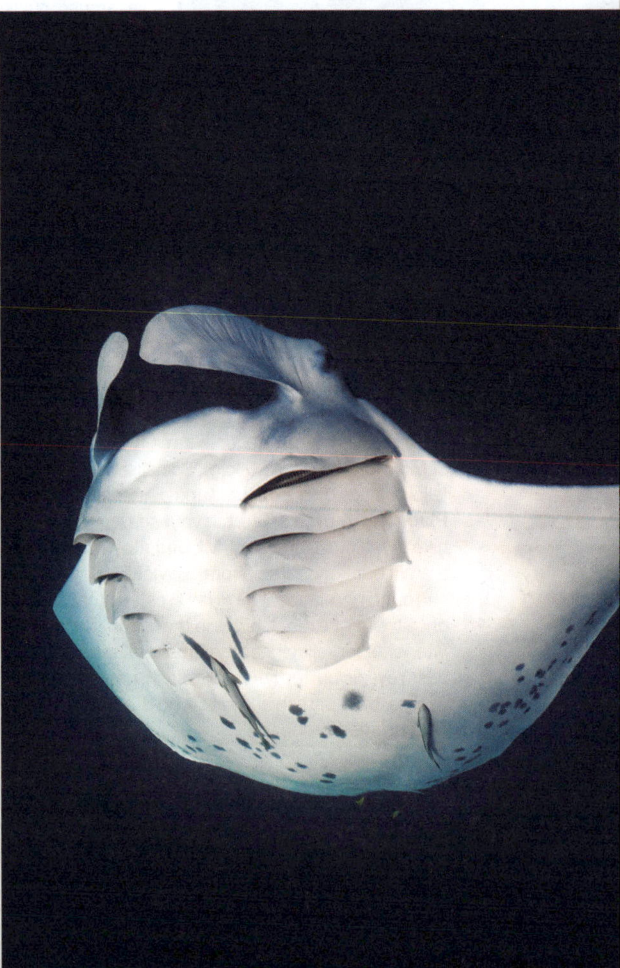

Insights from Luke Gordon, marine biologist and project leader at Manta Trust Fiji @lukegordonphotography

in the passage can be strong. Wearing a life vest and staying in sight of the tour boat is wise.

Into the Blue Lagoon

The coral seascape creates blues of every hue throughout the Mamanuca and Yasawa Islands, but the most striking tint is found at **Nacula's** southwestern lagoon. Under the sunlight, the sandy bottom and shallow water create colours your phone can't capture. Its calm waters make it a prime place for novice swimmers and families with little ones. Accommodations are concentrated in Nacula's south, with fewer options as you head north. Dive with sea turtles and reef shark, dip into the waters of a limestone cave at **Sawa-i-Lau** and laze away on an untouched beach. While the upper Yasawas evoke desert-island fantasies, they also offer a window into village life. Bring a *sevusevu* and experience Fijian hospitality; learn how to catch fish with a handline and the best place to harvest sea grapes.

Left Manta Ray, off Fiji **Below** Nacula Island **Bottom** Sawa-i-Lau

FAR LEFT: KATARINA LOEFFLER/GETTY IMAGES; LEFT: DON MAMMOSER/SHUTTERSTOCK

RANI ZERAFA/GETTY IMAGES

Kava Culture in Fiji

FIJI'S STRESS-RELIEVING ELIXIR

Kava is Fiji's drink of choice and a ubiquitous influence in social settings, no matter how formal. More than just a beverage, the ritual of drinking kava while gathered around a *tanoa* (wooden bowl) is how many of the nation's strongest connections are made. Get ready to drink, connect and *talanoa* (converse).

Left Kava Ceremoni **Centre** Kava roots **Right** A *bilo* filled with kava

IGNACIO MOYA CORONADO/SHUTTERSTOCK

The Kava Connection

Kava, *yaqona* in Fijian, is made from the root of a pepper plant. It's thought to have originated in Vanuatu and spread throughout the Pacific by seafarers, integrating itself into many Pacific Island cultures. The naturalist onboard Captain Cook's 1770s HMS *Endeavour* expedition named kava *Piper methysticum*, meaning 'intoxicating pepper'. This is arguably a misnomer. Kava contains kavalactones, a psychoactive ingredient known to relieve anxiety. The psychological effect of kava is usually relaxation, not inebriation. Someone who has consumed too much kava can be found snoozing in the corner or keeled over with a sore stomach.

A kava plant takes at least three years to mature and grows up to 2m tall. Cyclones and droughts can wipe out kava plants, impacting one of the region's most lucrative cash crops. Bringing in around FJ$38.1 million in 2024 with 501 metric tonnes exported, it's one of the nation's most lucrative agricultural exports.

In Fiji, the kava plant root is harvested, dried and ground into a fine powder. You'll often see a tangle of brown roots laid on a corrugated metal sheet, drying under the equatorial sun. The metronome thump, thump, thump you'll hear around the islands is the sound of men pounding kava into its powder form with a heavy rod and large metal mortar *(tabili)*.

When it's time to drink kava, the powder is filtered through a cloth, mixed with water and served from the *tanoa*. A *bilo* (coconut shell) filled with kava is passed around and enjoyed in turn. It has an earthy, peppery flavour. Kava starts with a tingling sensation in the mouth, followed by

JANTIRA NAMWONG/SHUTTERSTOCK

ED SLOANE/WORLD SURF LEAGUE VIA GETTY IMAGES

a sense of calm. Other Pacific Island nations, like Vanuatu, consume kava in fresh root form, and the potency tends to be stronger. Some communities in the South Pacific grind their kava by chewing it, though this is losing popularity.

Rooted in Respect

While it seems like the point of drinking kava is for its psychological effects, it's seen as a facilitator of discussion. Seated on even ground, consuming a substance known to make people more agreeable, it's no wonder kava is integral to settling conflicts and finding compromises within the South Pacific. Workplaces often host kava sessions to find resolutions, even in political settings.

> Drinking kava in Fiji has ritualistic practices that vary from community and setting

Friends drink it amongst themselves to swap stories and strengthen bonds. It's rare to attend a ceremony and not find kava, no matter the reason. Sporting events often have a stall where fans enjoy kava (their circle's cheer emerges a little after the general crowd's).

Drinking kava in Fiji has ritualistic practices that vary from community and setting. Drinking at a kava bar or as part of a hotel activity is informal, and tourists are not expected to know kava customs. Whenever you visit a new village, it's customary to bring a gift of kava, traditionally in its root form *(waka)*, found at most major markets. The kava is presented to the village elders as a *sevusevu*, followed by a ceremony inviting you to enter the village. This genuine hospitality usually extends indefinitely, and you'll be welcome to return.

Kava Etiquette 101

You'll quickly pick up the group's kava drinking rituals. If in doubt, clap once before taking the *bilo* with both hands. Drink it in one draught. Return the *bilo* and clap thrice before saying *vinaka* (thank you) or *maca* (empty). Tell your host in advance if you prefer not to drink kava. Accepting the first round and politely declining or asking for 'low tide' on subsequent rounds is okay.

Dress modestly. Men and women should cover their legs with a sarong *(sulu)*. Avoid wearing anything on your head. A smile and apology smooths most snafus.

Listings

BEST OF THE REST

Flavours of Fiji

Red Pepper Restaurant & Bar, Nadi $$

Flavourful curries and tandoori meats are found within the unassuming walls of what's perhaps Nadi's best Indian restaurant. Order *panipuri* (pockets of vegetables and spices) with a dollop of tamarind chutney.

Vasaqa Fiji, Wailoaloa $$$

Take your pick of barbecued meats like spit-roasted pork or smoked brisket at this seaside favourite. Palusami pasta or toasted cumin vegetable wraps tempt vegetarians.

Nadina Authentic Fijian Restaurant, Port Denarau $$$

Try Fijian classic dishes and platters of fresh seafood on the marina waterfront. Try any variation of *rourou* (taro leaves cooked in coconut milk) and *kokoda* made with *walu*.

Sails, Port Denarau $$$

Dress your best and watch yachts cruise through Port Denarau. Upscale Fijian and Indo-Fijian dishes grace the menu. The *kokoda*, mud-crab curry and marinated baked fish are worthy picks.

Crab Shack Fiji, Korotogo $$$

Ocean views await at this assembly of picnic tables on Korotogo's Sunset Strip. Go with the mud crab wok-fried in garlic and butter or baked mussels soaked in sauvignon blanc.

Ashiyana, Suva $$

Opt for the balcony and people watch over Suva's main road. Share bowls of fiery Indian curries, tandoori meats, and a plate of potato 65 – fried potatoes smothered in spices.

Eden Bistro & Bar, Suva $$$

Fijian food with fine-dining flair in Suva. Stick to the local side of the menu for fresh seafood and salads made from wild fern (*ota*) and sea grapes (*nama*).

Kanalevu Kitchen, Suva $$

Kanalevu means 'huge appetite' in Fijian – bring yours here. Enjoy Indian and Fijian classics in an open-air restaurant next to the rugby stadium. The seafood platters are great value. Don't skip dessert.

Govinda, Suva $$

For the best value, go for the thali at this all-vegetarian Indian cafeteria. Chickpea, paneer, pumpkin and jackfruit curries accompany soft roti. Save room for their sweets.

Surf and Turf, Savusavu $$

A humble shopfront hides one of Savusavu's best restaurants for seafood and breezy sea views. If rock lobster or seared ahi tuna makes an appearance on its everchanging menu, you're in luck.

International Bites

Byblos, Denarau Island $$$

Reserve an oceanfront table for sunset and share decadent platters with your choice of meat and hummus, falafel, fatayer and salads. Located at the Raddison Blu on Denarau Island.

Veggie Restaurant, Suva $$

One of the most inventive menus in Suva is found at this cosy vegetarian restaurant. Come for sizzling tofu stir-fries, plump burgers, woodfired pizzas, huge salads and heartwarming soups.

Rudy's Italian Trattoria and Grill, Suva $$$

This Suva restaurant serves the best Italian food in Fiji – chef Bruno Bettinazzi ensures its authenticity. Breads, pastas, sauces and gelato are made in-house. Wine is imported from Italy.

Jee's Hand Pulled Noodles, Suva $

There are three Jee's around Suva doling hearty Chinese dishes. They're known for their noodles, but the wontons, dumplings and steamed buns are bound to hit the spot too.

Fish Bar, Momi Bay $$$

Reserve a table for stunning sunset views at Marriott Momi Bay's seaside restaurant and bar. One of the top spots for steak and seafood. Ask for a table near the water.

Fiji Food Truck $$

Roaming between Suva and Nadi, dine on takeaway treats of burgers, wraps, fries, salads and barbecued meats. Track the food truck down on Instagram @thefijifoodtruck.

Cool Cafes

Broady's Bar and Cafe, Nadi $$

A hip spot that's open for all meals, but breakfast is what they do best. If there's a rugby game on, come for commiseration or celebration. Live music on Fridays.

Coffee Hub, Suva and Nadi $$

With a fully loaded brunch menu, coffees made correctly and a welcoming atmosphere, this is where you come to stay a while. Peek at the pastry display before placing your order.

Mana, Suva $$

Come to this popular cafe in the morning for coffee and in the afternoon for kava. Suva's changemakers often host cultural events and swap stories over all-day breakfasts, burgers and curries.

CHANTAE REDEN

Crab Shack Fiji

Projects Collective, Korolevu and Nadi $

Delicious coffee and sweet treats served at a stylish boutique filled with locally made products. Located in Nadi and Coral Coast; the latter is better if you wish to linger.

Cafe Planet, Korotogo $

Good coffee is surprisingly hard to come by – you'll find it here. The tiny cafe is a perfect short stop for long Queens Hwy drives. Juices, cold brews and smoothies available.

Dive Cafe, Taveuni $$

Wake up with an iced coffee, smoothie or fresh juice at this beach cafe off Matei. Reef fish cruise the shallows underneath the cafe balcony searching for stray morsels.

Cold Beers, Kava & Cocktails

Ed's Bar, Nadi $

Fiji's nightlife scene is rather scant, but there's likely something happening at Ed's bar. Tourists and locals intermingle over cold beers, cocktails and kava.

Club 57, Wailoaloa $$$

The 6th-floor rooftop bar offers panoramic ocean views, making it the perfect spot of a sundowner. It's a little more upscale than other Wailoaloa offerings – feel free to dress up.

Boatshed Restaurant and Sunset Bar, Viseisei $$$

The Boatshed has a convivial vibe on the marina's edge, with yachties and locals coming to sip drinks at sunset. Hearty pastas, pizzas and burgers ensure you won't leave hungry.

Cloud 9, Mamanuca Islands $$$

Rotate between the bar, your lounge chair and turquoise waters while floating on a wooden platform in the Mamanucas. DJs playing chill house music add to the island vibes.

Malamala Beach Club, Mamanuca Islands $$$

Grab a cocktail or coconut and cool off in the infinity pool. This private island has white sands, spacious lounge chairs, chill house music, private cabanas and hot showers.

Musket Cove Yacht Club Island Bar, Malololailai $$

Plop into a plush couch under the thatched-roof bar and eavesdrop on yachties telling tall tales. Tropical cocktails, beers and wines grace the drinks menu, with the frozen mango slushie as a highlight.

Hilltop, Suva $

Groove to bowls of kava or pints of beer at Suva's no-frills rooftop bar. Check the Instagram account @hilltopbeergarden for updates on live music and events.

Copra Shed Marina, Savusavu $$

Surprised-they're-floating sailboats and superyachts sail into the waters in front of Copra Shed Marina. Clink glasses with visiting yacht crew, boat owners and local salties. Exceptionally friendly staff.

Traditional Stays

Namosi Eco Retreat, Viti Levu

Both the road and the power grid end at the river you'll cross on foot to reach the retreat. Spend your days swimming, trekking and harvesting. Spend your nights stargazing.

Private Island Paradises

Tavarua

A heart-shaped private island resort for keen surfers who can commit to a week of surfing, snorkelling, kayaking and fishing. The iconic wave of Restaurants (p50) is within paddling distance – no boat required *(tavarua.com)*.

Kokomo Private Island Resort

Live your private island paradise at this five-star resort on the fringe of the Great Astrolabe Reef (p65). Indulge in a spa treatment, customise your meals, dive with mantas and return via seaplane *(kokomoislandfiji.com)*.

Outdoor Thrills

Rivers Fiji, Navua

Bumble over the rapids of Viti Levu's Navua River in a trusty rubber raft. Paddle by misty waterfalls and quiet villages, and through the towering walls of an ancient gorge.

Ecotrax Fiji, Cuvu

What once was a sugarcane train railway is now an exciting eco-adventure in Sigatoka. Pedal along the railway on a mounted electric bike, called a velocipede *(ecotrax.com.fj)*.

DON MAMMOSER/SHUTTERSTOCK

Lavena Coastal Walk

Lavena Coastal Walk, Taveuni

Hike 5km along the flat trail of Lavena Coastal Walk or catch a boat ride to Wainibau Waterfall on Taveuni, where waterfalls and a large natural swimming pool beckon.

Tavoro Waterfalls Falls, Taveuni

Tread lightly over jungle vines to a trio of waterfalls, each getting more spectacular with altitude. Sights like this are how Taveuni earned its reputation as Fiji's 'Garden Island'.

Sigatoka Sand Dunes, Sigatoka

The view atop Sigatoka's sweeping coastal dunes is worth the trek. Feel the sea's energy as waves lap against the dunes, watch endemic birds flit about, and search for Lapita-era artifacts hidden in the sand.

Garden of the Sleeping Giant, Nadi

A trail weaving past gargantuan monstera leaves, hundreds of orchids, lily ponds and tropical plants leads to a lookout point with views spanning to the Mamanuca islands *(gosg.com.fj)*.

iBike Fiji, Nadi

Buzz around the foothills of Sabeto on a four-hour guided electric bicycle tour. A local guide leads you through rolling grasslands, sugarcane fields and villages to panoramic lookouts *(landandseatours.com.fj)*.

Snake God Cave (Nakoroloaloa), Wailotua

Follow your guide's torchlight through a cave named after six snake-like stalactites. You'll reach a natural amphitheatre with blossom bats clinging to its ceiling.

Aquatic Adventures

Moon Reef, Silana, Viti Levu

Wild spinner dolphins perform out-of-water acrobatics alongside the tour boat in the calm waters of this crescent reef 5km offshore, 30 minutes by boat. Pack your snorkel gear and peek at the corals.

Great Astrolabe Reef, Kadavu

The second-largest fringing reef system in the world. Snorkel and dive with manta rays, sea turtles, sharks and critters who call the reef's vibrant corals home. Stay on Kadavu.

Sawa-i-Lau Cave, Yasawa Islands

Swim in the cool, teal pool inside an ancient limestone cave. Sunlight shining from the cave's windows dances across the water. Brave travellers swim through to another dark chamber.

Beqa Adventure Divers, Beqa Lagoon

Plunge into the deep and witness bull sharks cruise through the blue – no cage required. If you're lucky, a tiger shark might join the spectacle.

Historical Sights

Fiji Museum, Suva

Fiji's largest museum highlights the Pacific's seafarers with a replica *drua*, a double-hulled sailing canoe, and 3700-year-old artifacts. Includes an exhibit on Fiji's indentured labourers from India *(fijimuseum.org.fj)*.

Levuka, Ovalau

Fiji's first capital, a UNESCO World Heritage Site, has false-front shops, colonial-era buildings, a burned-down Masonic temple and produce markets. Welcoming locals always seem to have time to chat.

Lovoni, Ovalau

The villagers of Lovoni share their shadowed past, when residents were kidnapped and sold into slavery. Experience their warmth through a traditional kava ceremony, singing and dancing, and a feast of freshwater prawns.

VANUATU
DIVING | CEREMONIES | VOLCANOES

VANUATU
Trip Builder

Vanuatu – a constellation of 83 islands situated in Melanesia and united by their adherence to the ancient cultural code of *kastom* – is arguably one of the most remarkable enclaves of Indigenous tradition in the world. For centuries, these islands have been sculpted by fire and sea. Imbued with mythology, Vanuatu's islands offer off-the-grid adventures that stretch far beyond its beachfront resorts.

Santa Maria

Port Olry

Espiritu Santo

Lugan

Deep dive into Vanuatu's role in WWII at the South Pacific **WWII Museum** (p86).
50mins from Port Vila

Get a taste of kava in **Port Vila** (p73).
5mins from downtown Port Vila

South Pacific Ocean

0 200 km
0 100 miles

Poum

NEW CALEDONIA

Maewo
Aoba
Sanasom
Laone
Pentecost
Lonorore
Craig Cove
Ambrym
Lakula
Ulei
Lamap
VANUATU
Epi
Lamen Bay
Valesdir
Makura
Mataso
Efate
Port Vila

See what inspired the invention of modern-day bungee jumping on **Pentecost Island** (p76).

1hr from Port Vila

Surrender to enchantment witnessing the ancient art of sand drawing at the **Vanuatu National Museum** (p85).

5mins from downtown Port Vila

Learn how ancient technologies have been preserved at **Ekasup Cultural Village** (p75).

20mins from Port Vila

Dillons Bay
Potnarvin
Ipota
Erromango
Tanna
Futuna

Venture to the rim of one of the world's most accessible active volcanoes, **Mt Yasur** (p81).

1hr from Lenakel's White Grass Airport

Port Patrick
Mystery Island

Practicalities

LASZLO MATES/SHUTTERSTOCK

ARRIVING

Bauerfield International Airport Travellers typically arrive at Port Vila's airport, the country's main gateway. Direct flights are available from Australia, Fiji, New Caledonia and the Solomon Islands. Taxis to central Port Vila are available outside the arrival terminal, with fares starting at around 2000VT. Most resorts and hotels also offer airport transfers or shuttles.

Cruise Ship Port If arriving by cruise ship, it is a five-minute drive (3km) by taxi to central Port Vila.

HOW MUCH FOR A

Shell of kava 50–100VT

Local meal 750–1000VT

Handmade craft 1000–2000VT

GETTING AROUND

Air Travel The country's domestic carrier, Air Vanuatu, faced bankruptcy in 2024 but resumed service towards the end of the year. Private charters are available but are in high demand so booking well in advance is recommended.

Public Minibuses Public minibuses operate without fixed routes – you simply tell the driver where you need to be dropped off. In Port Vila and Luganville, fares are between 150VT and 200VT within city limits.

Public Ferries Available, but not the best or most reliable option.

WHEN TO GO

APR–JUN
The only time to experience the Land Diving Festival in Pentecost (p76).

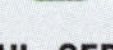

JUL–SEP
The cool season. The country comes alive with *kastom* festivities for Independence Day celebrations in July.

NOV–MAR
Cyclone season sees fewer travellers. Travel is far cheaper, but rain presents a challenge.

EATING & DRINKING

Vanuatu's cuisine reflects the ni-Vanuatu people's relationship with both land and sea, with fresh, organic ingredients. Staples include yam, taro and manioc, traditionally baked in an earth oven to prepare *laplap* – Vanuatu's national dish made with grated root vegetables, coconut cream and chicken or fish. Coconut appears in the bulk of ni-Vanuatu dishes, both savoury and sweet. Fresh seafood – lobster, tuna and coconut crab – is abundant and often grilled or steamed with local spices. Seasonal fruits like pawpaw (papaya), banana and pineapple are staples too.

Best seasonal fruits **Port Vila Market** (p73)

Must-try kava **Kava Lounge** (p73)

CONNECT & FIND YOUR WAY

Wi-fi Access is limited but occasionally available in Port Vila and Luganville; there is free wi-fi at hotels and some cafes.

Mobile phones Coverage (Digicel or Vodafone) is reliable in populated areas, but patchy on remote islands. Physical and e-SIMs available on arrival at the airport.

Navigation For navigation, offline maps are recommended, as road signage is nearly non-existent.

WHERE TO STAY

Vanuatu's lodging offerings are vast in their range: from beachfront villas in Efate to homestays in traditional *kastom* villages. Families can enjoy Santo's resorts, while more rustic adventurers can unplug at community-run bungalows on Pentecost or Tanna.

Town/Island	Pro/Con
Port Villa, Efate	Vanuatu's capital is the most developed and accessible part of the archipelago.
Luganville, Santo Espiritu	Santo offers both culture and comfort. Accommodation here ranges from homestays to high-end resorts.
Tanna Island	Homestays, bungalows and *kastom* villages near Mt Yasur make for a unique cultural immersion.

2024 EARTHQUAKE

In December 2024, Vanuatu was hit by a 7.3 magnitude earthquake, causing widespread destruction across Port Vila. Reconstruction is ongoing. Contact your tour operator or accommodation to confirm their status.

MONEY

Vanuatu's currency is the vatu (VT). Convert or withdraw the money you will need in Port Vila. ATMs are scarce elsewhere in the country and there are very few places outside of the resorts that take cards.

06 Adventures Around THE CAPITAL

MARKETS | KAVA | SAND DRAWING

Port Vila is more than just a stopover en route to the more rural islands. A day exploring the town allows you to blend in history, craftsmanship and a slice of adventure – not to mention the world's strongest kava.

Community Nakamals

Nakamals are communal meeting places that originated as ceremonial centres for *kastom* protocol – once the exclusive domain of chiefs, these communal areas now function as kava bars in Port Vila. *Nakamals* are foundational to the capital's social landscape, serving as refuges where people can decompress from the stress of modern living.

How to

Getting around: Central Port Vila is walkable, but taxis and public transport are also easily accessible.

When to go: Time your walk to finish at sunset with a drink at the Kava Lounge.

For shell beginners: Pace yourself at the kava bar!

01 Hideaway Island Start with a visit to the world's one and only underwater post office, which is just a 10-minute boat ride from Mele Beach, at Hideaway Island. Entry fees include a day pass to the island.
Hideaway Island (7.6km)
Quartier Français
FROM LEFT: IGNACIO PALACIOS/GETTY IMAGES, THOMAS COCKREM/ALAMY
CHAMPAGNE
Route de la Teouma
02 Hebrida Market Place (pictured) Take a cab to this market buzzing with sewing machines as local women craft hand-painted, made-to-order clothing and accessories. You can purchase authentic ni-Vanuatu handicrafts directly from artisans here.
R Bougainville
Lini Hwy
R Carnot
R de Paris
Ave du General de Gaulle
TASSIRIKI
Vila Bay
Independence Park
03 Port Vila Market (pictured) Open 24 hours from Monday to Saturday, this bustling centrally located market is the best place to get a taste of Vanuatu's fresh fruit and local cuisine.
Ave Edmond Colordeau
Iririki Ferry
Rue Dartois
Rue Cornwall
Kumul Hwy
Iririki
SEASIDE
700
Rue Picarde
Captain Cook Ave
Erakor Lagoon
NAMBATU
04 Vanuatu National Museum Take a walk through 3000 years worth of Vanuatu's history. There are daily sand drawing (p84) demonstrations with Edgar Hige – one of Vanuatu's most renowned sand-drawing artists.
Rue d'Anjou
05 Kava Lounge There is no shortage of kava bars in town but Kava Lounge just south of central Port Vila is a resounding favourite amongst locals and visitors alike.
Wharf Rd
Elluk Rd
0 500 m
0 0.25 miles

07 Cultural TRADITION

HERITAGE | HISTORY | STORYTELLING

In Bislama (Vanuatu's local pidgin language), *kastom* encompasses the protocols of ni-Vanuatu, covering everything from economics and governance to art and magic. As you journey through Vanuatu, pay special attention to *kastom*; be it through *kastom* stories – (legends and folktales that preserve communal histories or *kastom tabu)* – objects and gestures of sacred significance.

THOMAS COCKREM/ALAMY

How to

When to go: Efate comes to life in Fest'Napuan Melanesian music festival (p86) each October.

Getting around: Public minivans travel around Efate Island without predesignated stops (you tell them where you're headed when you board) and offer an adventurous, affordable alternative to taxis.

Tip: Tempting as it may be to capture every moment in a photo, consider taking time before bringing out your camera – presence goes a long way towards forging a meaningful understanding of *kastom*.

RICHARD I'ANSON/GETTY IMAGES

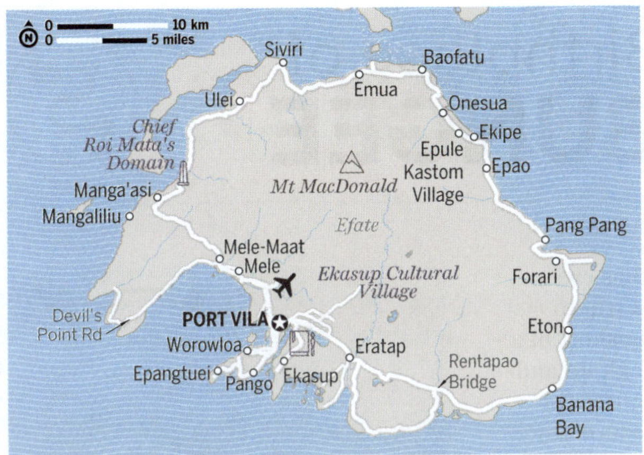

Immerse in Kastom

Steeped in Heritage **Ekasup Cultural Village**, a 20-minute ride from Port Vila, is a living museum cloaked in *kastom*. Ekasup is the ideal half-day experience to kick off your immersion into ni-Vanuatu ways of life. Run by a local family who hail from Futuna, one of the archipelago's smallest islands, Ekasup offers educational immersive tours that invite visitors into a microcosm of ni-Vanuatu culture – advance bookings are encouraged, but not necessary.

Make the Most of It There are two two-hour-long group tours at Ekasup scheduled from Sunday to Friday. On Friday nights, the village offers a 'Feast Night' with entertainment and plenty of kava on tap. For a more intimate experience, however, you can drop in or call to request a private tour. Entry fees are around 3000VT, and tipping is encouraged. Guides are generous in narrating the wisdom of *kastom*: How to weave stories into mats, How to trap wild boars and preserve food through the winter using Indigenous technology, and How to heal with forest herbs. Budget enough time to take in each of the tour guides' immersive lessons, and be sure to take a moment to meditate inside the giant banyan tree on site.

Beyond Efate There is no shortage of cultural villages across the archipelago. Vanuatu's tourism website *(vanuatu.travel/en/stay/by-type/village-experiences)* offers an up-to-date database of various homestays where you can explore and arrange overnight *kastom* immersions.

Rising to the Occasion

Over seven centuries ago, a formidable leader named Chief Roi Mata became the first to successfully unite the numerous warring tribes across present-day Vanuatu. The legacy of Roi Mata's enduring *kastom* governance has been preserved in three main sites across Efate and its surrounds: Mangaas, Lelepa and Eretoka. Collectively known as **Chief Roi Mata's Domain**, these landmarks were the first in Vanuatu to be designated as UNESCO World Heritage sites. Mangaas is the site of Roi Mata's residence; while Fels Cave on Lelepa Island is home to rock art tied to his reign; and Eretoka is where Roi Mata was laid to rest.

08 Birthplace of BUNGEE

CEREMONY | SPORT | TRADITION

If bungee jumping has ever been on your bucket list, a trip to Pentecost Island is nothing short of a pilgrimage. The annual Naghol Land Diving Ceremony here inspired AJ Hackett to develop the modern-day daredevil activity. A remarkable ritual, the Naghol features young men leaping over 30m with only tree vines tied around their ankles.

How to

When to go: The Naghol only takes place on Saturdays between April and June. Plan in advance, as the ceremony is one of Vanuatu's most popular attractions.

Getting here & around: Most people come on an organised tour. There is no public transport on Pentecost Island. The only ways to get around are by private trucks or hitchhiking – the latter is often expensive.

Money: Locals in South Pentecost are well aware of the value of their cultural ceremony and prices are steep. Tours can be upwards of 50,000VT (US$400).

Jumping to Anything but Conclusions Pentecost Island is a rural paradise that serves as a visceral reminder that Indigenous culture forms the backbone of what many revere about 'modernity'. In the annual Naghol Land Diving ceremony, hundreds of young men in South Pentecost look fear in the eye – climbing upwards of 30m on platforms made exclusively from tree branches, with vines tied around their ankles.

Organised Tours The easiest way to immerse in this ceremonial spectacle is through an organised tour with local operators such as Vanuatu EcoTours *(vanuatuecotours.com/tours/pentecost-vanuatu-land-diving)*. Tour operators arrange local charter

Top right and bottom right
Naghol Land Diving ceremony

PVINCE73/SHUTTERSTOCK

Conscious Protocols

As the young men performing the Naghol's daring land dives scale to steeper heights, only one thing is forbidden: looking back. Having reached the top, they usher themselves into manhood with one brave leap at a time. Vanuatu's government banned commercial filming of the Naghol in 2006 in order to protect the ceremony's cultural integrity. Recreational photography and video is allowed, but each visitor is encouraged to ask before filming. Permission to film can cost upwards of 15,000VT – considered a token of appreciation for the local community.

flights to Pentecost's **Lonorore Airport** via Air Taxi Vanuatu, or Unity Airlines, as well as lodging via homestays, which are the only form of accommodation available on the island. After catching the 45-minute flight from Port Vila, arriving in Pentecost you will be met by a lush landscape where *kastom* is king. A weekend-long trip is around 130,000VT.

Independent Travel If you opt to arrange your own trip, be prepared to spend 15,000–30,000VT a day on a car/driver hire. Make sure to coordinate transport and local lodging in advance. A 4WD car and local driver is essential, owing to the island's road conditions and lack of road markings.

STEVE DAVEY PHOTOGRAPHY/ALAMY

09 Chasing Shades OF BLUE

BEACHES | WATERFALLS | CAVES

Vanuatu's shores and aquatic enclaves glisten in immaculate shades of blue – from spirited waterfalls like Efate's Mele Cascades to Tanna's Blue Cave, the archipelago's waters offer adventure and refuge in tandem. Vividly imbued with Vanuatu's *kastom* stories and well stewarded by locals whose reverence for nature is paramount, these beaches and caves are the epitome of ecological treasures.

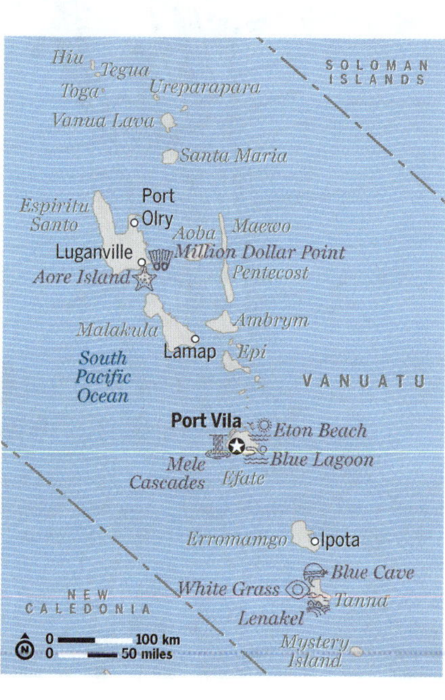

How to

Getting here & around: Daily flights connect Port Vila and Tanna/Espiritu Santo; minibus services run on these three islands. Elsewhere hire a car (10,000–15,000VT).

When to go: The dry season (May–October) is best for calm seas and less rain.

Money: Some beaches and caves ask for a small entry fee; bring cash (2000–3000VT) with you.

Accessibility: Vanuatu's waterfalls, caves and beaches usually require a bit of hiking – keep this in mind if you are travelling with kids or have mobility constraints.

Caves, Coves & Cascades

Efate From Port Vila, make your way to the **Mele Cascades**, a 30-minute drive from town followed by a 25-minute hike through rainforest. The water at these tiered waterfalls tumbles into crystal-clear pools that are nothing short of purifying. The **Blue Lagoon** on Efate's southeastern coast en route to **Eton Beach** is famous for its rope swings.

Tanna The **Blue Cave** on Tanna is etched into cliffs on the island's northwest coast, a one- to two-hour drive from **Lenakel** or 30-minute boat ride from **White Grass**. Most accommodation providers offer guided trips to these sites for an additional cost.

Top right Blue Lagoon **Bottom right** Blue Cave

MARTIN VALIGURSKY/SHUTTERSTOCK

VIKRAM VILASAGARAM/GETTY IMAGES

WWII's Afterlife in Vanuatu

World War II thrust Vanuatu – at the time called the New Hebrides – into the spotlight. In 1942, the US established military bases on Efate and Espiritu Santo to counter Japanese advances, and by the end of the war, over 500,000 troops had passed through. The war left a dual legacy: the rapid militarisation disrupted traditional life, but it also catalysed the development of infrastructure and seeded international solidarities, as ni-Vanuatu formed relationships with the African American troops stationed there.

Espiritu Santo Million Dollar Point, close to central Luganville's accommodation offerings, is a dive site steeped in ecological tragedy – at the end of WWII, the Americans dumped all of their excess construction materials here. A snorkelling expedition is bittersweet, with the world's largest underwater dump site now cloaked in coral and teeming with marine life.

Dugongs These endangered creatures are abundant in Vanuatu's azure waters. Amid climate change and the degradation of their seagrass habitat, they are most easily spotted from June to September around **Aore Island**.

10 Erupting with CULTURE

VOLCANOES | FESTIVALS | MYSTICISM

Tanna Island is equal parts raw and captivating – where volcanoes, mysticism and traditional villages converge. From the ever-present rumble of Mt Yasur to enchanted villages where the eclectic John Frum cult thrives, Tanna offers an unparalleled portal into Vanuatu's spiritual and natural worlds.

DAVID KIRKLAND/DESIGN PICS EDITORIAL/UNIVERSAL IMAGES GROUP VIA GETTY IMAGES

How to

Getting here: Tanna's **White Grass Airport** is an hour-long flight from Port Vila.

When to go: The best time to visit is during the dry season (May–October), when the weather is mild. There are fewer travellers during the off-season (November–March) but be prepared for the rain to interrupt your volcano expedition.

Where to stay: Lenakel is Tanna's main town, and home to most of the resort accommodation. The bulk of the offerings (bungalows and homestays) are near Mt Yasur.

PAUL HARDING 00/SHUTTERSTOCK

Pilgrimage to a Volcano

There are very few places where you can be driven 150m away from the mouth of a cinematically active volcano, but Tanna is one of them. One of the world's most accessible active volcanoes, **Mt Yasur** is a site of immense spiritual significance to Tanna's Indigenous inhabitants. With no railing separating lava pilgrims from the volcano's mouth – known for its belching, molten lava and lunging hot rocks – a voyage to Mt Yasur is as treacherous as it is thrilling.

With the support of a guide and driver arranged through your organised tour or local accommodation, you can make your way to the rim by car, opt for a 45-minute walk up from the main road, or make your way up on horseback. After paying the 9750VT entrance fee, you walk up to the top – the

PETER UNGER/GETTY IMAGES

Tanna on the Big Screeen

Yakel Village is the setting of Vanuatu's most famous film: *Tanna* (2015). Filmed by a crew of only two Australian filmmakers who spent six months living in the community, the Romeo-and-Juliet tale inspired by true events was the first film set in Vanuatu to be nominated for the Oscars.

Far left and botom left Mt Yasur **Above** Tanna Island

driver will wait until you are ready to return to your accommodation. For an added dose of adventure, consider ashboarding (think snow-boarding, but on soft volcanic ash) on your way back down the slope. Be sure to bring along a face covering to protect yourself from volcanic ash, and keep up to date with local eruption advisories in advance of your visit.

Black-Sand Beaches

Tanna Island's black-sand beaches, such as **Louniel Beach** on the northeast coast and **Iwaru Beach** south of **Lenakel**, owe their unique sands to Mt Yasur's volcanic activity. On Tanna's eastern coastline lies **Lowakel's Cove**, a secluded black-sand beach framed by jungle and volcanic rock formations. These beaches are accessible via 4WD vehicles (which can be arranged through your accom-modation) and a short hike. Local folklore speaks of ancestral spirits inhabiting these shores, with legends of Yasur's eruptions be-ing manifestations of these spirits' emotions.

The Birth of John Frum

The John Frum phenomenon first surfaced on Tanna in the 1930s amidst rising discontent with colonial taxation and Christian missionaries. By the early 1940s, the arrival of American troops who came bearing radios, Coca-Cola and unanticipated generosity fuelled the belief in a mysterious saint named John Frum – a figure associated with the Americans – who would one day return to bring abundance and restore Indigenous ni-Vanuatu autonomy. The stark contrast between local scarcity and military excess sparked dreams of liberation and political self-determination, which led locals to start holding nighttime rituals – building mock airstrips and donning makeshift uniforms in the hopes of summoning Frum's promised 'cargo'.

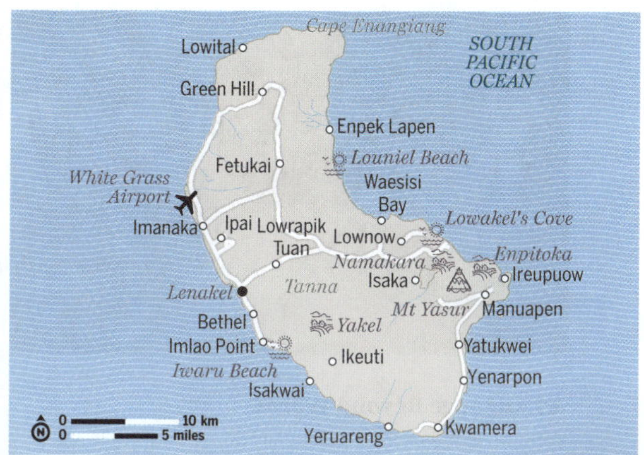

Left Followers of John Frum **Below** Iwaru Beach

Syncretised Spectacles

Held annually on 15 February, **John Frum Day** is a most eclectic cultural spectacle rooted in Tanna's cargo cult traditions. Birthed out of a complex history of Western influences from WWII syncretising with local mysticism, this holiday consists of local **Namakara** villagers donning military-style attire, performing synchronised marches, and raising the American flag. On Friday nights, Namakara hosts big dances and welcomes visitors to join in as witnesses to the spectacle.

Celebrating Reconciliation

In the 1700s, a gathering at **Enpitoka** village's *nakamal* in East Tanna celebrating the end of a conflict between two neighbouring tribes led to the birth of what would come to be one of the island's most remarkable ceremonies: the **Nekowiar** (also known as the Toka). At the (occasionally irregular) behest of local *kastom* chiefs, people from across the island come together for three days and three nights in this bonanza of reconciliation. The celebrations feature traditional *napen napen* and *toka* dancing, and culminate in the Niel – an exchange of kava and pigs that symbolises the mending of any past quarrels or disputes. Contact a local tour operator via one of the Vanuatu Tourism offices to plan your visit.

Sand Drawing

AN ANCIENT MEMORY-KEEPING TRADITION

At surface level, Vanuatu's sand drawings are precisely what their name suggests: drawings etched in sand. But there are multitudes encrypted within this ancient practice. Each one is a cultural library – cataloguing genealogies, environmental protocols, oral histories, healing traditions and community ethics.

Left Men sand drawing, Vanuatu **Centre** Completed A sand drawing **Right** Sand drawing, Vanuatu

HEMIS/ALAMY

A Language Beyond Words

Vanuatu is the most linguistically dense country in the world. Despite its small population of under 400,000, this nation's archipelago is home to over 130 different vernaculars. The most universal expressive medium between these islands, however, is not a spoken language – it is an ancient artistic practice: sand drawing. A Raga chief once explained to a visiting researcher that sand drawing preceded spoken language because the ni-Vanuatu believed that the Earth spoke for itself. On beaches and beneath jungle canopies, skilled practitioners use their fingertips to incant motifs in volcanic ash or coral sand with just a single continuous line. The resulting artworks are more than just whimsical designs – they express encoded wisdoms carried through generations as a living archive of folklore, relational protocol and Indigenous mythology.

Preserving the Intangible

The storied swirls and grids definitive of sand drawing represent a form of Indigenous technology as eloquent as it is ephemeral; after each etching, the sand drawings are erased. With much of ni-Vanuatu culture being passed down through oral storytelling, the consistency of sand drawing designs and the folktales that accompany them across Vanuatu's many islands is a testimony to the durability of *kastom* as a cultural infrastructure. Despite there being no written record of the full library of sand drawings, some expert practitioners have upwards of 400 designs memorised. In 2008, UNESCO added Vanuatu's sand drawings to its list of Intangible Cultural Heritage – a promotion intended to preserve this graphic tradition's

CYOSHI/GETTY IMAGES

ERIC LAFFORGUE/ART IN ALL OF US/ CORBIS VIA GETTY IMAGES

importance as one that demands rigorous safeguarding. At the **Vanuatu National Museum** in Port Vila, renowned sand drawing artist Edgar Hige leads daily demonstrations of this mesmerising craft.

Cultural Encoding

In recent decades, academics in the field of ethnomathematics have been captivated by the logic present in Vanuatu's sand drawings. When American mathematician and ethnomathematics pioneer Marcia Ascher embarked on a study of sand drawings in the 1980s, her findings established that the sand drawings embodied foundational principles in advanced graph theory. Through interpretations of sand drawings' recursive motifs and meticulous designs, Ascher's findings contested Western assumptions about the origins of mathematical knowledge. Bearing eerie similarity to Celtic sigils and geometric designs in Tamil Nadu, Vanuatu's sand drawings suggest a constellation of algorithmic kinship expressed through sacred arts across the Indigenous world.

> Through interpretations of sand drawings, Ascher's findings contested Western assumptions about the origins of mathematical knowledge

A Plurality of Tongues

Language is a map of encounters, and Vanuatu's linguistic landscape is a testimony to this. From 1906 to 1980, Vanuatu was governed by the Condominium – an unusual joint administration by both the British and the French – during which time Port Vila bore the weight of two colonisers imposing separate systems on one land. This arrangement resulted in dual systems of governance, law and education, with separate courts, police forces and even health services for British and French residents. While British and French residents operated in silos, ni-Vanuatu forged a creolised path, blending European languages with their Indigenous tongues to create Bislama. Today, Port Vila's trilingualism – English, French and Bislama – persists as a manifestation of the sum of these influences.

Listings

BEST OF THE REST

Kastom Villages

Leweton Cultural Village, Espiritu Santo

Water drumming is a sacred spectacle performed by ni-Vanuatu women that you can witness at this traditional centre that showcases arts from the Banks Islands.

Emiotungun Village, West Ambrym Island

This village is the site of ancient carvings. Polipetagever villagers perform everything from Rom dances and sand drawing demonstrations to string-band performances and magic shows.

Toak Village, East Ambrym Island

Home to a unique Maritime Mobility project that aims to establish a cargo vessel to service the entire Ambrym region *(toaklink.vanuatucloud.com)*, Toak is another great place to witness the Rom dance and local magic shows.

Yaohnanen Village, Tanna Island

This cargo cult village regards the late Prince Phillip as a deified figure whose origins trace back to the island as a descendent of their mountain spirit. His visit to Vanuatu in 1974 continues to reverberate in its spiritual landscape.

Laone Village, North Pentecost Island

Laone village is the birthplace of Vanuatu's founding father and first prime minister, Walter Lini. Laone Guesthouse has three guest rooms that can accommodate up to six guests.

WWII Landmarks

South Pacific WWII Museum, Luganville

The exploitation of Vanuatu during WWII due to its geopolitical significance is nothing to celebrate, but this museum offers useful context through its artifacts, photographs and narratives from that era.

Quonset Huts, Espiritu Santo

Vanuatu was the US's largest WWII outpost, second only to Pearl Harbor. Remnants of are scattered across Espiritu Santo, including this group of semi-cylindrical structures built by US forces that have been repurposed by locals.

SS President Coolidge, Luganville

Once a luxury liner, this vessel now rests as a haunting relic in the waters off Luganville. It is considered one of the world's most accessible shipwreck sites. Aore Adventures *(aore adventures.com)* in Espiritu Santo offers dives to each of Santo's shipwreck sites.

USS Tucker, off Espiritu Santo

This US Navy destroyer struck an Allied mine in 1942 near Malo Island. It was the first ship to be made predominantly from stainless steel. At around 115m long, this vessel's remains are now broken in two and covered with coral.

MV Henry Bonneaud, off Espiritu Santo

A coastal trader sunk during WWII, the MV *Henry Bonneaud* wreck lies at a depth suitable for recreational divers and is known for its intact structure and the vibrant marine ecosystem it supports.

Tui Tawaite Coastal Trader Shipwreck, Segond Channel

This ship from New Zealand was used for oil salvage on the SS *Coolidge* and was intentionally sunk in the 1980s to serve as a dive wreck site. It's located in the Segond Channel, between Santo and Aore Islands.

Festivals & Traditional Celebrations

Fest'Napuan, Port Vila

Held in October, this music festival is Vanuatu's biggest cultural event showcasing contemporary and traditional sounds. Local artists come together to celebrate Melanesian music alongside international genres like reggae.

Yam Festival, South Malekula

Known locally as the Yanarawia Festival, this bonanza involves ceremonies dedicated to Majikjiki, the spirit believed to bless the harvest. Offerings such as bananas, taro and fish are presented in the *nakamal* (village meeting place) as tokens of gratitude.

Big Nambas' Erpnavet, Malekula Island

Big Nambas men lather themselves in coconut oil and charcoal, adorn their hair with feathers, and invoke the spirit of a hawk in this captivating ceremony.

Nalawan Festival, Malekula Island

This festival in Malekula Island's southwest bay features participants adorned in elaborate Nalawan masks, hand-carved with intricate patterns. Storytelling, drumming and traditional dance punctuate the festivities.

Back to My Roots Festival, North Ambrym

Held in August, this multiday festival celebrates ni-Vanuatu traditions, through performances of the Rom dance, intricate sand drawings and demonstrations of traditional craftsmanship such as wood carving.

Natural Marvels & Sacred Landscapes

Aoba/Ambae Volcano

This otherworldly volcano's summit features a crater lake that enchants locals and visitors alike in its mineral-induced magic tricks which change its colour from blue to bright red. According to local *kastom* Chief Virenaliu Paul Vuhu, this volcano and its lakes are the sacred paradise where spirits take residence after death.

BRANDI MUELLER/GETTY IMAGES

USS Tucker

Aneityum, Mystery Island

Mystery Island – a picture-perfect sandy islet just off of Aneityum – is believed to be home to ghosts, which render it uninhabitable to locals, but mystically compelling to curious visitors.

Champagne Beach, Espiritu Santo

Champagne Beach is renowned for its powdery white sands and inviting turquoise waters. The beach gets its name from the effervescent bubbles that rise from the volcanic sea floor during low tide, which create a champagne-like effect.

Mount Marum & Mount Benbow, Ambrym Island

These two volcanoes are a strenuous trek away from Ranon Village (one day) or Port Vatu (multiday). Intrepid travellers who solicit the help of a local guide can brave these two volcanoes and be rewarded by the beauty of their bubbling lava lakes.

Turtle Bay Beach, Tanna Island

Located on Tanna Island's southeast coast, Turtle Bay Beach is renowned for its tranquil waters and opportunities to spot sea turtles.

Lake Letas, Gaua Island

This freshwater lake in northern Vanuatu is located inside Gaua Volcano's caldera and is the largest lake in Vanuatu.

NEW CALEDONIA
BEACHES | ADVENTURE | CULTURE

NEW CALEDONIA

Trip Builder

New Caledonia, with the world's largest lagoon and continuous coral reef, offers stunning beaches and vibrant reefs. It's a haven for nature lovers. The Kanak culture thrives with deep-rooted traditions, while French influence adds a European charm.

Enjoy a snorkel at **Baie des Citrons** in Noumea.

LEFT TO RIGHT: NORINORI303/SHUTTERSTOCK, MATHILDE RECEVEUR/GETTY IMAGES, DAMSEA/SHUTTERSTOCK, DELPIXEL/SHUTTERSTOCK. PREVIOUS SPREAD: DAMSEA/SHUTTERSTOCK

LOYALTY ISLANDS
0 50 km
0 25 miles
SOUTH PACIFIC OCEAN
Ouvéa
Fayaoué
Wé
Lifou
La Roche
Tadine
Maré
a Côte Oubliée
anala
Thio
Boulouparis
PROVINCE SUD
Tontouta
Païta
Dumbéa
Mont-Dore
NOUMEA
Yaté
Prony
Port Boisé
Vao
Hike and swim amongst the natural wonders of **Parc Provincial de la Rivière Bleue** (p105).
1½hrs from Noumea
Windsurf, Kayak or snorkel the azure waters of **Îlot Maître** (pictured above, p105).
15mins from Noumea
Take in the breathtaking marine wonders of **Amédée Lighthouse** (p105).
10mins from Noumea
Visit stunning beaches and marine life of the **Île-des-Pins** (pictured, p96).
1hr from Noumea

Practicalities

MTCURADO/GETTY IMAGES

ARRIVING

Tontouta International Airport Noumea's primary gateway (pictured) is 45 minutes from Noumea. There are regular shuttles running from the international airport into Noumea which can be booked online though Arc en Ciel or in person. Some accommodation also arranges airport transfers or you can hire a rental car.

Port of Noumea Cruise ships anchor here. Shuttle buses take passengers to the Cruise Ship Terminal where there are waterfront dining options.

HOW MUCH FOR A

Beer
400–600 CFP

Croissant
500–600 CFP

Medium portion of sashimi
1500–3500 CFP

GETTING AROUND

Car Renting a car is an easy way to explore the mainland of New Caledonia. A great option to visit remote beaches and natural reserves off the beaten track. Driving is on the right-hand side of the road.

Boat & Plane If you are planning to explore the smaller islands taxi boats and tours operate. Flights You can fly from Magenta Airport in Noumea to Île-des-Pins and the North Province (Koné).

Tour operators Kunié Island Services has guided minibus tours of the Île-des-Pins; South Pacific Tours has excursions throughout New Caledonia; Noumea Discovery has cruise ship excursions, including trips to Amédée Lighthouse; Private Custom Tours & Transfers has luxury options.

WHEN TO GO

JAN–MAR
The hottest months in the rainy season with lovely warm water.

APR–JUN
Cooler drier months. Ideal for exploring and hiking.

JUL–SEP
The coldest drier months. Perfect for exploring the natural areas on land.

OCT–DEC
The start of the rainy season with hot days and warm water.

EATING & DRINKING

The food of New Caledonia is a delightful blend of French and Pacific tropical cuisine. The best is the speciality *poisson cru* (pictured), a traditional Polynesian dish made with raw fish marinated in coconut milk, lime and vegetables like tomatoes and cucumbers. You'll find it in both fancy restaurants and the simplest eateries, eaten for lunch or as a starter. Follow it with the local cocktail Ti'Punch (pictured, short for 'petit punch'), combining white rum, sugar cane syrup and a splash of lime over ice.

Best poisson cru
Le Roof (p104)

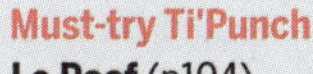

Must-try Ti'Punch
Le Roof (p104)

CONNECT & FIND YOUR WAY

Wi-fi There are a number of free hotspots, though the connection can be spotty.

Connect The best to get connected is to rent a pocket wi-fi device (at the airport) or buy a SIM card (at the post office or airport).

SAFETY

In 2024, New Caledonia experienced political unrest, with tensions between French and Kanak groups. For safety, steer clear of protests and follow your government's guidance.

WHERE TO STAY

New Caledonia is pricey, but there are plenty of attractive options. Pick somewhere near where you plan to spend the most time.

Neighbourhood	Pro/Con
Noumea City Centre	Local markets, French-style cafes, vibrant nightlife and near the waterfront.
Anse vata	Calm beach, waterfront restaurants and close to Noumea's main attractions.
Baie des Citrons	Vibrant atmosphere, bustling nightlife, waterfront dining and near main attractions.
Magenta	Quiet ambience, easy airport access and close to nature reserves and small local beaches.
Île-des-Pins	Stunning beaches, lagoons, hiking trails and a slower pace of life.
Lifou	Coral reefs, remote beaches, Kanak culture and ecotourism experiences.
Hienghène	Limestone formations, hiking trails and a deep immersion in New Caledonia's natural beauty.

MONEY

The official currency of New Caledonia is the Central Pacific Franc (CFP). Cards can be used in many places in Noumea, but carry some cash because they're accepted everywhere.

TOP: EQROY/SHUTTERSTOCK

Tropical DELIGHTS

SNORKELLING | CULINARY DELIGHTS | CORAL

Spending a day in Noumea? Stroll the promenade and savour tropical and French-inspired cuisine. Then explore pristine coral reefs, diving into crystal-clear waters for a snorkel.

WESTEND61/GETTY IMAGES

How to

Getting here/around: Downtown Noumea is easy to walk around; take a short ride in a taxi to Anse Vata to stroll the promenade and visit restaurants overlooking the water.

When to go: In the evenings and on weekends, the local community gathers to swim, play beach volleyball and socialise, creating a lively atmosphere.

Top Tip: Following a few shark incidents, shark nets have been installed to ensure safer swimming in designated areas.

The Taste of the Land

For an authentic local experience, try Kanak-inspired dishes like *bougna*, a traditional meal made with meat or seafood, root vegetables and coconut milk, wrapped in banana leaves and slow-cooked in a Kanak oven. This earth oven method uses heated stones to infuse the dish with smoky flavour and moisture.

01 Start your day at the lively **Port Moselle Market** (pictured), where you will find a vibrant array of tropical fruits and locally grown produce. Refresh yourself with a chilled coconut.

02 Enjoy a quintessentially French breakfast at **Au Péché Mignon** bakery. Try the irresistible *choux à la crème* (crispy pastry filled with luscious cream), a delightful melt-in-your-mouth experience.

03 Embark on a snorkelling excursion at **Baie des Citrons**, exploring vibrant coral reefs and colourful tropical fish (pictured).

04 In the afternoon, indulge in a scoop of gelato from **Amorino**, a local favourite. Enjoy it along the beach on the promenade, the perfect sweet treat while soaking in the coastal beauty.

05 End your day with dinner at **Le Roof**, enjoying dishes that blend local flavours with French flair, while watching schools of fish and occasional dolphins.

FROM LEFT: SERGE MELESAN/GETTY IMAGES, KAT CLAY/GETTY IMAGES

12 Island HOP

BEACHES | NATURE I CORAL

Embrace the slow pace of Island life and visit the **Île-des-Pins**. Whether you're diving with marine life, hiking through untouched landscapes, or simply marveling at the wonders of the coral reef and beautiful beaches, you will be surrounded by pristine nature. Discover new experiences as you explore hidden coves and enjoy the serenity that comes with being off the beaten path.

How to

Getting here and around: You can either fly or embrace the journey and go by the rapid catamaran, the *Betico*. The catamaran travels from Noumea to the Île-des-Pins in two and a half hours. Flights are from the domestic airport, **Magenta** and take 20 to 25 minutes.

When to go: Lovely all year.

Tip: The *Betico* operates on the weekends and only some weekdays, depending on the season.

Pirogue Trips Board a traditional pirogue in the tranquil **Bay de Upi** and drift past colossal coral boulders that seem to float in the air. Spot turtles, dolphins and manta rays gliding through the waters. You can organise your pirogue excursion with your accommodation provider. Alternatively, contact the Île des Pins tourist office to be put in touch with a *piroguier*. The departure point for the excursion is in the **Baie de St Joseph**.

Marine Wildlife Surrounded by towering columnar pines, dive into the crystal-clear waters of **Oro Bay**, a marine sanctuary teeming with corals and a rainbow of fish. For those wanting to delve deeper into the marine world, embark on a diving adventure with **Kunié Scuba Center**. It has all the equipment you need and great

Top right Oro Bay **Bottom right** Grotte de la Reine Hortense

Marine Wonders

New Caledonia is home to a vast lagoon, encircled by a stunning 1600km coral reef – the third most extensive reef system in the world. This vibrant marine realm boasts an exceptional diversity of coral and fish species. The waters of New Caledonia also provide habitats for numerous threatened marine species, including turtles, whales and dugongs; in fact, the world's third-largest population of dugongs can be found here. Additionally, giant reef manta rays can be spotted at several sites across the archipelago, including the picturesque Île-des-Pins.

guides. Dive in the awe-inspiring **Ouaméo Bay**, where coral reefs and a kaleidoscope of fish and turtles await.

Cave Adventures Discover the fascinating **Grotte de la Reine Hortense**, a cave adorned with giant stalactites, bats and tangled banyan roots. Sites such as this represent the spiritual connection to ancestors and spirits to the indigenous Kanak people. If you want to explore the tunnel as far as its air shaft, don't forget to bring a torch. Bring cash to pay the entry fee (500 CFP).

Cycling While the Île-des-Pins is comparatively small, the attractions are not within walking distance. Rent a bicycle (or a car) to get around.

13 Wild West of the PACIFIC

RIDING | BEACHES | WILD WEST

Immerse yourself in the Wild West. Horse ride and take part in a cattle drive, but also find time to simply sit on the beach and watch the light play over the largest lagoon in the world.

YAN CAZABAN/SHUTTERSTOCK

How to

Getting here & around: The best way to get around this expansive area is to have your own wheels. It is easy to hire a car, and the drive is pleasant on well-maintained roads.

When to go: This area is lovely all year. In the hotter months, the ocean is warmer. April–September is cooler for hiking and horse riding.

Tip: Keep an eye out for fresh in-season produce like watermelons on the side of the road, a great addition to a picnic.

JIM/FLICKR/CC BY-NC-ND 2.0

Lagoon Experiences

Experience the clear, calm waters and striking geological formations at **La Roche Percée** and the expansive, lagoon-like beauty of **Plage de Poe**. The beach is renowned for its long, wide stretch of white sand that meets a shallow, calm lagoon. The lagoon of Poe Beach lies within the **New Caledonian Reef Marine Park**, as a result, the waters are teeming with marine life.

The highlight of swimming at La Roche Percée is the opportunity to swim near the famous pierced rock itself. As you approach the rocky formation, you can see how the ocean has eroded the stone over millennia, creating a natural archway that towers above the water. Depending on the tide, it's possible to swim through the arch. This location has dramatic rock formations, offset by the blue

ANDREW BAIN/ALAMY

The Bossards

The Bossards, or Broussards, live in Grande Terre's rural regions. Hailing from the west and north plains, they proudly embrace a unique identity shaped by a turbulent history and diverse influences. Their culture blends traditions of hunting, fishing, livestock breeding, agriculture and far-west heritage.

Far left Plage de Poe **Left** Domaine de Deva (p100) **Above** La Roche Percée sea, and the lush green hills. The **Baie des Tortues** (Turtle Bay) is a stunning beach. It is named after the many loggerhead turtles that come here to lay their eggs every year between November and February. The bay's unique feature is its many columnar pine trees, which are native to New Caledonia. Despite the beauty of this beach and its spectacular waves, the rollers can be dangerous. You are therefore advised to go to La Roche Percée or Poe to swim.

Deva, an Adventurer's Paradise

Explore 158km of marked trails for hiking, horse riding and mountain biking which run through 1700 hectares of dry forest. When you enter **Domaine de Deva** nature reserve make sure to look out for the traditional wood-carved totems of the Kanak.

For a quick but spectacular 15-minute hike, go to **Oua Koue** viewpoint. From here you can look down at the Shark Fault. This small hike has clearly marked tracks from the huts a few

Kanak, People of the Land

The Kanak people of New Caledonia have a rich cultural heritage deeply rooted in tradition, spirituality and connection to nature. Central to their culture are wooden totems, known as *gongs*, which are sacred symbols of clan identity and ancestral spirits. Carved from wood, these totems often represent important figures, animals or natural elements that embody the tribe's beliefs. Each totem is intricately designed with symbols and patterns that communicate stories, values and spiritual connections to the land. They are revered objects that play an integral role in ceremonies, rituals and the transmission of oral history, preserving the Kanak legacy for future generations.

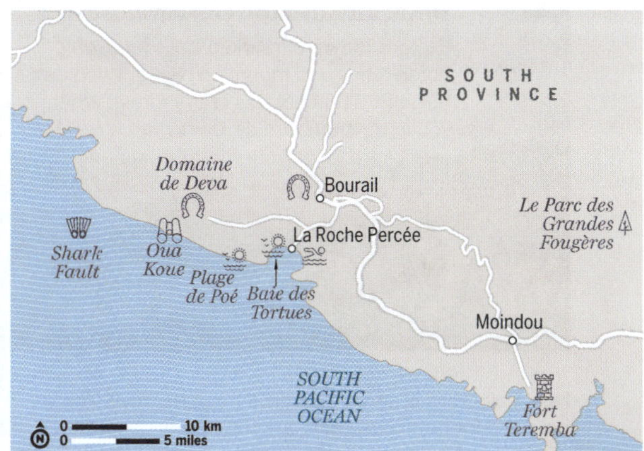

Left Kanak carving, New Caledonia
Below Boussards, New Caledonia

metres before the Sheraton Deva entrance. Follow the arrows up the trail. There is not much shade so head up in the early morning or late afternoon and avoid the heat in the hotter months.

The **Shark Fault** connects the lagoon to the reef. The site is home to exceptional biodiversity. Divers can spot turtles and different species of sharks, rays and fish. If you get up high – either by taking one of the Domaine de Deva's hiking trails or a microlight flight – you will be dazzled by the magnificent palette of colours below. The colours are accentuated by low tide.

Ride with Cowboys

Bourail's natural beauty is best experienced on horseback. The region is known for its sprawling cattle ranches, and several local operators offer horse-riding tours in the surrounding countryside. These tours take you through vast grassy plains, along rivers and up into the hills for panoramic views of the coastline and mountains.

For the full Wild West experience reside with the local Boussards (French cowboys) and embrace the bush culture. You may be lucky enough to join in the incredible spectacle of a cattle drive, when cattle are mustered by riders across the rolling plains. To find authentic homestay experiences, reach out to New Caledonia's tourism offices.

Wonders of New Caledonian Nature

ENDLESS HORIZONS, VIBRANT REEFS, NATURE'S BEAUTY.

New Caledonia is a haven for unique and extraordinary species. Many of these creatures, plants and reptiles are found only on this small island, making it a biodiversity hotspot with species that exist nowhere else on Earth.

Left Rivière Bleue **Centre** Leach's giant gecko **Right** Cagou

AURELIEN DUCOS/SHUTTERSTOCK

New Caledonia is a true biological treasure trove. This paradise for botanists holds a rich diversity of species, with 75% of its plant species found nowhere else on Earth. The island's isolation and varied climates, which range from tropical rainforests to arid zones, have fostered the evolution of plants in fascinating and unique ways. These conditions have led to a stunning variety of endemic species that thrive in the island's diverse landscapes.

In places like the Rivière Bleue, the terrain is a striking blend of vibrant green rainforest trees and rich red soil. This area is home to a wealth of plant life, including delicate orchids that climb to the canopy, releasing subtle scents of vanilla and fruit into the air. On the forest floor, more unusual plant species, such as carnivorous plants with unusual smells and colours to attract, lie in wait. These plants have evolved intricate traps – sticky, acidic surfaces or snap-shut leaves – to capture insects. The insects are absorbed provide the nutrients not found in the surrounding poor-quality soil. A very clever solution.

New Caledonia's natural wonders aren't limited to plants; the island also supports a remarkable array of animal species. The cagou, a long-legged, white bird with a distinctive crest, is one of the most iconic symbols of New Caledonia.

Among the island's reptiles, giantism – a phenomenon where species grow larger than their relatives on the mainland – is evident. New Caledonia is home to 67 species of geckos, including the New Caledonian giant gecko, the largest of its kind in the world. These geckos often live high

LAUREN SURYANATA/SHUTTERSTOCK

THE ASAHI SHIMBUN VIA GETTY IMAGES

in the forest canopy, though they can be heard chirping loudly to each other in their search for mates. In addition, the island is home to giant monitor lizards and giant skinks, which can often be seen basking on warm rocks under the sun.

Unfortunately, New Caledonia's natural wonders face growing threats. Invasive species, brought to the island over the years, have wreaked havoc on the delicate ecosystem. Feral cats, in particular, pose a significant risk, preying on the giant geckos, cagou birds and flying foxes. Rats also cause major damage, raiding bird nests and destroying eggs and chicks, while disrupting essential ecological processes like pollination and seed dispersal. Meanwhile, deer, introduced from France, graze on over 130 plant species, preventing young trees from growing and making it difficult to replace aging forests.

Unfortunately, New Caledonia's natural wonders face growing threats – invasive species, brought to the island over the years, have wreaked havoc on the delicate ecosystem

To ensure the survival of New Caledonia's unique flora and fauna, controlling and eliminating invasive species has become a crucial step in conservation efforts. Without these actions, the island's rich biodiversity, which has developed over millions of years, could be lost forever. By addressing these environmental challenges, New Caledonia's native treasures may have a better chance of thriving allowing us the thrill of discovering these natural wonders.

Giant Geckos

New Caledonia is the home of the largest gecko in the world. Leach's giant gecko, measures 35.5cm long and weighs between 227g and 340g. At this size, you might think they are easy to find. However, members of the species camouflage themselves like chameleons, changing the colour of their pigment cells to match the bark of trees.

Listings

BEST OF THE REST

Restaurants

Marmite et Tire Bouchon, Noumea $$$

Dine in elegance; the place to get dressed up for a special occasion and splash out on a three-course French Pacific fusion culinary experience. Every meal is exquisite.

Fun Beach Restaurant & Grill, Noumea $$

Stylishly simple, enjoy the full carnivore experience with a stunning location overlooking the ocean. Grill your own steak at the table or try steak tartare for a rawer experience.

Le Roof, Noumea $$$

An exquisite location over the water. It is the perfect spot to have a glass of wine and a meal while you spot dolphins or a small shark gliding below.

Parfums de Olive, Baie des Citron $$

With warm lighting overlooking Baie des Citron, this simple but enchanting restaurant features Lebanese food with live music in the evenings.

MV Lounge, Baie des Citron $

A great spot for an evening drink with your toes in the sand of Baie des Citron. If you feel like extending your evening, there is often dancing.

Table des Gourmets, Baie de Magenta $$$

Home-cooked French style with representative French food. For the full Pacific French experience, try the duck or snails.

Bouche des Gouts, Baie des Citron $$

Conveniently located in Baie des Citron, the restaurant looks simple, but the food is anything but. The food is creative, with a menu to tempt all palates.

L'Ed'Zen, Noumea $$

With an exquisite setting away from the main strip, feast on organic fusion food in the shady little garden. Enjoy the lovely atmosphere for breakfast or dinner.

Petit Café, Noumea $$

A great atmosphere and an excellent menu that changes every week based on the seasonal fresh produce available. The homemade passionfruit cheesecake is a must.

West Food and Bar, Noumea $$

With a small but delicious menu and a lovely atmosphere, this is a relaxing place for a drink or one of the best meals in Noumea. Try the fresh tuna for a taste of the Pacific.

Cafes, Bakeries & Tasty Treats

Malongo, Noumea $

A delightful place to have a French *café au lait* and croissant in the morning or at lunch. The outside area has a lovely view of the ocean and a pleasant breeze.

Amorino, Noumea $$

The optimal way to cool down. These ice creams cannot be beaten. The biggest problem is selecting which combination of flavours to have. The mango and coconut are favourites.

L'Atelier Gourmand, Noumea $$

For a gorgeous pastry in the morning or what some call the best French baguette for lunch. Take your meal and eat it on the promenade overlooking the sea. Excellent value and delightful flavours.

Au Péché Mignon, Noumea $

For some truly delightful pastries, cakes, sandwiches and salads. On the weekends, there is a lovely breakfast area at the back. Get a takeaway pastry to eat at the waterfront.

Gourmet Heaven, Noumea $$

French gastronomy inspired pastry chefs are very busy here. There are all sorts of bread and croissants, *pain au chocolat*, and the must-taste *canelés* and *chaussons aux pommes*.

Hikes

Parc Provincial de la Rivière Bleue, southeast of Nouméa

A botanical treasure trove, this is a top location for biologists and environmental enthusiasts to explore the diversity of New Caledonia's flora and fauna. Also great for swimming with a range of trails.

Madeleine Waterfalls, near Sarraméa

Nestled in the lush landscapes of Noumea, this short hike is worth the effort. The river, surrounded by greenery and red earth, is a pleasant walk with beautiful vegetation.

Parc des Grandes Fougères, La Foa

Great Ferns Park is spread across 4535 hectares of tropical rainforest. Explore scenic walking trails in this lush, tropical landscape surrounded by ferns. Discover panoramic views, coursing waterways and rainforests.

Pic Malaoui, near Yahoué

Also known as Chapeau de Gendarme, this great half-day walk close to Noumea traverses a range of environments, from tropical forest to low heath. It culminates in brilliant sweeping views over Noumea's coast from the summit of Pic Malaoui.

Mont-Dore Peak, South Province

To combine physical effort with majestic sea and mountain scenery, take this hike! A 7.3km trail to an 800m summit offering breathtaking views of Noumea, the lagoon and the Great South.

Pic Malaoui

Top Snorkel Sites

Baie des Citrons, Noumea

Great for beginners with free shore access. Lovely coral with a reef drop-off, lots of fish species and turtles. Surrounded by a shark net.

Îlot Maître, Noumea

A beginner-level snorkel site in the heart of a 500-acre nature reserve protecting its reefs and lagoon. Lovely coral reefs and seagrass meadows, with green sea turtles, rays, sharks and reef fish.

Îlot Hienga

The underwater trail is a safe and enjoyable way to discover this lesser-known spot boasting rich biodiversity with surgeonfish, clams, butterflyfish and a variety of corals.

Pléiades, Ouvéa

Guides lead snorkellers to observe turtles and sharks; the highlight is the breathtaking sight of manta rays being cleaned by smaller fish.

Amédée Lighthouse, Amédée

One of the island jewels of the lagoon. Perfect for swimming, snorkelling, kitesurfing or diving. This is the perfect place to swim with turtles.

Jokin Cliffs, Lifou

Stunning views with clear waters, caves and towering cliffs. Snorkellers can encounter butterflyfish, parrotfish, clams and other marine life.

Îlot M'Bo, Noumea

A small island north of the lagoon of Noumea. A great setting for exploring the underwater world. Sharks, turtles and rays visit the drop-off, the reef is covered with colourful corals and colourful fish.

Dive into Kanak Culture

Hienghène, Hienghene

Get an authentic glimpse into the indigenous Kanak culture, traditions and lifestyles. Learn about traditional fishing techniques and local customs and rituals.

Perfect Family Fun

Baie des Citrons, Noumea

Calm sandy shores perfect for building sandcastles and splashing in the warm water. For older children, the snorkelling to the left of Citrons is great and a safe place to experience the marine life.

Parc Zoologique et Forestier, Noumea

Enjoy a picnic beneath the shade of magnificent trees, explore aviaries, and see the national bird, the kagu. As you stroll along the butterfly path, be on the lookout for the striking blue New Caledonian butterfly.

Aquarium des Lagons, Noumea

Find refuge from the heat or rain in this wonderful marine world. Get close up to sharks and turtles and see some marine species you did not know existed. Great for both adults and kids.

Festival Fun

Yam Festivals

The yam has great importance in New Caledonia, particularly to the Kanak people. There are several yam festivals across the country between February and April (specific dates vary by village), when each village celebrates the harvest. The Noumea yam festival features a parade, carnival, exhibitions, concerts, dancing and tastings.

Omelette Festival, Dumbéa

Held in the second week after Easter (usually in April), this festival revolves around the creation of a giant omelette in remembrance of the time Napoleon ordered a giant omelette be made for his soldiers by the townspeople of Bessieres.

Festival de la Musique, Noumea

This vibrant festival celebrates music from around the world from late May to early June, featuring performances by local and international artists across various genres, uniting New Caledonia's diverse cultural communities.

Fête de la Calédonie, Noumea

Celebrated on 24 September, this national holiday honors New Caledonia's unique identity. It includes cultural events, music and dance,

DE AGOSTINI VIA GETTY IMAGES

Aquarium des Lagons

highlighting the island's indigenous Kanak traditions and French heritage.

Kuna Festival, Hienghène

This is a traditional celebration of Kanak culture, taking place every two years, typically in October. It showcases music, dance and storytelling, emphasising local customs and spiritual practices.

Noumea Carnival, Noumea

Colourful parades, street performances, costumes, music and lively dancing. This family-friendly event celebrates New Caledonia's multicultural heritage, blending local traditions with French and Pacific influences. Held in late November or December (dates may vary each year).

Great Lagoon Regatta

The New Caledonia Great Lagoon Regatta is an international boating event open to all types and sizes of boats. The regatta is a celebration of Melanesian culture and traditions. The various stops include tropical islets and feature parties with traditional food, music and dancing. Exact dates vary annually.

New Caledonia Triathlon

The New Caledonia Triathlon is a major sporting event, attended by an excess of 300 athletes from around the world. The race takes place in May. To coincide with the fun, there are pasta parties and entertainment such as music and dance shows.

Bastille Day, Noumea

Bastille Day, held on 14 July each year is the national holiday in France and New Caledonia, marked with a military parade, fireworks, music and dancing.

Avocado Festival, Maré

The Avocado Festival offers the possibility of a homestay experience within the tribe. Numerous leisure activities, such as tastings, music and traditional dance are held to celebrate the avocado in late October.

Bourail Fair, Bourail

The Bourail Fair is a three day agricultural and craft fair held annually in October (dates can vary). Each stand at the fair showcases the best local offerings from stock-car racing, motocross, tasting of local specialties, sheep dogs, wood chopping, horse riding and the very popular rodeo.

Blackwoodstock Festival, Fort Téremba

The Blackwoodstock Rock Arts and Music Festival offers music-lovers three days of open-air concerts in the fabulous setting of Fort Téremba. Festival goers can camp onsite for an immersive experience or opt for comfort with accommodation in nearby La Foa. Held in late November (dates may vary).

Vanilla Festival, Lifou .

Lifou is well known for its vanilla plantations. During the Vanilla Festival, visitors can experience choral singing, Kanak concerts, traditional dancing, vanilla plantation visits and guided hikes on this beautiful island. Held in July or August (exact dates can vary).

Goro Nickle Fest, Goro area

Goro Nickel Fest is a two-day cultural festival held in the southern region of New Caledonia in April (dates may vary). The festival celebrates the rich cultural diversity of the region with a specific focus on music and dance.

Nengone Village Festival, Maré

The highlight of the event is the captivating display of traditional music and dance performed by the local villagers. The rhythmic beats of the drums resonate through the air as the performers, adorned in traditional attire, execute intricate dance routines. Held in November (exact dates may vary).

COOK ISLANDS

BEACHES | CULTURE | FOOD

COOK ISLANDS
Trip Builder

Encompassing droplets of land scattered across almost 2 million sq km of the Pacific Ocean, the Cook Islands are simultaneously remote, traditional, accessible and modern. Cafe- and beach-hop on relaxed Rarotonga before venturing north to Aitutaki's sublime lagoon.

Take in reef and lagoon views on Rarotonga's **Cross Island Trek** (p121).
5mins from Avarua

Learn about Cook Islands history while biking along Rarotonga's ancient **Ara Metua** (p122).
40mins from Avarua

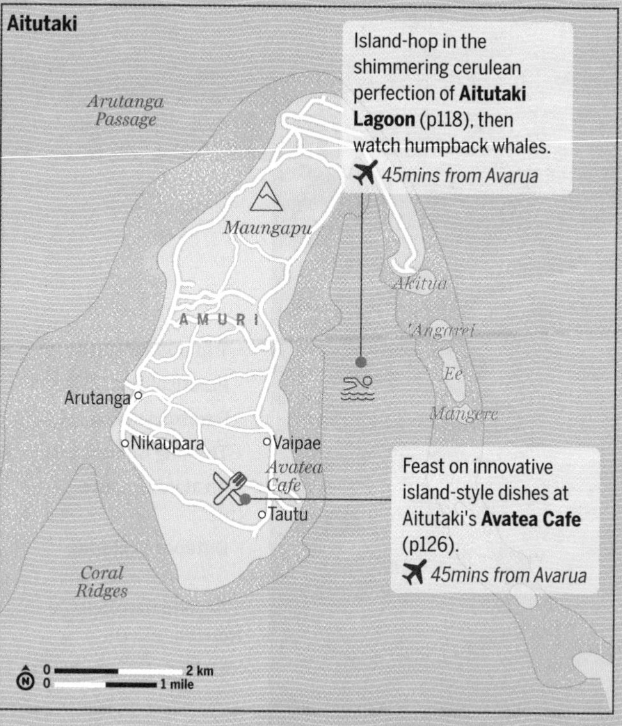

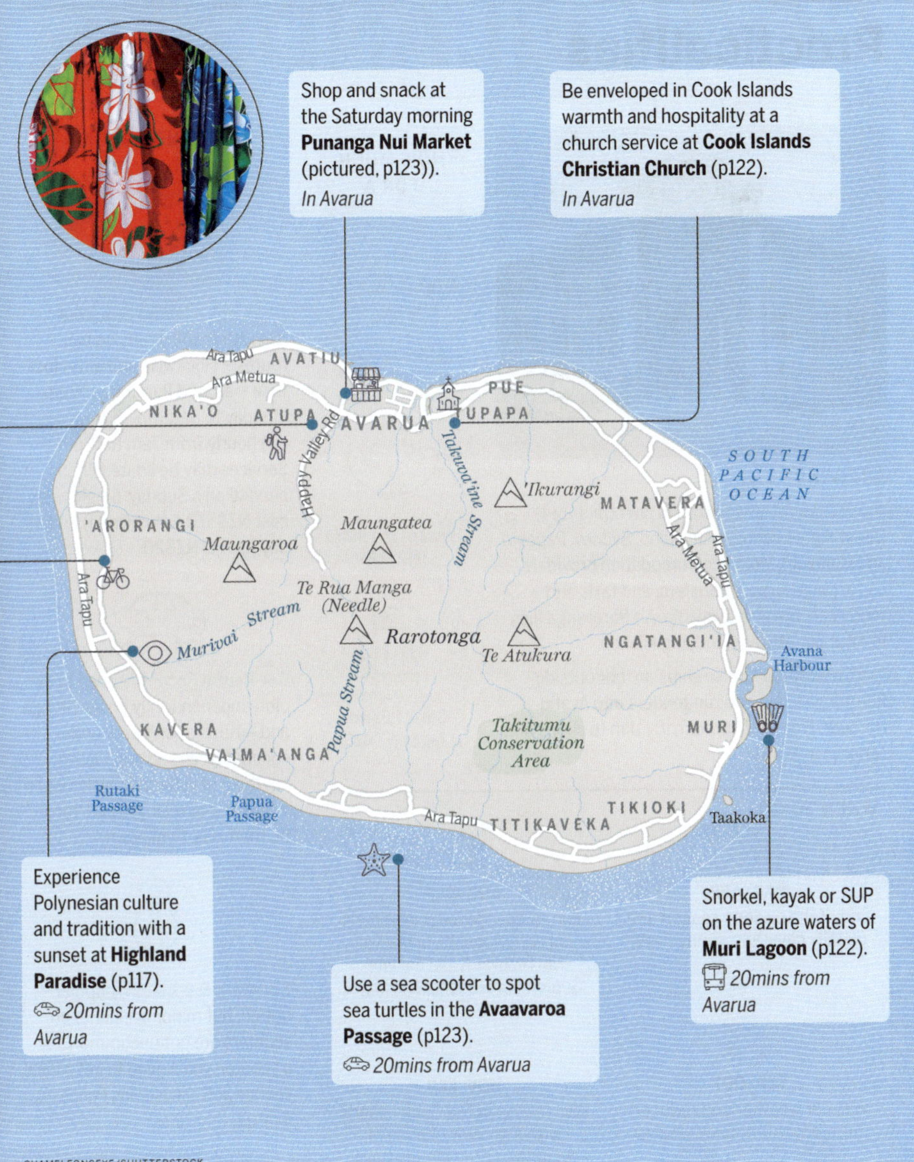

Shop and snack at the Saturday morning **Punanga Nui Market** (pictured, p123)).
In Avarua

Be enveloped in Cook Islands warmth and hospitality at a church service at **Cook Islands Christian Church** (p122).
In Avarua

Experience Polynesian culture and tradition with a sunset at **Highland Paradise** (p117).
20mins from Avarua

Use a sea scooter to spot sea turtles in the **Avaavaroa Passage** (p123).
20mins from Avarua

Snorkel, kayak or SUP on the azure waters of **Muri Lagoon** (p122).
20mins from Avarua

Practicalities

MTCURADO/GETTY IMAGES

ARRIVING

Rarotonga International Airport (pictured) Direct flights connect Auckland, Sydney, Papeete and Honolulu. Most accommodation providers can arrange airport transfers, and taxis and rental cars are also available. Air Rarotonga flies to Aitutaki, 'Atiu and outlying islands.

Avatiu Harbour Cruise ships anchor outside Rarotonga's reef and run tenders into Avatiu Harbour. From the harbour, it's 1km to shops and services in Avarua.

HOW MUCH FOR A

Muri Lagoon cruise NZ$45

Bowl of *ika mata* NZ$18

Cook Islands lager NZ$10

WHEN TO GO

MAR–APR
End of the cyclone season and usually clear and sunny days.

AUG–SEP
Join independence celebrations at early August's Te Maeva Nui Festival. Avoid the late-September NZ school holidays.

SEP–OCT
Warmer weather and reduced humidity; humpback whales can be spotted Jul–Oct.

NOV–FEB
Wet season in the Cook Islands with a greater chance of cyclones. Often cloudy days.

GETTING AROUND

Bus Cook's Island Bus *(cookislandsbus.com)* runs on two routes – clockwise and anti-clockwise – around Rarotonga. From Monday to Saturday, buses run hourly from 7am to 10pm. Services may be limited or suspended on a Sunday. Single rides cost NZ$5/3 (adult/child) and a day pass is NZ$20.

Car Rental Recommended to explore independently on Rarotonga and Aitutaki. Don't park under coconut trees and don't leave anything of value in vehicles when swimming or hiking. Opportunistic theft is not unknown.

Scooters & e-bikes A popular option, but minor accidents on scooters are not uncommon. For a scooter, you'll need to get a local licence at Cook Islands Police in Avarua.

EATING & DRINKING

Seafood is often served as *ika mata* (pictured, raw fish marinated in coconut milk and lime juice) or sashimi. Sandwiches with grilled tuna or *mahi mahi* are also popular. Tropical fruit smoothies feature at cafes and markets, and sunset happy hours offer good discounts on cocktails and beer. Local dishes include grilled *māroro* (flying fish) and *rukau* (pictured, young taro leaves and caramelised onions cooked in coconut cream). Avarua's Soul Cafe even does a *rukau* eggs Benedict.

Best fish tacos
Avatea Cafe, Aitutaki (p126)

Must-try drink A fresh *nu* (drinking coconut) at the **Punanga Nui Market** (p127), Avarua

TOP: SNOOPAYA/GETTY IMAGES

CONNECT & FIND YOUR WAY

Wi-fi Apart from a few accomodation providers, free wi-fi is uncommon in the Cook Islands. Higher-end properties offer fast paid access via the Starlink network.

Mobile service Vodafone Cook Islands provides mobile services with local SIM cards. This includes around 100 exclusive wi-fi access points around Rarotonga and Aitutaki. Vodafone has branches in Avarua and the airport arrivals area.

SOUTH PACIFIC TIME TRAVEL

Travelling to Rarotonga from New Zealand and Australia, flights cross the international date line, arriving in the Cook Islands on the previous day. Double-check your accommodation bookings.

WHERE TO STAY

Accommodation ranges from rustic self-contained beach bungalows through to luxury adults-only resorts. Renting a holiday home is recommended for families and groups.

Area	Pro/Con
Avarua	Rarotonga's compact capital. Close to shops, the Punanga Nui Market and restaurants, but often lacking beach access.
Arorangi	Larger family-focused resorts near cafes and activities. Good sunset views and a quieter Rarotonga west coast location.
Muri	Rarotonga's east coast travellers' enclave has smaller, upmarket resorts and good-value beach bungalows.
Titikaveka	Quieter Rarotonga south coast district with good holiday-home rentals and adjacent beach access. Most cafes are a drive away.
Aitutaki	Pricey resorts and affordable bungalows. No public transport. A car or scooter is needed to get around the island.

MONEY

Credit and debit cards can be used at most shops, cafes and restaurants. The New Zealand dollar (NZ$) is the Cook Islands' official currency. For market stalls, bring cash from New Zealand, or withdraw it from ATMs on Rarotonga and Aitutaki.

14 Rarotonga LOOP

MARKET | HISTORY | GARDENS

Meander around Rarotonga along this easygoing coastal route where you're guaranteed reef, lagoon and Pacific horizon views. Fuel up on island eats at Avarua's Saturday morning market before setting off. En route, there are other spots for relaxation and replenishment.

MVALIGURSKY/GETTY IMAGES

How to

Getting around: Rent an e-bike, car or scooter, or buy an all-day pass and catch the bus in a clockwise or anti-clockwise direction. You choose.

When to go: Saturday morning for the Punanga Mui Market is best, but on other days the bus will be less busy.

Dress sense: A collared shirt for men and a dress for women is appropriate for church on a Sunday morning.

South Pacific Street Art

Around 1km north-east of Black Rock, the **Marae Moana Mural** was completed in early 2024, and at 562m is the South Pacific's longest mural. Colourful images of *vaka* (canoes), and stories and legends from all of the Cooks' 15 islands feature along the vibrant and hand-painted oceanside seawall.

01 Punanga Nui Market Skip breakfast on a Saturday morning and feast on coconut buns and fruit smoothies. Lots more eating and drinking options, and you can book activities with local tour operators.

02 Cook Islands Christian Church Crafted from coral limestone, Avarua's white-washed church was built in 1853. The main service is at 10am Sunday, and visitors are welcome to stay for morning tea with the congregation.

03 Avana Harbour Reputedly where ocean-going *vaka* (canoes) departed in earlier centuries for Aotearoa (New Zealand). A stone-circle garden commemorates the seven great canoes of NZ's Māori tribal histories.

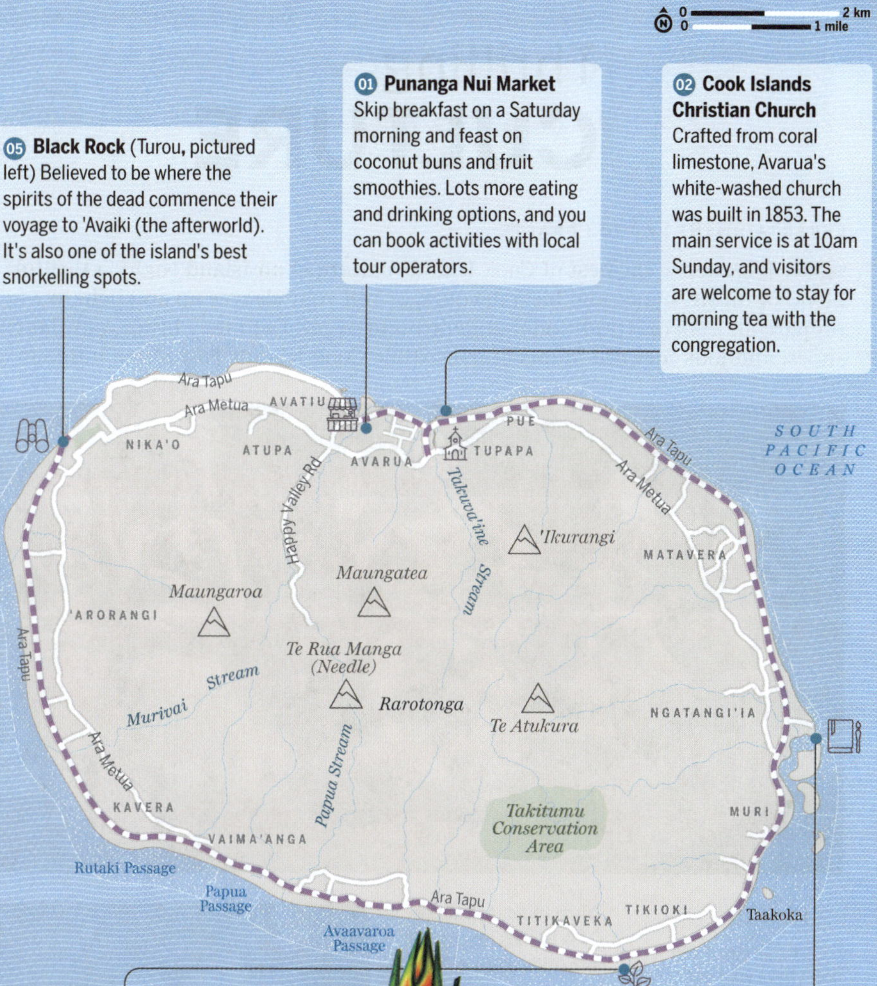

04 Maire Nui Gardens (pictured) After exploring tropical gardens featuring shaded lily ponds and mountain views, relax in the cafe to try the gardens' own organic produce and herbs. Order the cheesecake.

05 Black Rock (Turou, pictured left) Believed to be where the spirits of the dead commence their voyage to 'Avaiki (the afterworld). It's also one of the island's best snorkelling spots.

0 – 2 km
0 – 1 mile

Ara Tapu
Ara Metua
AVATIU
NIKA'O
ATUPA
AVARUA
PUE
TUPAPA
SOUTH PACIFIC OCEAN
Happy Valley Rd
Takuva'ine Stream
'Ikurangi
MATAVERA
Maungatea
Maungaroa
'ARORANGI
Te Rua Manga (Needle)
Murivai Stream
Rarotonga
Te Atukura
NGATANGI'IA
Papua Stream
KAVERA
VAIMA'ANGA
Takitumu Conservation Area
MURI
Rutaki Passage
Papua Passage
Avaavaroa Passage
TITIKAVEKA
TIKIOKI
Taakoka

DAVID WALL/ALAMY

15 Thrilling CULTURE

ENTERTAINMENT | FOOD | CRAFTS

Experience the best of Cook Islands culture at an Island Night, a thrilling blend of music, dance and local flavours, or roll your sleeves up and help to prepare an *umukai* (traditional underground oven). Definitely bring your dancing shoes, and look forward to lots of irresistible Cook Islands Polynesian humour.

CHAMELEONSEYE/SHUTTERSTOCK

How to

Getting there: If you don't have your own vehicle, ask if transport – either free or paid – is available to get you to and from Island Night venues.

When to go: Ask at the Cook Islands tourist information office in Avarua for a weekly schedule of Island Nights around Rarotonga.

Getting moving: Audience participation at Island Nights is encouraged. Good luck learning a few local dance moves.

NIK WHEELER/CORBIS VIA GETTY IMAGES

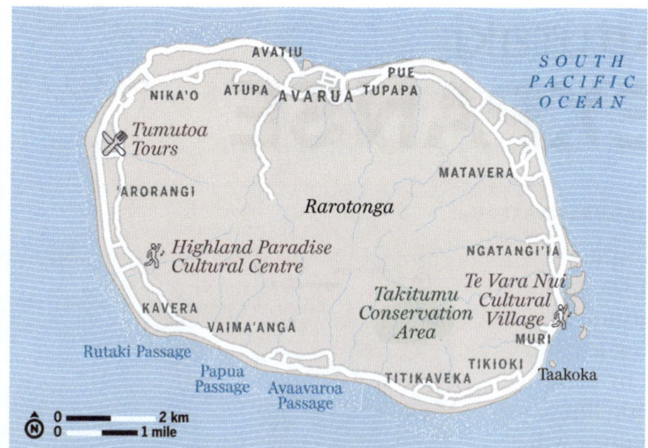

Far left Traditional entertainment, Island Night **Bottom left** Umukai

Island Nights Raro-Style

At resorts on Rarotonga and Aitutaki, the Cook Islands' traditional form of evening entertainment is the **Island Night**, a spectacular blend of dance and music *(karioi)* teamed with a lavish buffet of local food *(kai)*. Dancing, drumming and singing always feature, with fire-juggling, acrobatics and storytelling added into the entertaining mix. Food cooked on the hot volcanic rocks of the *umukai* includes *rukau* and tender parcels of fish and pork.

Lagoon-Side Legends

At **Te Vara Nui Cultural Village** *(tevaranui.co.ck)*, spectacular Island Nights take place on set around rock gardens and above an artificial lagoon. Telling the story of **Tongaiti**, a legendary Polynesian explorer, shows include an *umukai* buffet. Day experiences include learning about traditional medicine, and arts and crafts.

Sunset Celebrations

Above Arorangi on Rarotonga's west coast, **Highland Paradise Cultural Centre** *(highlandparadise.co.ck)* stands on the site of the old Tinomana village. Featuring panoramic coastal views, sunset **Ka'ara** (Drums of our Forefathers) celebrations are action-packed shows with superb island harmonies. Performers include members of the Pirangi family, all descendants of the first *ariki* (chief) of Tinomana. Day tours of the site include an *umukai* lunch.

Help Prepare an Umukai

Book an *umukai* experience with Ngame and Mānia from **Tumutoa Tours** *(tumutoatours.com)*, helping them to prepare the feast, or embark on a village **walking tour** learning about local ingredients, traditional medicinal plants and Cook Islands culture.

Dance Like Everyone's Watching

As well as being authentic celebrations of Cook Islands culture, groups performing in Island Nights also use them to practise for two very important festivals on the country's events calendar. Held from late July to early August, **Te Maeve Nui** celebrates the Cook Islands' independence from New Zealand in 1965. Dance competitions culminate with the finals at the National Auditorium, an extravaganza attracting performers from right across the nation's far-flung islands. Held during April, **Te Mire Ura** concludes with the celebration at the National Auditorium of 'Dancer of the Year' across three different age categories.

16 Aitutaki EXPANSE

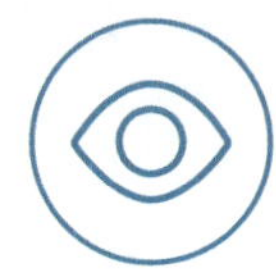

LAGOON CRUISES | FISHING | RELAXATION

Seen from above, Aitutaki's lagoon is one of the South Pacific's most stunning sights, a turquoise islet-studded expanse arcing around a low-slung island framed by palm trees. After a few days snorkelling, fishing and relaxing, Rarotonga will feel like a bustling metropolis when you reluctantly return south to the mainland.

How to

Getting here/around: Air Rarotonga has 45-minute flights from Rarotonga. Book ahead to rent a scooter or car with Aitutaki Car & Bike Hire *(aitutakicarhire.com)*.

When to go: May to October for clear skies and lower humidity.

One-day wonder: From April to September, Air Rarotonga day trips from Rarotonga include an island tour and a lagoon cruise. Consider a longer stay on Aitutaki to relax and really experience the destination.

Lagoon Adventures

Day cruises on **Aitutaki Lagoon** stop at pearl-drop *motu* (islets) including **Maina**, a haven for tropicbirds, and **Tapuaeta'i** (One Foot Island), where barbecue lunches are served, and there's snorkelling in a channel separating Tapuaeta'i from **Tekopua**. Beyond lagoon trips, Quinton Schofield at **Wet & Wild Aitutaki** *(wetnwild-aitutaki.com)* can arrange kiteboarding, spearfishing, and swimming with humpback whales.

Beyond the Lagoon

Fishing in the deeper cobalt-blue waters beyond Aitutaki's turquoise lagoon is also popular. Hook up with **Black Pearl Charters** *(blackpearlaitutaki.com)* for a pre-dawn departure. **Dive Aitutaki** *(diveaitutaki.com)*

Top right Tapuaeta'i (One Foot Island) **Bottom right** Cook Islands Christian Church

WIRESTOCK CREATORS/SHUTTERSTOCK

A South Pacific Stopover

In the 1950s, Aitutaki lagoon was used as a refuelling stopover for TEAL's (Tasman Empire Air Lines) Coral Route service from Auckland to Tahiti. The predecessor to Air New Zealand, TEAL's luxury service in Solent flying boats stopped on Akaiami *motu*. Passengers on the 30-hour island-hopping journey also including Samoa and Fiji could disembark for a swim, or relax under the palm trees lining Akaiami's shoreline. Hollywood acting legends John Wayne and Cary Grant both enjoyed the experience.

can arrange diving experiences in the **Aratunga Passage** and also snorkelling with humpback whales when they swing by from July to October.

Aitutaki's Sleepy Downtown

On the southwestern edge of Aitutaki's main island, **Arutanga** is a laidback collection of a store, bank and government offices. Boat trips leave from its harbour, including fishing boats negotiating Aratunga Passage to deeper waters. Sitting above the harbour is the whitewashed **Cook Islands Christian Church**, built in 1828, and the country's oldest church. Restored in 2010, features include carved wood panelling and a shimmering stained-glass window. Sunday services are very welcoming.

Outdoor EXPLORING

HIKING | CYCLING | WATERSPORTS

Relaxation comes very easily to visitors to Rarotonga, but the island also offers outdoor activities exploring both on the land and on the water. Earn your sunset cold beer or cocktail by hiking right across the island, biking on an ancient coral inland road, or *motu*-hopping by kayak on Muri Lagoon.

JUERGEN_WALLSTABE/SHUTTERSTOCK

Getting here: Most of Rarotonga's outdoor activity operators are based either near Muri Lagoon or around Arorangi on the west coast. A few have stands at Saturday morning's **Punanga Nui Market**.

When to go: Humpback whales visit from July to October. Whale-watching trips are available on Rarotonga. Head to Aitutaki to swim with them.

Renting a scooter?: Keep your legs away from the hot exhaust to avoid getting a 'Raro tattoo'.

CHAMELEONSEYE/GETTY IMAGES

Hike from North to South

Traversing the island's forested heart via the 413m-high **Te Rua Manga (The Needle)**, the **Cross Island Trek** is Rarotonga's most popular hike. Completing the 6km, three- to four-hour walk from north to south is recommended as there's less chance of straying off the trail and you can finish with a cooling swim at **Papua (Wigmore's) Waterfall** or the nearby lagoon. Framed by boulders and tangles of tree roots, the track is a challenging and sometimes steep uphill/downhill workout, and it can be muddy and slippery after rain. Fixed chains and ropes provide final optional access up the 20m-high Needle. Follow the orange trail markers carefully to do the hike independently or join a guided walk with **Maunga Tours** *(maungatours.com)*.

BLUEORANGE STUDIO/SHUTTERSTOCK

Rarotonga for Kids

The Cook Islands are one of the South Pacific's best family destinations. There's safe snorkelling at **Tikioki Marine Reserve** (aka 'Fruits of Rarotonga') on the south coast, and kayaking around **Muri Lagoon** is a good way to build confidence on the water. Tropical fruit smoothies always go down a treat.

Far left Te Rua Manga (The Needle) **Left** Kayaking around Muri Lagoon **Above** Papua (Wigmore's) Waterfall

Muri Lagoon Adventures

Studded with four compact *motu*, **Muri** is the most beautiful section of the lagoon encircling Rarotonga. Sheltered with calm waters around a metre deep, it's a great place for swimming and watersports. Hire a kayak or SUP from **KiteSUP** (kitesup.co) or join their spectacular Fire on Water after-dark SUP experience. Kiteboarding and wing-foiling lessons are also available. For snorkelling, a barbecue lunch on a tiny *motu*, and entertaining Cook Islands humour, embark on a lagoon tour with **Captain Tama's Lagoon Cruizes** (*captaintamas.com*) or **Koka Lagoon Cruises** (*kokalagooncrusies.co.ck*). Both companies have glass-bottom boats so everyone can check out the wonders below.

On Two & Four Wheels

Leisurely three- to four-hour biking experiences along Rarotonga's **Ara Metua** inland backroad with **Storytellers Eco Cycle Tours** (*storytellers.co.ck*) include insights into

A Local's Highlights

My favourite spot for snorkelling and swimming is a place locals refer to as 'Fruits of Rarotonga'. Look for the parking space and beach opposite **Cafe Puretu**. If walks are more your thing, and you want to venture inland, take a wander up Avana Valley Rd at the northern end of Muri Lagoon. Further along Rarotonga's south coast, an interesting historic building is the **Titikaveka Cook Islands Christian Church**, hand-built from coral over a period of six years. For delicious *kai* (food) and a coffee, check out **Beluga Cafe** in Arorangi.
Kia manuia! (Good luck!)

Insights from Corrina Tucker
Owner/operator of Storytellers Eco Cycle Tours, storytellers.co.ck

Left Titikaveka Cook Islands Christian Church **Below** Raro Safari Tours

Cook Islands history and culture. Look forward to sampling seasonal tropical fruits along the way, and lunch and an optional swim in the lagoon after the tour. Starting after the weekly **Punanga Nui Market**, 90-minute Saturday afternoon walking tours of Avarua township are also available.

To get higher into Rarotonga's rugged and forested interior, jump aboard a 4WD trip with **Raro Safari Tours** *(rarosafaritours.com)*. Even more exciting are drive-yourself experiences with **Raro Buggy Tours** *(rarobuggytours.com)*, drifting around tight corners and getting down and (very) dirty on a slipping and sliding off-road track.

Exploring Avaavaroa Passage

Like a scene from a James Bond movie, an underwater sea scooter is the best and safest way to negotiate the waters of the **Avaavaroa Passage**. Guided experiences with **Ariki Adventures** *(arikiadventures.com)* use the devices on their Turtle Adventures, providing up close viewing of *onu* (sea turtles) and eagle rays cruising through the passage's deeper waters. Scooter-free swims are also available, but participants must be experienced swimmers to deal with the passage's sometimes strong currents.

To go fishing outside the reef, or see humpback whales from July to October, contact **Wahoo Fishing Charters** *(wahoofishingcharters.net)*.

FROM LEFT: CHAMELEONSEYE/GETTY IMAGES, MATTHEW WILLIAMS-ELLIS TRAVEL PHOTOGRAPHY/ALAMY

Beyond Rarotonga's Horizon

STORIES AND ANECDOTES FROM AN IMPROBABLY EXPANSIVE ISLAND NATION

Pa enua, only two short words in Cook Islands' Māori – a close relation of New Zealand's *te reo Māori* – is a concise phrase representing 14 other islands beyond Rarotonga's administrative and commercial hub. Welcome to a diverse nation arrayed over almost 2 million sq km of wild Pacific blue.

Left Palmerston **Centre** Cook Islands black pearls **Right** *Kakerori* (Rarotongan flycatcher)

GALAXIID/ALAMY

Land of the Birds

Around 220km northeast of Rarotonga, 'Atiu bucks the trend of pristine lagoons elsewhere in the Cook Islands. Formed of volcanic *makatea*, it's a raised coral atoll, ringed by cliffs, and peppered with subterranean caves. Descend past the gnarled banyan tree roots at the entrance to 'Atiu's Anatakitaki cave, and the clicking you'll hear is *kopeka*, rare 'Atiuan swiftlets using bat-like echolocation to negotiate the darkness. 'Atiu's alternative name is Enua Manu ('Land of the Birds'), and amid the island's dense forest, attractions for birdwatchers making the 45-minute flight from Avarua include the *kakerori* (Rarotongan flycatcher), only reintroduced from Rarotonga in 2010. Elsewhere in the forest, shaded glades host sunset *tumunu* (bush-beer drinking clubs), technically illegal, but welcoming of visitors staying in 'Atiu's collection of accommodation.

A Divided Church

'Atiu's (formerly) clandestine *tumunu* are a legacy of when Christian proselytisers from the London Missionary Society banned *kava* drinking in the 19th century, and on Ma'uke, another *makatea* island 82km east of 'Atiu, the island's Cook Islands Christian Church still harbours the legacy of an 1882 disagreement between the villages of Areora and Ngatiarua.

With no agreement on how the interior would be decorated, a wall was built down the middle. The wall has now been removed, but each village has its own entrance, and the villagers still sit on their own side and take turns singing hymns. The contrasting decorations were restored in 2008, and during services the minister stands astride a dividing line down the middle of the pulpit. There's a handful of accommodation on Ma'uke and 50-minute twice-weekly flights from Rarotonga.

CHAMELEONSEYE/SHUTTERSTOCK

CHARLESJSHARP/WIKIMEDIA/CC BY-SA 4.0

James Cook's Only Island Landing

Despite having the islands named after him by Russian cartographers in 1823, the 18th-century British explorer James Cook never actually sighted Rarotonga, and the atoll of Palmerston 366km west of Aitutaki was the only island he actually walked on.

It remained uninhabited after Cook visited in 1777 on the HMS *Resolution*, but William Masters, a carpenter from Gloucester, England arrived in 1863 with his two Polynesian wives, and went on to establish an island lineage which still exists today. Residents of Palmerston (population: circa 30) are all related to Masters – now spelt Marsters – and still speak with a slight tinge of his Gloucester accent. That makes Palmerston the only island in the Cooks where English is the native language. Getting to Palmerston involves hitching a ride on a supply freighter or on a private yacht.

That makes Palmerston the only island in the Cooks where English is the native language

Nice Pearls, Nice Hat

Go shopping in downtown Avarua or at the **Punanga Nui Market**, and what you're buying may have come from the Cook Islands' far-flung Northern Group. Manihiki, 1046km from Rarotonga, is where most of the country's black pearls are farmed, all carefully harvested around the atoll's magnificent lagoon, fully enclosed and studded with almost 40 tiny *motu*. More than 350km further northeast, Penrhyn also harvests pearls around the Cooks' biggest lagoon, so huge that two villages on opposite sides can barely see each other. Hats and fans lovingly crafted in *rito* (coconut fibre) are exported from Rakahanga, 1300km north of Rarotonga.

Marae Moana

Established in 2017, **Marae Moana** *(maraemoana.gov.ck)* covers all of the Cook Islands' EEZ (Economic Exclusion Zone), and at more than 1.9 million sq km is one of the planet's biggest marine protected areas. Also known as the Cook Islands Marine Park, it reflects the nation's commitment to marine conservation and sustainable utilisation of ocean resources. As a multi-use area, the traditional livelihoods of local communities are protected, and Marae Moana also includes specific zones for fishing and sustainable tourism. Under its charter, sustainable mining of the seabed may also be permitted, and debate over this is a key environmental issue in the Cook Islands.

Listings

BEST OF THE REST

Local Flavours

Charlie's, Titikaveka $$

Lagoon and reef views go well with pizza, sashimi and a pint of Cook Islands lager. Ukulele-driven music kicks off around 6.30pm.

Antipodes, Avarua $$$

Elevated ocean views near Black Rock combine with Mediterranean flavours and Pacific ingredients. Good shared platters.

Beluga Cafe, Arorangi $$

Modern cafe with good brunch dishes and local arts and crafts for sale. Just maybe Raro's best coffee, too.

Waterline Restaurant & Outrigger Beach Bar, Arorangi $$

Book for just before sunset to enjoy a cocktail, before graduating to a restaurant table for calamari, prawns and Thai curry.

Tamarind House, Avarua $$$

Sprawling seafood platters and Med- and Asian-inspired mains served in a gracious colonial building with a breezy verandah.

Soul Cafe, Avarua $$

Delicious tropical fruit smoothies, ocean-fresh tuna and healthy salads. There's also a handy onsite barber if you need a trim.

Muri Night Market, Muri $

Barbecue, seafood curries and stir-fries served from stalls and food trucks on Tuesday, Wednesday, Thursday and Sunday from 5pm. Occasional live music.

Progressive Dinner $$$

Eat your way around Rarotonga during this progressive feast held in locals' homes. Dishes include *ika mata* and papaya salad. Book online at *cookislandstours.co.ck*.

Avatea Cafe, Aitutaki $$

One of the Pacific's best cafes with dishes crammed with local ingredients. Try the legendary fish tacos with Aitutaki's very own Ru's Brew craft beer.

Koru Café, Aitutaki $$

Breezy Aitutaki cafe offering all-day breakfasts and good coffee. Ask about picnic lunches and barbecue packs to take away.

Refreshing Beer & Sunset Cocktails

Rarotonga Brewery, Arorangi $

Try refreshing Cook Islands lager in local bars and restaurants, or visit the brewery for tours, tastings and to fill up reusable 1L bottles. Also kombucha and ginger beer.

Trader Jacks, Avarua $$

Iconic Cook Islands watering hole with ocean views and the choice of the raffish bar or a (slightly) more formal dining area. Good food including pizza, sushi and sashimi.

Shipwreck Hut, Arorangi $$

A rustic spot with an absolute waterfront location, good bar food and regular live music. Schedule a visit for a superb west coast sunset.

21.3 Vaiana's Bar & Bistro, Avarua $$

Fast track into an island state of mind with loping Pacific reggae, bar snacks, burgers and cold beer at this relaxed beachside bar that's a locals' favourite.

Special Raro Stays

Ikurangi Eco Retreat, Matavera

Safari-style glamping tents with private outdoor showers and breezy high-ceilinged bungalows. Located inland with mountain views.

Ocean Escape Resort & Spa, Matavera

Oceanfront views from two-storey self-contained studio apartments. Solar power and UV-treated rainwater reinforce sustainability. Adults-only relaxation awaits.

Motu Beachfront Art Villas, Takitimu

Luxury bungalows set in a palm-shaded garden enlivened with spectacular Pasifika art installations. Look for the giant red *moai* statue outside.

Kura's Kabanas, Muri

Excellent family option with spacious self-contained bungalows right on Muri Lagoon. Complimentary kayaks are great for a pre-breakfast paddle.

Around the Island & Underwater

Tik-e Tours

E-bike hire and guided e-bike tours. A great way to explore the 32km road encircling Rarotonga.

Raro Reef Sub, Avatiu Harbour

Take in underwater views of giant trevally and a shipwreck from this bright yellow vessel departing from Avatiu Harbour. Definitely one for Beatles fans.

Rainy-Day Options

Te Ara – Cook Islands Museum of Cultural Enterprise, Muri

Galleries showcasing traditional Polynesian carving, maritime navigation and the environmental challenges facing the South Pacific. Also a good gift shop with local arts and crafts.

Pare rito, Punanga Nui Market

Discover Marine Wildlife and Eco Centre, Arorangi

Learn about the Cook Islands' environmental initiatives. Also focused on the rehabilitation of *onu* (sea turtles) and sea birds.

Papua (Wigmore's) Waterfall, Takitimu

Cooling and cleansing haven, especially after completing the Cross Island Trek or getting extremely muddy with Raro Buggy Tours (p123). Also a good option in warm tropical rain. Expect a few mosquitoes.

Pearls & Pare Rito

Bergman & Sons Pearl Store, Avarua

Cook Islands black pearls crafted into unique and modern settings including necklaces, rings and bracelets.

Tivaevae Collectables, Avarua

Vibrant and colourful Cook Islands *tivaevae* (hand-sewn quilted fabrics) made into bedspreads, cushion covers, tablecloths and women's clothing.

Punanga Nui Market, Avarua

Arts and crafts, handmade ukuleles, and finely crafted *pare rito* (hats made of coconut fibre) from the Cooks' far-flung Northern Group.

Common Ground Spanning the South Pacific

THE WORLD'S BIGGEST OCEAN BACKGROUNDS A SHARED HISTORY ACROSS MANY COUNTRIES

Spread across the countries and cultures of Micronesia, Melanesia and Polynesia, it's estimated more than 1500 different languages are spoken across the West and South Pacific's scores of islands. Despite the cultural, linguistic and geographical diversity of this sprawling region, key struggles, challenges and opportunities feature in their shared past, present and future.

Left Recruiting islanders, Vanuatu, 1891
Centre Protests, New Caledonia
Right Kokoda Track

The Impact of Colonialism

Throughout the South Pacific, European colonial powers including Britain, France and Germany left a legacy of political and economic structures at odds with traditional land ownership and established cultural and linguistic boundaries. Scope for developing a capacity for local government was often hamstrung, and European diseases had a devastating impact. It is estimated many Polynesian island populations were halved, while some islands of Vanuatu dropped to just 5% of their original populations.

Forced Economic Abductions

Blackbirding was a 19th-century practice whereby Pacific Islanders were recruited – sometimes at gunpoint against their will – to work as cheap (read: slave) labour in mines and plantations in Australia, Fiji, New Caledonia and Peru. Many islands' populations were devastated by blackbirders. Tiny Tokelau lost almost half its population to Peruvian slave ships in 1863, while Penrhyn in the Cook Islands was almost totally depopulated. It was once the Cooks' most populous atoll with around 2000 residents before European contact; only 88 remained after blackbirding raids. People were also taken as slaves from Niue, Tonga, New Caledonia, Vanuatu and the Solomon Islands. Most never returned to their home islands.

Across the Last Century

More recent impacts of colonialism include the United Kingdom, the United States and France using the South Pacific for nuclear testing. This stretched from US tests at

THEO ROUBY/AFP VIA GETTY IMAGES

ANDREW PEACOCK/GETTY IMAGES

Bikini Atoll in 1946 to France's last nuclear test in the Tuamotu Archipelago in 1996. Migration for economic opportunities, especially to Australia, New Zealand, Tahiti and France, continues to risk outer-island depopulation for the Cook Islands, Samoa, Tonga and French Polynesia.

Christian faiths continue to dominate in the region, but communities across the Pacific are also reclaiming and celebrating older ways of worship, reinforcing a deep understanding and environmental respect for their ocean and island homelands. Other recent initiatives for Pacific Islanders to reassert their traditional culture include 2024 social unrest supporting greater autonomy for New Caledonia from France.

The Cook Islands signed a strategic partnership agreement with China, asserting greater autonomy from New Zealand, their close constitutional partners

South Pacific Soft Power

Soft power in the South Pacific includes the US government-funded Peace Corps, and in 2022, the Solomon Islands signed a security agreement with Beijing. This gave China the option to station naval forces near vital international shipping lanes. Local opposition to the agreement saw rioting and the looting of Asian businesses in the Solomons' capital of Honiara.

In early 2025, the Cook Islands signed a strategic partnership agreement with China, asserting greater autonomy from New Zealand, their close constitutional partners. The Marshall

Authentic Local Solutions

Sustainable and regenerative tourism activities are helping to balance the impact of climate change. These initiatives are often rooted in authentic local values and traditional cultural practices, offsetting the homogeneity of modernisation and globalisation. One example is the Kokoda Track Authority supporting sustainable and managed development along the WWII mountain trail in Papua New Guinea. In the Cook Islands, reservoirs of traditional knowledge are being maintained by local tourism hosts including Tumutoa Tours and Highland Paradise, while tiny Niue is diversifying to become an exporter of sustainable and organic vanilla and honey.

Islands, Palau and Tuvalu all continue to recognise Taiwan.

To balance China's growing strategic investment, governments in Washington, Canberra, Wellington, Tokyo and Paris continue to reinforce their influence with South Pacific countries. Key initiatives include developmental aid, disaster relief and support for combatting climate change.

Fighting Back Against Rising Sea Levels

Across the Pacific, the sea level has risen from 5cm to 15cm across recent decades, more than twice the global rate from 1993, and is most urgently experienced as an existential threat in smaller western Pacific countries including Kiribati, Tuvalu and the Marshall Islands. Already, the window to evacuate some low-lying atolls is closing faster than previously envisaged.

In 2024, supporting an initiative first introduced by islands including Tuvalu and Barbuda in the Caribbean, the International Tribunal for the Law of the Sea (ITLOS) ruled that greenhouse gases absorbed by the world's oceans should be considered marine pollution. Also in 2024, Vanuatu, Fiji, Papua New Guinea and the Solomon Islands brought a case to the Hague's International Court of Justice arguing the impact of climate change on sea levels was the responsibility of industrialised nations.

The magnitude of severe weather events is projected to impact more on South Pacific nations

Extreme Events

The magnitude of severe weather events is projected to impact more on South Pacific nations in the future. The frequency of hurricanes is not increasing, but warmer waters means their intensity is becoming greater.

JESSICA LOCKHART

MAXAR VIA GETTY IMAGES

WESTEND61/GETTY IMAGES

The region is also framed by the Pacific Ring of Fire, and the 2022 eruption of Hunga Tonga-Hunga Ha'apai, an undersea volcano near Tonga, caused tsunami waves of up to 20m. Across recent centuries, it's thought only 1883's Krakatoa eruption rivalled the atmospheric disturbance produced by the event, and it's currently the 21st century's biggest volcanic eruption. In December 2024, a magnitude 7.3 earthquake struck near Vanuatu, causing significant damage and loss of life in the nation's capital city, Port Vila.

Protecting the Oceans

Recent initiatives to protect the South Pacific's marine environment include the Cook Islands' Marae Moana, Niue's Moana Mahu, and Te Tai Nui a Hau near the Marquesas Islands. All are marine protected areas limiting fishing and mineral extraction, and promoting sustainable development in line with traditional Polynesian values.

Left Yessie Mosby, climate change protester **Centre** Earthquake damage, Vanuatu **Above left** Hunga Tonga-Hunga Ha'apai **Above** Humpback whales, Tonga

Protecting the Pacific's Ocean Giants

From July to October, humpback whales visit the warm waters of the South Pacific, returning annually to give birth and nurse their calves. In 2024, a treaty to protect the whales was signed by respected elders from the Cook Islands, Tahiti, Tonga, Hawai'i, New Zealand and Rapa Nui (Easter Island).

Dubbed He Whakaputanga Moana (Declaration for the Ocean), the treaty accords whales legal personhood, giving them the same legal standing as humans if harmed. Based on the treaty, it's hoped South Pacific governments will establish legislation to further protect whales, and also redirect shipping lanes away from their seasonal migratory routes.

TONGA
PRISTINE | SCENIC | TRADITIONAL

Go for a spot of quality beach time to the coastal island of **Pangaimotu** (pictured, p143).

10mins from Nuku'alofa

Drive to Tongatapu's northwest coast and see the awesome blowholes of **Mapu'a 'a Vaea** (pictured, p142).

45mins from Nuku'alofa

TONGA
Trip Builder

Located in the heart of South Pacific's marine wilderness, Tonga's oceans are the roaming grounds of leviathan humpback whales. Its towns and villages, on the other hand, thrive on the quaint charms of rustic life, built around the nation's devotion to the church and family. Tongatapu, the country's main island where the capital Nuku'alofa is located, is home to spectacular coastal scenery, and attracts nature lovers with some of the most intriguing creations of nature's all-conquering forces.

0 200 km
0 100 miles

Niuafo' ou

Tafahi

Niuatoptapu

Niua group

SOUTH PACIFIC OCEAN

Snorkel in the stony wonderland of submerged **Swallows Cave** (pictured, p146)

1hr from Vava'u

Fonualei

Vava' u group

Vava' u

Neiafu

Late

Kapa

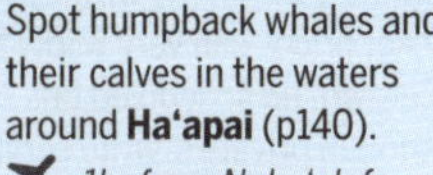

Spot humpback whales and their calves in the waters around **Ha'apai** (p140).

1hr from Nuku'alofa

Kao

Ha' ano

Tofua

Pangai

Foa

Lifuka

Ha' api group

Tungua

Ride the wind on a kitesurfing session in the lagoons off **Uoleva** (p146.)

1hr from Nuku'alofa

Nomuka

Nomuk'iki

Telekivava' u

Hunga

Marvel at the mysterious 'stonehenge' monument of **Ha'amonga 'a Maui** (p143.)

45mins from Nuku'alofa

NUKU'ALOFA

Ha'amonga 'a Maui Trilithon

Tongatapu

Tonga Trench

Tongatapu group

Count crashing waves from the dizzying and precipitous rim of **Hufangalupe Archway** (p143).

30mins from Nuku'alofa

Spy on maroon shining parrots in the forests of **'Eua** (pictured, p146).

10mins from Nuku'alofa

Practicalities

REBECCA HARDING/GETTY IMAGES

ARRIVING

Fua'amotu Airport The airport in Nuku'alofa connects with Nadi, Sydney, Auckland and Apia. Ticket prices can vary wildly through the year. There are no scheduled bus services into town, although private shuttle services pick up and drop off at major hotels. There's a self-drive rental kiosk at the airport, outside the arrival hall.

Cruise ports Cruise ships visiting Tonga drop anchor in the port of Nuku'alofa, Neiafu in Vava'u and off Uoleva in Ha'apai.

HOW MUCH FOR A

Midrange hotel room T$150–200

Airport shuttle T$30

Bottle of beer T$8

WHEN TO GO

JAN–MAR
Warm and wet days mark the lean season for travel.

APR–JUN
Oceans begin to cool. The first whales arrive from Antarctica.

JUL–SEP
Height of the whale-watching season across the country.

OCT–DEC
Tourists depart, but expat Tongans return home for Christmas.

GETTING AROUND

Air Noisy twin-otter aircraft connect the capital to Ha'apai, Vava'u and 'Eua, among other island groups. Book ahead – tickets go fast between June and October.

Self-Drive Car The best option for getting around the main island of Tongatapu. Rent cars at the airport or in Nuku'alofa for about T$100 a day, including basic insurance but excluding fuel. Driving licences issued in your home country usually suffice, as long as they are printed in English.

Ferry The Inter-island Ferry Terminal in Nuku'alofa has ferry services to 'Eua (two hours), a'apai (10 hours) and Vava'u (eight hours). Tickets are cheap and usually sold for cash only. Boat schedules change frequently.

TOP: JASON EDWARDS/GETTY IMAGES

EATING & DRINKING

Experiencing an authentic Tongan meal ranges from trying a Sunday pit-roast made in the traditional *umu* oven to eating in one of Nuku'alofa's many popular restaurants serving local dishes. Tongan cuisine relies heavily on coconut cream, onion, tomato (pictured), chilli (pictured) and lemon to impart seasoning, flavour and texture to many signature dishes. Most of the fare is robustly non-vegetarian, but vegetarians will find a fair number of preparations – derived from pumpkin, eggplant or native flora such as taro leaves and edible varieties of hibiscus – to feast on.

Must-try seafood
Chef Zero (p147)

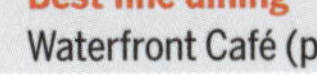

Best fine dining
Waterfront Café (p147)

CONNECT & FIND YOUR WAY

Wi-fi Wireless connectivity is scarce in Tonga. Some resorts in Nuku'alofa will hand out daily vouchers to resident guests for about T$20, but don't expect to be connected in cafes or restaurants.

Mobile Phones Digicel and U-Call are Tonga's largest and most reliable providers. SIM cards can be picked up at the airport or in Nuku'alofa.

WHERE TO STAY

Where you choose to stay in Tonga will depend purely on your interests and the plan of action for your vacation. Each place has its own offerings and limitations.

Place	Pro/Con
Nuku'alofa	Biggest urban centre. Widest choice of hotels, restaurants and amenities. Quick connections by air to other countries.
Ha'apai island group	Few choices and limited conveniences. Pristine nature makes it a preferred choice for those who want to be close to wilderness.
Vava'u island group	A good selection of lodges and resorts despite the remoteness. Can get crowded during the whale-watching months of June to September.

OFFLINE MAPS

Download a map of Tonga on your phone before you arrive – mobile connectivity is weak or absent in several remote areas.

MONEY

Tonga uses the Tongan *pa'anga* (T$). If you're heading to the outer islands, carry a sufficient amount of cash to cover daily expenses. Settle major payments like accommodation and tours online when you book.

18 Walking NUKU'ALOFA

HISTORY | ARCHITECTURE | CULTURE

A charming capital characterised by colourful markets, quaint streets, lofty heritage buildings (many of which trace their history to Tonga's regal tradition), a scenic waterfront and a delightfully relaxed grain of Pacific island life, Nuku'alofa is a delight to explore on foot.

IKT COLLECTIONS/SHUTTERSTOCK

How to

Getting here: Most landmarks and sights are located within or around the grid formed by Laifone Rd, cutting through the town centre, and Vuna Rd, the main coastal thoroughfare.

When to go: Early mornings are best for taking pictures, and late afternoons for socialising with residents and getting a sense of the local grain of life.

How long: You can easily take in all the major sights within two hours, including a coffee break.

Afternoon Splash

The public **Saltwater Swimming Pool**, created by damming a square section of sea east of Nuku'alofa's ferry terminals on Vuna Rd, is a fantastic place to go for a dip and a splash in the late afternoon, and shoot the breeze with the town's residents. It's free to access, and remains open until dusk.

0 — 500 m
0 — 0.25 miles

SOUTH PACIFIC OCEAN

Royal Palace

American Pier

Vuna Rd
Salote Rd
Wellington Rd
Albert St
Sipu Rd
Siulikutapu Rd
Vaha'akolo Rd
Tu'i Rd
Taufa'ahau Rd
Laifone Rd
Mateialona Rd
'Unga Rd
Fatafehi Rd
Railway Rd
Lavinia Rd

01 Watch the tide roll in and out while strolling along the promenade of **Vuna Wharf**, where ships dock upon arrival in Nuku'alofa and locals go for walks.

02 A plethora of fruits, vegetables, groceries and other daily commodities line the alleys of **Talamahu Market** (pictured), offering ample photo-ops and a few good purchases.

03 Intricately crafted Tongan souvenirs can be found at **Langafonua Handicrafts Centre**, including woven baskets, mats, textiles, jewellery and wooden artifacts.

04 The **Sai'one Centenary Church** is one of many lofty churches in town, but it's the only one where royals come to pray.

05 The stately **Royal Tombs** (pictured) of Mala'e Kula have served as the burial grounds for Tongan royalty since the late 19th century. Visitors must dress modestly.

19 Whale Wonders IN HA'APAI

BOAT TOUR | WILDLIFE | BEACHES

Ever dropped your jaw to the spectacle of a 40-ton humpback whale breaching the ocean with the energy of a playful puppy, then crashing back in the water with the blast intensity of a freight truck in free fall? The remote Ha'apai archipelago is Tonga's frontline for up-and-close encounters of the cetacean kind – while doubling as one of the country's best beach getaways.

WILDESTANIMAL/SHUTTERSTOCK

How to

Getting here & around Lulutai Airlines operates several flights daily between Ha'apai and Nuku'alofa.

When to go June to October is the broad window for whale sightings in Tonga. Visitor numbers tend to peak in August and September.

Where to stay The central islands of Lifuka (where the airstrip is located) and Uoleva are where you will find most of Ha'apai's resorts and amenities. The two islands are connected by a 10-minute boat ride.

BY WILDESTANIMAL/GETTY IMAGES

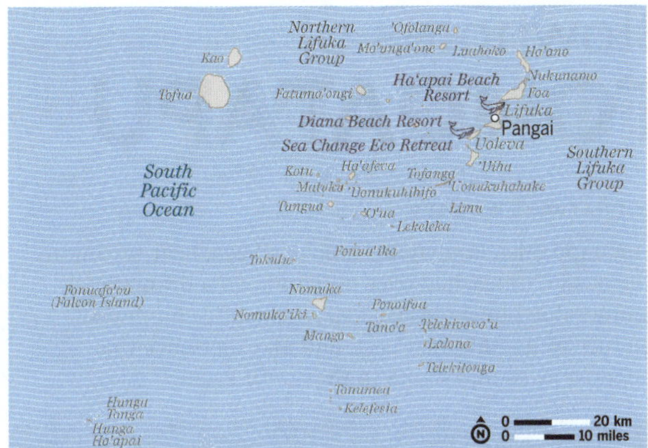

Safe Haven Protected by royal decree, the territorial waters of Tonga have traditionally been a refuge for humpback whales, who swim up from Antarctica at the start of the southern winter in search of warmer waters. During their time here, the animals mate, give birth, and rear their calves until the young ones are strong enough to make the long journey back to Antarctica.

Advantage Ha'apai The lagoons of Ha'apai have minimal boat traffic compared to Tonga's other popular whale-watching spots, such as Vava'u or Nuku'alofa. The idyllic waters allow whales to forage close to shore, thus often allowing some fantastic sighting opportunities and photo-ops from the comfort of your seaside resort. For beach bums, there are some excellent sands to be found on the southern tip of Lifuka, as well as along the western side of Uoleva.

Know the Pod Whales may be sighted swimming alone, in pairs or in greater numbers. Once a female whale has given birth, the mother and calf stick together, and are often accompanied by a male escort. Once in a while, whales may be seen engaging in a 'heat run', where males pursue females in an act of courtship.

Boat Tours Resorts usually run excursions around the reefs surrounding the islands on a half- or full-day basis. Typically, travellers purchase boat tours from the same resort they stay in. Advance reservations are strongly recommended. **Ha'apai Beach Resort** on Lifuka boasts a vantage location between the airstrip and the main village of **Pangai**, while on Uoleva, **Diana Beach Resort** and **Sea Change Eco Retreat** offer accommodation and tours in more rustic surroundings.

Far and bottom left Ha'apai

How Close Is Close?

Whale watching is a strictly regulated activity in Tonga. Licensed operators are obliged to ensure that whales are never chased or disturbed, that boats venture no closer than 50m to the animals, and that only one boat is allowed to approach a sighted pod at any given time. With such regulations in place, Tongan authorities go as far as allowing visitors to enter the water to snorkel alongside whales. No more than four swimmers are permitted entry at a time, and duck diving is forbidden. Of course, there is still a chance that the whales may be disturbed or threatened by a human presence, so it's best to use your own discretion and awareness if you choose to engage in this activity.

20 Blowholes of TONGATAPU

ROAD TRIP | PHOTOGRAPHY | NATURAL WONDER

The blowholes of Tongatapu, also known as Mapu'a 'a Vaea, bear testimony to the relentless forces of the ocean, unleashed over millennia on a dramatically sculpted coast to create innumerable blowholes that spew gigantic columns of water into the sky. This is nature at its untamed best, and an experience that easily qualifies as one of the most awesome sights in the South Pacific.

NANA TRONGRATANAWONG/SHUTTERSTOCK

How to

Getting there It's a 45-minute drive from Nuku'alofa to the main viewing platform past Houma village. Consider self-driving, or hiring a tourist vehicle from town.

When to go The blowholes can be visited year round. There are two main viewpoints for different blowhole clusters, both open from dawn to dusk.

Daypack checklist Carry bottled water, snacks and sturdy shoes with grippy outsoles if you wish to walk around on the slippery rocks.

DON MAMMOSER/SHUTTERSTOCK

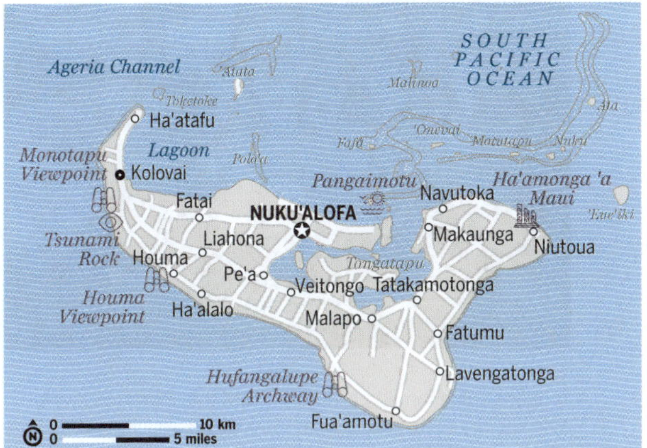

Far left Blowholes of Tongatapu
Bottom left Hufangalupe Archway

Houma Viewpoint The blowholes are essentially a network of channels bored by saltwater into a wall of submerged volcanic rock, which stretches almost 5km along the northwestern shoreline of Tongatapu. The most impressive cluster of blowholes can be seen from the viewing platform near Houma, a vantage spot that's so close to the action you will be soaked by the thick spray of water that dissipates from the chutes. There's a walking track going northwest from the car park, which runs parallel to the blowholes and allows visitors to stroll along the rocky shore for several hundred metres.

Monotapu Viewpoint An alternative viewpoint for a different cluster of blowholes is by the secluded Monotapu Beach, a 10-minute drive from Houma. The highlight here is a short but immaculate strip of golden sand, where you can enjoy a dip in the sea while admiring the blowholes exploding on the reef about 200m away.

Tsunami Rock On a grassy pasture near Monotapu Beach, you will find this herculean 10m-high rock that – according to popular lore – was supposedly ripped out of the sea and flung on the shore by a tsunami thousands of years ago. It's a curious photo-op, and a 10-minute wander from the sands.

Best Time to Visit Unsurprisingly, the blowholes are most stunning at high tide, when they spew water almost 20m into the air. However, timing your visit with the falling light of day can be a good idea, as the dramatic afternoon sun renders the blowholes in a magical shade of auburn.

Offbeat Tongatapu Sights

Ha'amonga 'a Maui
An ancient stone trilith located in Niutoua village, 45 minutes from town, which marked the official seat of the Tui Tonga kings. It is also believed to have been used to measure the summer solstice.

Pangaimotu An island accessible by a 10-minute ferry ride from Nuku'alofa, with stunning beaches and some good snorkelling around a shipwreck.

Hufangalupe Archway
Created by the collapse of what once used to be a coastal cave, 30 minutes from town. The viewpoint is perched on the rim of the collapsed roof, from where you can peer down at waves crashing on limestone cliffs.

■ **Lilieta Soakai, native Nuku'alofan and sailing crew member of Uto Ni Yalo Trust, Fiji,** *facebook.com/lilieta.soakai.5*

Sundays in Tonga

A TIME FOR REST AND REPAST

A devoutly Christian nation, Tonga adheres to the divine word each day of the week. No surprises, then, that Sundays bring about a blanket shutdown of public life across the nation. While outsiders may find this peculiar, it all makes perfect sense to the Tongan way of life.

Left An *umu* **Centre** Christian church, Tonga **Right** Twraditional Tongan dress

JANIS APELS/SHUTTERSTOCK

Tongans value family, community and the church as invaluable social assets and Sundays are exclusively earmarked as a time to devote oneself to these congregations. This is no light matter: even the constitutional law of the land stipulates that Sunday is to be set aside as a holy day. This is when, barring essential services like hospitals and the police, the entire nation takes their hands off any work commitments, whether commercial or personal. Supermarkets, fuel stations, restaurants, cafes and entertainment venues all pull down their shutters. The roads become eerily devoid of transport or pedestrians. Even airports remain shut through the day, halting all commercial flight operations. Hotels advise their international guests to pack cold meals and shop for rations on Saturday evening, just so that they are adequately stocked to get by until at least Sunday evening, when traces of life slowly begin to creep back into Tonga's civic arteries.

This isn't to say, however, that Sunday is simply an excuse for Tongans to lie in bed and snooze away the idle morning hours. Daybreak is marked by the pealing of church bells across neighbourhoods, calling on people to rise and shine for Sunday mass. (Some people wake up even earlier to attend a pre-dawn church service.) Not long after, devout citizens assemble in their respective community churches to immerse themselves in solemn prayer and invocation. Choirs break into hymns, singing in immaculate pitch and four-part harmonies, their voices heard in every corner of town (or village) through the morning.

Very often, Tongans also welcome visiting foreigners to partake in their church services. For uninformed travellers who are blindsided by the sudden stalling of civic life, it is not uncommon to receive an invitation from their tour operator

MYSTIC STOCK PHOTOGRAPHY/SHUTTERSTOCK

DMITRY MALOV/GETTY IMAGES

or local liaison to join them in church on Sunday morning, and thereby gain an insight into this deeply spiritual dimension of Tongan culture.

Feast with the Family

Once church is over, it's time for Tongans to head back home and bond with their families over a hearty meal. In Tongan culture, repast on Sunday is typically prepared in a pit oven called *umu*. Similar to the Fijian *lovo* or the Maori *hāngī* culinary traditions, this involves digging a pit into the ground at dawn, and firing it up with coconut fibre, hot stones and coal. Chunks of taro, yam, plantain and potato are wrapped in layers of banana leaf (or cooking foil) and placed above the fiery embers. Cuts of chicken, fish, lamb and beef – rubbed with seasoning and drizzled with coconut cream – are encased in leaf containers called *lu* and placed on top of the root vegetables. The oven is then sealed with more layers of banana leaves, coconut leaves and loose earth, and left for the entire duration of the church service.

Tongans proceed to dig up the oven and extract the food, which has now been baked to delicate tenderness – this is then washed down with copious amounts of *otai*

Having returned home from church, Tongans proceed to dig up the oven and extract the food, which has now been baked to delicate tenderness. This is then washed down with copious amounts of *otai*, a pulpy beverage made from coconut and watermelon, to the accompaniment of laughter, merriment and good cheer.

Dress to Impress

Tongans literally dress in their Sunday best for church service. Men wear shirts and blazers, paired with a *tupenu* (traditional skirt) that falls below the knees. A woven ornamental mat called *ta'ovala* is worn around the waist above the *tupenu*, and is held in place by a belt called *kafa*. Women also wear a *tupenu* with a *ta'ovala* (though some may opt for a smaller girdle called *kiekie* woven from leaves or plant fibre instead of a *ta'ovala*), paired with a blouse. *Ta'ovala* are considered a family heirloom, often symbolic of a family's social standing, and some pieces are passed down several generations over decades.

Listings

BEST OF THE REST

Aquatic Thrills

Snorkelling in Swallows Cave

Don your mask, snorkel and fins to explore the stony underwater amphitheatre of Swallows Cave, or the technicolour coral reefs of Japanese gardens, both reachable by boat from Vava'u.

Kitesurfing in Uoleva

The windy lagoons in the vicinity of Uoleva are a fantastic location for some robust kitesurfing, and attract connoisseurs from around the world to surf the waters.

Scuba Diving in Vava'u

Famous dive sites include **Pelagic Pinnacle**, where giant fish, sharks and rays feed in strong ocean currents, and **China Town**, whose swim-throughs teem with myriad species of reef fish.

Surfing in Tongatapu

In the northwestern edge of Tongatapu, the reefs off **Ha'atafu Beach** boast some decent breaks for advanced surfers, with imaginative names such as Corners, Motels, Fishtraps and the Bowl.

Best of Nature

Birdwatching in 'Eua

Less than 10 minutes by air from Tongatapu, the lushly forested island of 'Eua is home to the *koki* or maroon shining parrot, believed to have originated in the islands of Fiji, Tonga's regional neighbour.

Hiking Mt Talau

Looming above Vava'u at 131m, the summit of Mt Talau is a brisk one-hour return hike from the town of Neiafu, and affords gorgeous vistas of the ultramarine ocean channels and harbours scattered around Vava'u.

Surfing in Tongatapu

In the northwestern edge of Tongatapu, the reefs off Ha'atafu Beach boast some decent breaks for advanced surfers, with imaginative names such as Corners, Motels, Fishtraps and The Bowl.

Offbeat Sights in Tongatapu

Fishing Pigs

The coast to the north of Mu'a village is home to Tonga's famed fishing pigs. When the tide is out, these porkers trot out into the shallows and snuffle around in search of seafood.

Flying Foxes

The village and neighbouring forest reserve of Kolovai, on the western end of Tongatapu, is a popular destination for nature lovers wishing to spot flying foxes (aka fruit bats), who hang upside down from tree canopies in the hundreds.

Abel Tasman Monument

On the far northwestern tip of Tongatapu stands a modest monument commemorating

ROBERT SZYMANSKI/SHUTTERSTOCK

Fishing pigs

Dutch explorer Abel Tasman's visit to Tongatapu in 1643, while making his way back to Batavia (present-day Jakarta) after bumping into Tasmania and New Zealand.

Captain Cook Landing Site

A modest cairn above a mangrove inlet near Holonga village marks the spot where British naval legend Captain James Cook came ashore in 1777 on his third trip to Tonga, and where Queen Elizabeth II paid a visit to commemorate it in 1970.

Nuku'alofa's Best Eateries

Chef Zero $

This understated restaurant located on a quiet street in Nuku'alwofa's ancient quarter serves delectable fish and crustacean preparations, such as grilled lobster, tuna carpaccio, sashimi spreads and *ota ika,* the local delicacy.

Friends Cafe $

This trendy and stylish cafe – housed in a charming heritage villa located on a prime Salote Rd plot – attracts young adults, office goers and travellers alike with its wide selection of meal platters, sandwiches, burgers, shakes, coffee and chilled beer.

Waterfront Café $$

The in-house multicuisine restaurant at the Waterfront Hotel, overlooking Nuku'alofa's ferry wharf on Vuna Rd, headlines the fine-dining scene with signature creations such as braised pork belly, tuna poke bowls, falafel bowls, blackened tuna and a line of creative desserts.

Billfish $

This long-standing, pub-style restaurant on Vuna Rd is a great place to meet and socialise with Nuku'alofa's residents as well as travellers over sumptuous servings of burgers, sandwiches, steaks and assorted finger foods, all of it washed down with chilled beer and cocktails.

DLERTCHAIRIT/GETTY IMAGES

View from Mt Talau

Vietnamese Cafe $

Cheap and delicious servings of signature Vietnamese items – such as phó, banh mi, spring rolls, seafood pancakes and rice noodles with grilled pork – fly thick and fast at this unassuming restaurant, located off Laifone Rd in the centre of town.

Emerald $

This in-house eatery at the Emerald Hotel on Vuna Rd is a good spot to tuck into a wide selection of authentic Chinese dishes, from a selection of fried rice and fried noodles to pork in black-bean sauce, steamed whole fish and an assortment of vegetarian sides featuring bok choy, tofu or mushrooms.

Little Italy $$

This seaside place on Vuna Rd boasts a long list of pizzas, ranging from the classic Margherita, Napolitana and *quattro formaggi* (four cheeses) to crowd pleasers such as the ham-and-pineapple Hawaiian and the pepperoni-laden 'godfather'.

TOP Restaurant $$

Offering great rooftop views of Nuku'alofa's business district and the ocean, this elegant restaurant is a good place to enjoy a sundowner, accompanied with tasty nibbles like pumpkin and potato fritters, stuffed mussels and devilled eggs.

TAHITI & FRENCH POLYNESIA
ISLANDS | LAGOONS | CULTURE

TAHITI & FRENCH POLYNESIA

Trip Builder

Ever dreamt of lazing about on a tropical island with a baguette in hand? Then French Polynesia is for you. From azure lagoons to lush jungles and its vibrant culture, there's a certain *je ne sais quoi* here that makes it unforgettable.

Dive with sharks in **Fakarava** (pictured, p159).
70mins from Tahiti

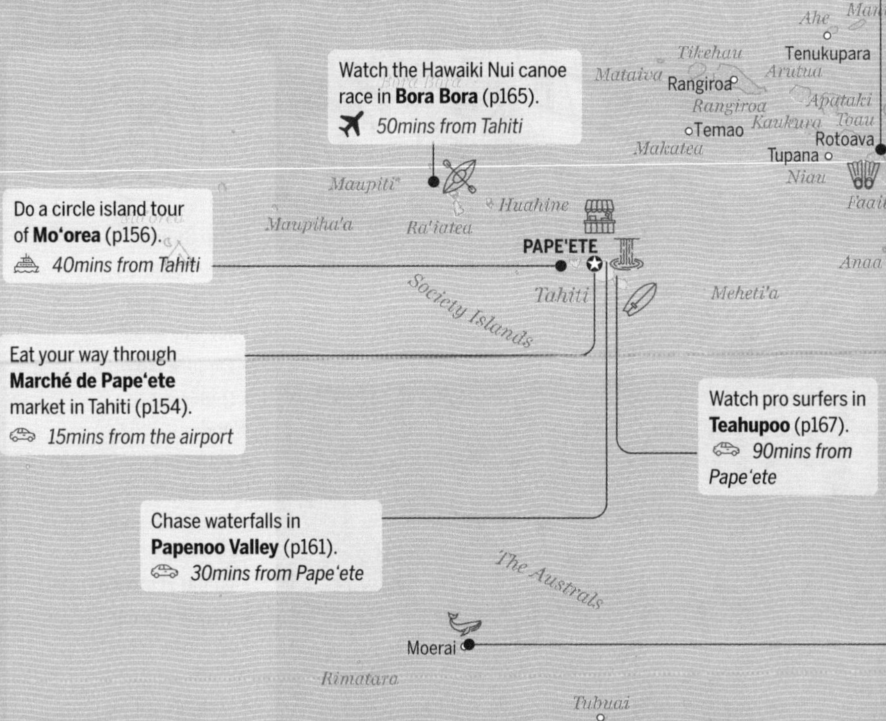

Watch the Hawaiki Nui canoe race in **Bora Bora** (p165).
50mins from Tahiti

Do a circle island tour of **Mo'orea** (p156).
40mins from Tahiti

Eat your way through **Marché de Pape'ete** market in Tahiti (p154).
15mins from the airport

Watch pro surfers in **Teahupoo** (p167).
90mins from Pape'ete

Chase waterfalls in **Papenoo Valley** (p161).
30mins from Pape'ete

Experience the Matavaa Henua Enana festival in the **Marquesas** (pictured, p166).

3¼hrs from Tahiti

Swim with whales in **Rurutu** (p170).

1½hrs from Tahit

Practicalities

EQROY/SHUTTERSTOCK

ARRIVING

Faa'a International Airport Located 10 minutes by car from the capital, Pape'ete. Direct flights from Auckland, Noumea, Nadi, Los Angeles, San Francisco, Honolulu, Rarotonga, Paris and Tokyo. Most accommodation providers can arrange airport transfers, and taxis and rental cars are also available at the airport. Buses run on weekdays to Pape'ete and down the west coast.

Pape'ete Cruise Terminal (pictured) Conveniently located five minutes from downtown Pape'ete on foot.

HOW MUCH FOR A

Casse croûte **(baguette sandwich) 500CFP**

Pareo **(sarong) 2000CFP**

Six-pack of Hinano beer 1600CFP

GETTING AROUND

Plane Quickest way to island hop. Air Tahiti and Air Moana offer domestic flights to over 40 islands. Air Moana is cheaper, but Air Tahiti services more islands and offers multi-island discount passes.

Ferry Inter-island ferries such as the Vaeara'i, Aremiti and Apetahi Express travel regularly from Tahiti to Mo'orea, Huahine, Raiatea, Taha'a and Bora Bora. Fares start at around 2600CFP round trip to Mo'orea, 18000CFP return to Bora Bora.

Land Transport Semi-reliable buses service Tahiti; they're non-existent on most other islands. Car rental is ideal in Tahiti and Raiatea, and scooters are great for smaller islands like Mo'orea and Taha'a. Hire a bike on the Tuamotu atolls, Maupiti and even Bora Bora.

WHEN TO GO

MAY–OCT
Dry season, sunny weather

JUN–AUG
Festival season and summer school holidays; popular time to visit

NOV–APR
Rainy season; hot and humid days, frequent downpours

SEP–OCT
Low season with pleasant weather; whales visit July–November

EATING & DRINKING

Tahiti's food scene ranges from French style haute cuisine to fire-roasted breadfruit served with canned corned beef – and everything in between. For a truly local experience, eat out at a *roulotte* (food truck, pictured) on a Friday or Saturday night. They typically serve huge portions of Tahitian favourites such as steak frites, chow mein and sashimi (pictured) for around 2000CFP a plate. If in doubt, follow the locals – if the *roulotte* is crowded, that's a good sign.

Must-try dish
Poisson cru at **Kfe Roti** (p171)

Best breakfast Marché de Pape'ete on Sunday morning (p154)

CONNECT & FIND YOUR WAY

Wi-fi Free hotspots in French Polynesia are rare and internet connections can be unreliable or non-existent, especially on more remote islands. The best way to stay connected is to rent a pocket wi-fi device (at the airport or online *tahitiwifi.com*), or buy a SIM card with a local provider – Vini has the best coverage *(vini.pf)*.

DRINKING WATER

The tap water is not always safe to drink in French Polynesia. If in doubt, ask your accommodation provider or drink bottled water.

WHERE TO STAY

French Polynesia is known for its luxury accommodation, but there's something here for every budget – from campsites and family-run guesthouses to Airbnb and five-star overwater bungalows.

Island/Town	Pro/Con
Bora Bora	Luxury resorts on private islands; pricey.
Tahiti – Pape'ete/ west coast	Range of accommodation options & cultural activities; can be noisy and crowded.
Tahiti iti	Quiet & close to nature; beautiful beaches, hikes, surfing etc; local-style accommodation.
Mo'orea	Great for families; wide range of accommodation and activities; can book out fast.
Tuamotu archipelago	Incredible diving and fishing; laid-back lifestyle; remote.
Austral archipelago	Natural beauty, authentic culture, beautiful handicrafts; slow-paced & remote.

MONEY

The currency is the Cour de Franc Pacifique (CFP). Tipping is not required. Bring some cash with you everywhere, as places such as roadside stalls and markets don't accept cards.

21 Breakfast at PAPE'ETE'S

FOOD | CULTURE | CITY

Where else in the world can you find buttery croissants, freshly made *poisson cru* (raw fish with coconut milk) and *pua'a rôti* (Chinese-style roast pork) all in one place? Every Sunday morning in Tahiti's capital, Pape'ete, the city market spills out into the surrounding streets as farmers and vendors from all over the island gather to sell their best fresh produce and local delicacies.

HOLGER LEUE/GETTY IMAGES

Getting here: Short walk downtown from anywhere in Pape'ete. Outside of the city, renting a car or scooter is easiest.

When to go: The market is open from 4am to 10am on Sunday mornings, but it's best to get there before 7am.

Don't forget: Bring an empty stomach and a reusable bag or three. It's useful to have different bags to separate fish, vegetables and cooked food.

WESLEY RIOU/SHUTTERSTOCK

FOROY/SHUTTERSTOCK

Go with a local The best way to experience the market is with someone in the know. Walking food tours of the **Marché de Pape'ete** are available in English with **Orama Mollimard** *(tahitiwithme.com)* or **Tahiti food tours** *(tahitifoodtour.com)*.

Sunday feasts The Sunday brunch or Sunday lunch is a Tahitian institution and families typically gather together after church to eat *ma'a* Tahiti (traditional Tahitian food) and sabbath-day favourites like *pua'a rôti*. There's no entrees, mains or desserts here; everything is piled onto a plate and eaten all together, with your hands. It tastes better that way!

Culinary legacies Tahiti has a unique food culture which reflects its history. Along with traditional Tahitian food, which is based on starchy vegetables, coconut and seafood, the islands' cuisine has also been shaped by its Chinese population, who first arrived in Tahiti in the late 1800s as labourers. French colonisers brought their food traditions to the island as well, and as a result modern Tahitian food is a delicious and sometimes surprising fusion of all three influences.

Do it yourself Arrive just before sunrise to beat the crowds and take your time. There aren't always labels on the food and produce, so don't be afraid to ask questions. If in doubt, follow the people – the best food stands can attract long queues and sometimes sell out before the crowds arrive.

Must-Try Market Foods

Firifiri Tahitian version of a doughnut made with coconut milk.

Pua'a rôti Chinese-style roast pork chopped into bite-size pieces.

Raw fish Try the classic *poisson cru*, which is raw fish and vegetables with coconut milk and lime juice or the *poisson cru au taioro*, raw fish with fermented grated coconut.

Po'e Sweet dish made with fresh fruit puree mixed with tapioca flour and covered in coconut milk. Popular variations include banana, papaya and pumpkin.

Starch Sweet potato, breadfruit, *fe'i* (plantain banana) and taro.

■Insights from Orama Mollimard,
food tour guide in Pape'ete
@tahiti.with.me

22 Explore MO'OREA

BEACHES | SIGHTSEEING | MOUNTAIN

The postcard-perfect island of Mo'orea, with its turquoise lagoon and jagged mountain peaks, is just a short ferry ride away from Pape'ete. It's just over 60km around the entire island, so relax and go at your own pace.

IPICS/SHUTTERSTOCK

Getting here: Ferries such as Vaeara'i *(vaearai.com)*, Terevau *(terevau.pf)* and Aremiti *(aremitiexpress.com)* run frequently to Mo'orea.

Getting around: Car and scooter rentals are close to the ferry wharf; e-bikes and bikes can be delivered to you.

When to go: August–November for whales, May–October for sunny weather.

Top Tip: Bring cash – chances are you'll want to stop at a roadside stall for fresh fruit or a coconut to drink.

Choose Your Adventure

Getting around Mo'orea Marché de Pape'ete is more fun with a rental, and there's a bunch to choose from:

Car Comfortable, fast, and air-conditioning is always a plus (7000+CFP per day)

E-bike Fun and eco-friendly (4000+CFP per day)

Scooter Get around like a local (5000+CFP per day)

Bike Exercise and appreciate the sights (3000+CFP per day)

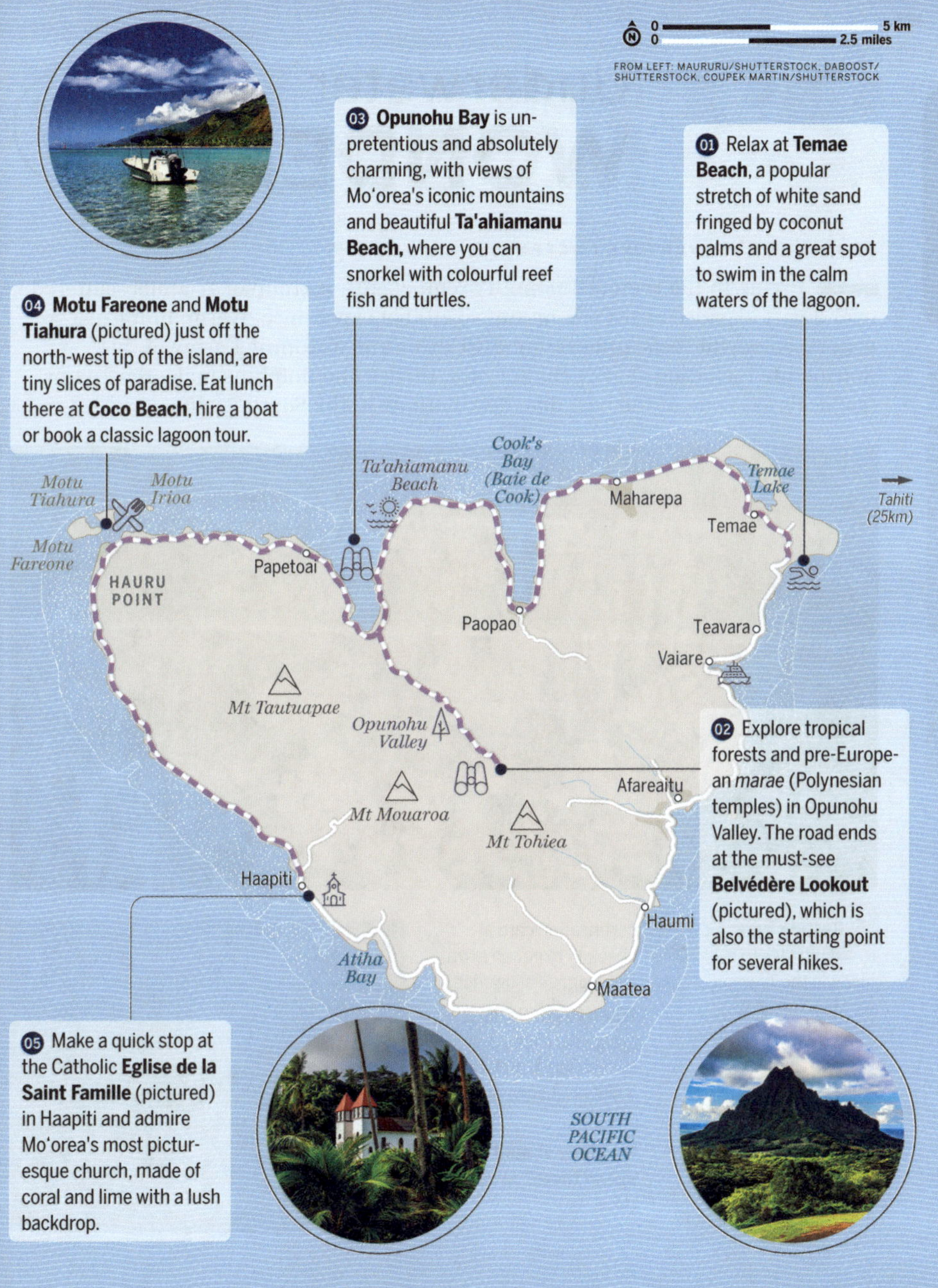

0 5 km
0 2.5 miles
FROM LEFT: MAURURU/SHUTTERSTOCK, DABOOST/SHUTTERSTOCK, COUPEK MARTIN/SHUTTERSTOCK
03 **Opunohu Bay** is unpretentious and absolutely charming, with views of Mo'orea's iconic mountains and beautiful **Ta'ahiamanu Beach,** where you can snorkel with colourful reef fish and turtles.
01 Relax at **Temae Beach**, a popular stretch of white sand fringed by coconut palms and a great spot to swim in the calm waters of the lagoon.
04 **Motu Fareone** and **Motu Tiahura** (pictured) just off the north-west tip of the island, are tiny slices of paradise. Eat lunch there at **Coco Beach**, hire a boat or book a classic lagoon tour.
Motu Tiahura
Motu Irioa
Motu Fareone
Ta'ahiamanu Beach
Cook's Bay (Baie de Cook)
Maharepa
Temae Lake
Temae
Tahiti (25km)
HAURU POINT
Papetoai
Paopao
Teavara
Vaiare
Mt Tautuapae
Opunohu Valley
Mt Mouaroa
Mt Tohiea
Afareaitu
02 Explore tropical forests and pre-European *marae* (Polynesian temples) in Opunohu Valley. The road ends at the must-see **Belvédère Lookout** (pictured), which is also the starting point for several hikes.
Haapiti
Haumi
Atiha Bay
Maatea
05 Make a quick stop at the Catholic **Eglise de la Saint Famille** (pictured) in Haapiti and admire Mo'orea's most picturesque church, made of coral and lime with a lush backdrop.
SOUTH PACIFIC OCEAN

23 Underwater WONDER

MARINE LIFE | ADVENTURE | OCEAN

Diving in the remote Tuamotu archipelago – a group of 77 atolls scattered over a vast expanse of sea – is an unforgettable experience. Warm, limpid waters, colourful reefs, unbeatable drift dives and a stunning array of 'big' marine life including sharks, manta rays, turtles and dolphins make the Tuams (as locals say) one of the best dive destinations in the South Pacific.

Getting here: Air Tahiti flies to over 20 atolls in the Tuamotu; Air Moana flies to Rangiroa only. Air Tahiti has a 'Tuamotu Pass', which allows tourists to visit all three atolls at a fixed, discounted price. Check out *airtahiti.pf* for specific dates and more info. Present your diving certification card at check-in to get an extra 5kg luggage allowance.

When to go: Diving is great year round, but December–March there's a higher chance of rain/storms.

How long should I spend there? At least three days.

Choosing an atoll Fakarava, **Rangiroa** and **Tikehau** offer world-class diving and great diving facilities. Fakarava is best known for its legendary Tumakohua pass, a drift dive known for the 'wall of sharks'. Rangiroa has a huge range of dive sites – something for every level – and offers a never-ending assembly line of marine life. Tikehau is renowned for its incredible numbers of fish, of every kind. Expect to see schools of Napolean wrasses, trevally, triggerfish and more.

Good to know The ocean is rarely cooler than 25°C, so a thin wetsuit is fine. Remember that on remote atolls, residents rely on rainwater for daily use; be mindful of your own water use while there. Good diving centres make all the difference; we recommend **O2 Fakarava** *(o2fakarava.com)*, **Rangiroa Diving Center** *(rangiroadivingcenter.com)* and **Coco Dive Tikehau** *(cocodivetikehau.com)*.

For Beginners Diving in the Tuamotus can be intimidating for inexperienced divers. If you're certified but feeling unsure, consider spending some time diving in islands such as Mo'orea or Huahine, where the conditions are easier and you can practise your skills before heading to Rangiroa. If you'd like to become a certified diver, courses in French Polynesia take three to four days and cost around 80,000CFP.

Diving cruises Dream of living on a boat and sailing to all the best diving destinations? Try **Aquapolynesie** *(aquatiki.com)* or **Miti charter** *(miticharterpolynesia.com)*.

Far left Coral Rangiroa **Bottom left** Tiger shark, Tuamotu

Expert Tips

Remember the Tuamotus are remote. Expect small dive centres, small boats and small groups of around four to eight people. Don't expect to find the comforts that come with big dive factories.

Many dives here are drift dives – they're not the same as calm reef dives.

The deeper you're able to dive, the more options you have. Getting down to around 30m will mean the current is slower in places like Fakarava's north pass.

Be prepared to have the best time of your life – there's nowhere else in the world like it!

■ **Insights from Thibault Gachon,** dive Instructor & founder, O2 Fakarava (o2fakarava.com)

24 Waterfall CHASING

HIKING | NATURE | ADVENTURE

There's nothing like the satisfaction of dipping your toes into a cool freshwater spring or gazing at a towering waterfall after trekking through lush tropical jungle. Too often underrated, Tahiti's awe-inspiring valleys, mountains and forests offer countless opportunities to appreciate nature at its absolute best. And with everything from 10-minute, family-friendly walks to multiday treks, there's something for everyone.

GERAINT TELLEM/ROBERTHARDING/GETTY IMAGES

Getting here: It's easiest to rent a car to get around Tahiti. If you hire a hiking guide they'll usually pick you up and take you to the trailhead.

When to go: Hiking is best and safest during the dry season, from May to October.

Hiking shoes: Many hikes involve walking through rivers or creeks. The classic local hiking shoes are jelly sandals: they're practical, cheap and can handle water!

IZANBAR/GETTY IMAGES

Top left Fa'aruma'i Waterfalls **Bottom left** Vaipahi Spring Gardens

Family-friendly waterfalls The **Fa'aruma'i Waterfalls** on Tahiti's east coast are the most impressive, easy-to-access falls. From the parking lot, it's a five-minute walk on a gravel path to **Vaimahutu Falls**, the first and highest one. For a small waterfall in a beautiful garden setting, head to the **Bain de Vaima & Vaipahi Spring Gardens** on the west coast for a quick stroll. This is also the starting point for a short, well-marked hike with nice lagoon views.

Two-day adventure For a spectacular two-day hike, **Te Pari** is unbeatable. Located on Tahiti Iti, the hike traverses the island's last wild, uninhabited coastline. Marvel at the spectacular natural landscapes, walk along coral reef, beaches, through forests and rivers, and discover hidden waterfalls and swimming spots.

Hiking guides Trails in Tahiti can be dangerous. They're often unmarked and difficult to find, with some trails requiring special permissions or equipment. Hiring a qualified hiking guide is the best way to find your way in Tahiti. They're locals, experts in the area, and you'll have the added bonus of learning about the flora, fauna and the history of the place you're visiting. Some good guides include Toanui Nena, who also does canyoning *(tetoahiking.com)*; Angelina Bordas, a well-established Tahiti-based guide *(tahitirevatrek.com)*; Hitinui, who specialises in Tahiti iiti hikes *(facebook.com/heeuriexplorer)*; and Asher Kora for Mo'orea hikes *(moorea-by-foot.com)*.

Best Waterfall Hikes in Tahiti

Fautaua Valley Trail Half-day hike to 150m waterfall in a history-filled valley; there's a beautiful swimming spot above the falls. Requires a permit and small fee from Pape'ete Town Hall.

Fara'ura Valley located in Hitia'a; there are five or six waterfalls on one trail, including beautiful twin waterfalls and lots of swimming spots.

Maroto Waterfalls Located in **Papenoo Valley**, this waterfall cascades down into a pool of brightest blue. Safe to swim.

My favourite hike The **Ahititera Summit hike** has no waterfalls, but the stunning 360-degree views of Papenoo Valley make up for it. Possible to swim at Maroto Falls on the return trail.

■ Insights from Toanui Nena, *hiking guide, facebook.com/toanui.nena*

FLORA
of French Polynesia

01 Cocotier (Coconut tree)
Perhaps the most revered tree in the Pacific, local legend has it that the tree sprouted from the buried head of the eel prince, as a final gift to his betrothed.

02 Tiare Tahiti
Once considered sacred, Tahiti's sweet-scented national flower is everywhere – in cosmetics, traditional medicine, tucked behind the ears and used as the logo for everything from the national airline to toilet paper.

03 'Aute (Hibiscus)
A favourite flower among French Polynesian women. If worn behind the right ear, it's a signal that she's single; behind the left means she's taken.

04 Tamanu

Most widely used today for its healing properties, the oil extracted from the nut – tamanu oil – is used to treat skin conditions.

05 Auti (Ti plant)
The *auti* is an important cultural plant with a myriad of uses – from cooking to decorating.

06 Tipanie (Frangipani)
A symbol of immortality, this tree with its stunning, fragrant flowers is a common sight, often planted in cemeteries.

07 Fara (Pandanus)
French Polynesians have perfected the art of processing and weaving pandanus leaves. Intricately woven hats, baskets and mats make beautiful souvenirs.

08 Vanille (Vanilla)
One of the countries' most prized exports, French Polynesia produces exquisite vanilla beans. They're grown almost exclusively on the island of Taha'a.

09 Re'a moeruru (shampoo ginger)
When squeezed, this pinecone-shaped flower releases a pleasant-smelling liquid, most commonly used as a natural shampoo or soap.

10 Pūrau (Cotton tree)
You know the grass 'hula' skirts everyone associates with Hawaii? Well, they're actually traditional dress from French Polynesia, and they're from the bark.

25 Island FESTIVALS

CULTURE | SPORTS | EVENTS

Tahitians love any excuse to celebrate and there's a range of vibrant cultural and sporting events throughout the year that showcase the best that Polynesian society has to offer – community, generosity and *mana*, a powerful natural energy that encapsulates the spirit of the islands.

GREGORY BOISSY/AFP VIA GETTY IMAGES

Getting here: For events in Tahiti, it's best to rent a car or be based in Pape'ete. For events on other islands, book plane or ferry tickets in advance to secure a place.

When to go: Culture lovers should visit in July, when the biggest festival, the Heiva, is held.

Top Tip: Brush up on your French, do some research beforehand or go with a local: events aren't always translated into English.

HEMIS/ALAMY

Heiva i Tahiti

French Polynesia's biggest, most joyous celebration of traditional culture is a spectacle not to be missed. Held mostly in Pape'ete, the festival, which takes place every July, lasts for three weeks and includes traditional sports competitions as well as a fire-walking ceremony, weaving demonstrations and more. The biggest draws, however, are the traditional dance and music competitions that take place over two weeks at **Place To'ata**, Pape'ete's outdoor amphitheatre. Both professional and amateur groups practise for months perfecting choreography and hand-making costumes, and the shows are always breathtaking. Tickets are available at *maisondelaculture.pf* and the program at *heiva.org*. Winning dance groups often do both free and paid performances after the

GREGORY BOISSY/AFP VIA GETTY IMAGES

Year-Round Tahitian Culture

Hotels host weekly traditional dance and buffet nights.

Smaller Heiva festivals are held in Mo'orea, Bora Bora and Raiatea late June.

Learn how to paddle a *va'a* (outrigger canoe) or surf.

Experience a traditional feast cooked in an *ahima'a* (underground oven).

Learn the Tahitian language with an immersion course.

Far left Heiva i Tahiti **Left** Hawaiki Nui Canoe Race (p166) **Above** A traditional dance night

Heiva – ask at the tourist office in Pape'ete to find out more.

Hawaiki Nui Canoe Race

Every year during the first week of October, the country stops to watch Polynesian outrigger canoe teams battle it out in a 128km race of endurance and teamwork, which starts on the island of **Huahine** and ends in Bora Bora's crystalline lagoon. While the three-day marathon is a men's event, there are also shorter-distance women's, amateur and youth races. The best place to witness this sporting prowess is at the finish line, from either **Matira Beach** in Bora Bora or on the lagoon. The atmosphere is festive and emotional as tired rowers are cheered on by the crowd and draped in flower leis by loved ones.

Miss Tahiti

A local institution, the Miss Tahiti pageant is one of the most anticipated events of the year, and the whole island gets behind the candidates. The pageant culminates in an

Other Notable Events

FIFO Pacific International Documentary Film Festival Hosted annually in February at the Maison de la Culture in Pape'ete. Showcases the best short films and documentaries from around the Pacific. *(fifotahiti.com)*

Matarii i ni'a Celebrates the arrival in November of the 'season of abundance' with traditional ceremonies in various locations around Tahiti.

Matavaa Henua Enana Spectacular culture and arts festival held every two years in December in the remote Marquesas archipelago. *(matavaa.org)*

Hura Tapairu Second in popularity only to the Heiva, this traditional dance competition is held in an intimate setting at the **Maison de la Culture de Tahiti** every November *(huratapairu.com)*.

Left Matavaa Henua Enana
Below Teahupoo

extravagant night hosted at the **Mairie de Pape'ete** (Town Hall) gardens, which involves dance and music performances, interviews and more. One of the highlights is the costume competition, where the candidates model lavish handmade gowns made entirely of natural materials such as leaves, shells and flowers. The final election is held in June and tickets are usually available in advance at *ticket-pacific.pf.*

Tahiti Pro

The best surfers in the world take on Tahiti's most powerful wave every August in **Teahupoo**, which recently hosted the Paris 2024 Olympic surfing event. Teahupoo is a small fishing village at the 'end of the road', and it's located about an hour and a half from Pape'ete by car. The population swells every year during major surfing events like the Tahiti Pro, so book accommodation early or look at staying in nearby towns such as **Vairao**. The best views are from the sea and numerous 'taxi boats' take visitors out for a fee.

FROM LEFT: SYLVAIN LEFEVRE/GETTY IMAGES, JEROME BROUILLET/AFP VIA GETTY IMAGES

Why is French Polynesia 'French'?

RESISTANCE, COLONIALISM AND NUCLEAR TESTS IN PARADISE

Flick through radio stations in French Polynesia and chances are you'll hear everything from the news in Paris to a Bible sermon in Tahitian or the latest Hawaiian reggae hit. What might seem at first like a random mix is actually rooted in the complex – and often bloody – history of 'paradise'.

Left Huahine island **Centre** Nuclear explosion, Mururoa **Right** Pouvanaa a Oopa

The Stage is Set for War

From the late 1700s tol the mid-1800s, Tahiti was an independent kingdom, ruled by the Pomare family. But during an age when European powers were busy carving up the world, the region we now call French Polynesia found itself torn between two great nations: England and France. By the mid 1830s the English protestant clergy had a strong foothold on the island of Tahiti, and the ear of the Tahitian Queen Pomare IV. French Catholic missionaries, however, had a foothold in the remote Gambier islands and Marquesas archipelago. Things came to a head in 1836 when French missionaries arrived in Tahiti to preach and were swiftly deported by order of the Queen. The incident gave the French the perfect excuse to retaliate, and they did so with guns blazing, effectively taking over Tahiti in 1842. Despite repeated pleas from the Tahitians and the English missionaries, England did not intervene.

The Franco-Tahitian Wars

By 1844, Queen Pomare IV had fled to a neighbouring island, and her key supporters were imprisoned or exiled. A rebellion broke out in Tahiti, Mo'orea and other islands against the French. The island of Huahine, known for its strong resistance to French rule, was bombed by the French military. The Franco-Tahitian Wars resulted in heavy casualties on both sides, but by 1847 the Polynesians, outgunned and under-resourced, had surrendered to the French, and a peace treaty was signed. Then in 1877, Queen Pomare IV passed away and was succeeded by her son, Pomare V. In 1880, France managed to convince Pomare V to cede his state to France, with the promise that Tahitians would be able to govern themselves according to their own traditions. Spoiler alert: they

MICHEL BARET/GAMMA-RAPHO VIA GETTY IMAGES

AFP VIA GETTY IMAGES

didn't keep their promise. Tahiti was officially annexed in 1880, and by 1901 the island of Rimatara in the Austral archipelago became the last island annexed in what was to become French Polynesia.

The Colonial Era & the Nuclear Era

From the late 1800s through to the 1950s, the islands developed an economy based on cotton, vanilla, mother-of-pearl and copra, some of which are still important industries today. Phosphate mining in Makatea proved lucrative. In 1957, the territory was officially named French Polynesia, and the majority voted to remain part of France. Then, in the 1960s, the islands became the testing ground that contributed to France's rise as a nuclear power. France would detonate close to 200 nuclear bombs on two atolls in French Polynesia, including 41 atmospheric tests. Despite rioting in Pape'ete, and protests internationally, French nuclear testing didn't end until 1996.

The islands became the testing ground that contributed to France's rise as a nuclear power.

Tahiti & French Polynesia Today

Today, French Polynesia mostly governs itself, although France is still in charge of defence, education and immigration. In 2023, pro-independence President Moetai Brotherson was elected after 10 years of pro-France politics, though this is unlikely to lead to a referendum on independence soon. While relations between France and its Pacific territory are cordial, islanders for the most part still consider themselves Tahitians first, and French second.

Pouvanaa a Oopa

Pouvanaa a Oopa is remembered today as an important political figure and the *metua* (father) of Tahitian nationalism. As a critic of nuclear testing with a growing following, Oopa was seen as a threat by French colonialists, who in 1958 falsely accused him of arson, inciting unrest. In 1959, Oopa was sentenced to eight years in prison and 15 years of exile in France. It wasn't until 41 years after his death, in 2018, that he was proven innocent. In Pape'ete today there's an avenue named Pouvanaa a Oopa, which leads, ironically, to the 'Place Jacques Chirac' – named for the president who restarted nuclear testing in the islands in the 1990s.

Listings

BEST OF THE REST

Off the Beaten Track

Nuku Hiva Island

Rugged and remote, with majestic bays, verdant valleys and towering cliffs, Nuku Hiva has a wild energy that's all its own. Think adventure: hiking, horse riding, diving and cultural discoveries.

Raivavae Island

Raivavae is a dream – its cerulean lagoon is unmatched, dotted with *motu* (islets) and sleepy villages, and warm locals add to the charm.

Mangareva Island

The rarely visited island of Mangareva in the Gambier islands is just one of a group of mountainous islands surrounded by a single reef. Beautiful environment, interesting Catholic history and welcoming people, who also produce some of French Polynesia's best pearls.

Makatea Island

For a unique experience, head to Makatea in the Tuamotu archipelago, accessible only by boat and known for its incredible limestone cliffs. It's paradise for climbers and lovers of the outdoors.

Historic Sites

Marae Taputapuatea, Raiatea

If you only see one *marae* (Polynesian temple) in French Polynesia, make it Marae Taputapuatea, French Polynesia's most important and sacred.

Iipona, Hiva Oa

Iipona is a fascinating archeological site near the village of Puamau in the Marquesas, known for its collection of well-preserved *tikis*.

Marae Arahurahu, Tahiti

Located in the district of Paea on Tahiti's west coast, this *marae* is a must-stop on a road trip around the island. Every year during the Heiva Festival, traditional dance shows are performed on the sacred grounds.

Te Fare Iamanaha, Puna'auia

A small museum with interesting artifacts, detailing the history and culture of the different archipelagos in French Polynesia, as well as other Polynesian islands such as Fiji and Hawaii.

Whale Encounters

Mo'orea

French Polynesia's most popular island for whale encounters, Mo'orea has a plethora of activity and accommodation options as well. Tour companies include WildMā (@wildma.expeditions) and Moorea Ocean Adventures (*moorea-ocean-adventures.com*).

Rurutu

This once relatively unknown island in the Austral archipelago has become one of French Polynesia's top destinations for humpback whale encounters, including swimming with whales. Book whale encounters through travel agencies or through your accommodation; Pension Teautamatea (*teautamatea.blogspot.com*) and Vaitumu Village (*vaitumuvillage.com*) are both good options.

Luxury Stays & Overwater Bungalows

Bora Bora

Ultramarine lagoon, towering green peaks and the iconic overwater bungalows. This is the island with the most options when it comes to luxury accommodation, and it never disappoints. The **Four Seasons Bora Bora Resort** (*fourseasons.com/borabora*) and **St Régis Resort** (*marriot.com*) are among the best.

Taha'a

Bora Bora's low-key cousin, Taha'a is less-developed, but just as appealing. Known for its vanilla plantations and locally made rum, it's also home to a couple of amazing resorts, such as **Le Taha'a by Pearl Resorts** *(letahaa.com)*, which has a range of beautiful suites and villas.

Tetiaroa

Holiday destination to the world's top movie stars and politicians, Tetiaroa is a privately owned atoll with an eco-resort known as the Brando *(thebrando.com)* that offers the best of remote island luxury, with prices to match.

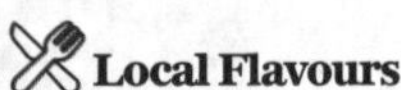

Local Flavours

WSK, Tahiti $

Sells baguette sandwiches every lunchtime filled with anything your heart desires – steak, chicken, chow mein, fish, fries, cheese and more. Two locations – one near **Pape'ete market** and the other in Faa'a.

Le Fournil Hautbois, Tahiti $

Classic French Boulangerie in multiple locations around the island. Best to go in the morning for fresh croissants, *pain au chocolat* and crunchy baguettes.

Kfe Roti, Pape'ete $$

Local-style breakfast cafe located close to Pape'ete Town Hall. Specialises in traditional Tahitian staples such as *firi firi* (coconut doughnuts), *poisson cru*, fried lagoon fish, taro and corned beef.

Snack Aoni, Faa'a $$

Hole-in-the-wall lunch place in Heiri serving up Tahitian-Chinese favourites such as lemon chicken, chow mein and one of the islands' best *ma'a tinito* (popular local dish made with macaroni, red beans, pork and vegetables).

Vini Vini Snacking, Tahiti $$

Open for lunch with multiple locations all over Tahiti. Specialises in fish – think sushi, sashimi, poke bowls, burgers and more.

Tropical Grill, Paea $$

Roulotte (food truck) on the main road. Big portions of local favourites such as steak frites, chow mein and raw fish.

Restaurant Le Moana, Pape'ete $$$

Go for great views of the port and Mo'orea and stay for fun vibes. Happy hour (4–6pm) has great deals, and they also do lunch and dinner.

L'O à la Bouche, Pape'ete $$$

Fine-dining restaurant in the heart of Pape'ete. Classic French dishes with a local twist.

Best Island Activities & Excursions

Lagoon tour

A version of this tour is available on just about every island. Usually involves a boat tour on the lagoon, with stops for snorkelling, and ends with a BBQ or traditional lunch on a *motu*. A winning formula that's always a good time.

Fenua Aihere & Teahupoo boat tours

Beyond the end of the road in Tahiti lies a wild coastline full of natural treasures. Tours will take you boating along the coastline with stops at **Teahupoo**'s famous wave, snorkelling spots, caves and waterfalls. Unforgettable adventure.

Tetiaroa Day Tour

A great way to see a beautiful atoll without having to fly to the Tuamotus. Catamarans leave Pape'ete to Tetiaroa and include breakfast, lunch, snorkelling and walking tours of the atoll.

Jet ski tour

It doesn't get much better than zooming awround on a jet ski over a turquoise lagoon on a paradisacal island. These tours are available on multiple islands.

MARKET
Food

01 Lolo
Fluffy coconut buns are a big hit in Fiji. Samoan *pani popo* are similar. Both are especially good straight from the oven.

02 Poi
Taro root mashed into a smooth paste and then fermented to be slightly sour is the Solomon Islands' favourite side dish.

03 Watery rose apple
Bright red, and with a refreshing flavour similar to watermelon or pear. Actually more related to guava than apples.

04 Laplap
In Vanuatu, coconut cream and breadfruit, taro or yam are wrapped in banana leaves and cooked in an underground oven. Added protein could include chicken or pork.

05 Island cabbage
Leafy vegetable popular around the Pacific. Used for salads and also to wrap fish and meat before cooking. Known as 'slippery cabbage' when steamed.

06 Māroro

Grilled *māroro* (flying fish) is a popular weekend treat at Rarotonga's Saturday morning Punanga Nui Market.

07 Firi firi

Partner these Tahitian deep-fried coconut dumplings with a weekend coffee.

08 Rukau

Rukau, young taro leaves steamed in coconut cream, is a Cook Islands favourite. In Fiji, ask for the local variation, *rourou*.

09 Breadfruit

Starchy fruit that's mixed with coconut cream. Along with fried taro and sweet potato, also made into crispy chips.

10 'Ota 'ika

Raw fish marinated in lime juice coconut milk in Samoa and Tonga. Called *ika mata* on Rarotonga, *kokoda* in Fiji and *poisson cru* in Tahiti.

11 Nem

Vietnamese-style spring rolls are popular in Tahiti. Other Asian-inspired treats are *chao pao* (steamed buns) and *lope pan* (rice dumplings).

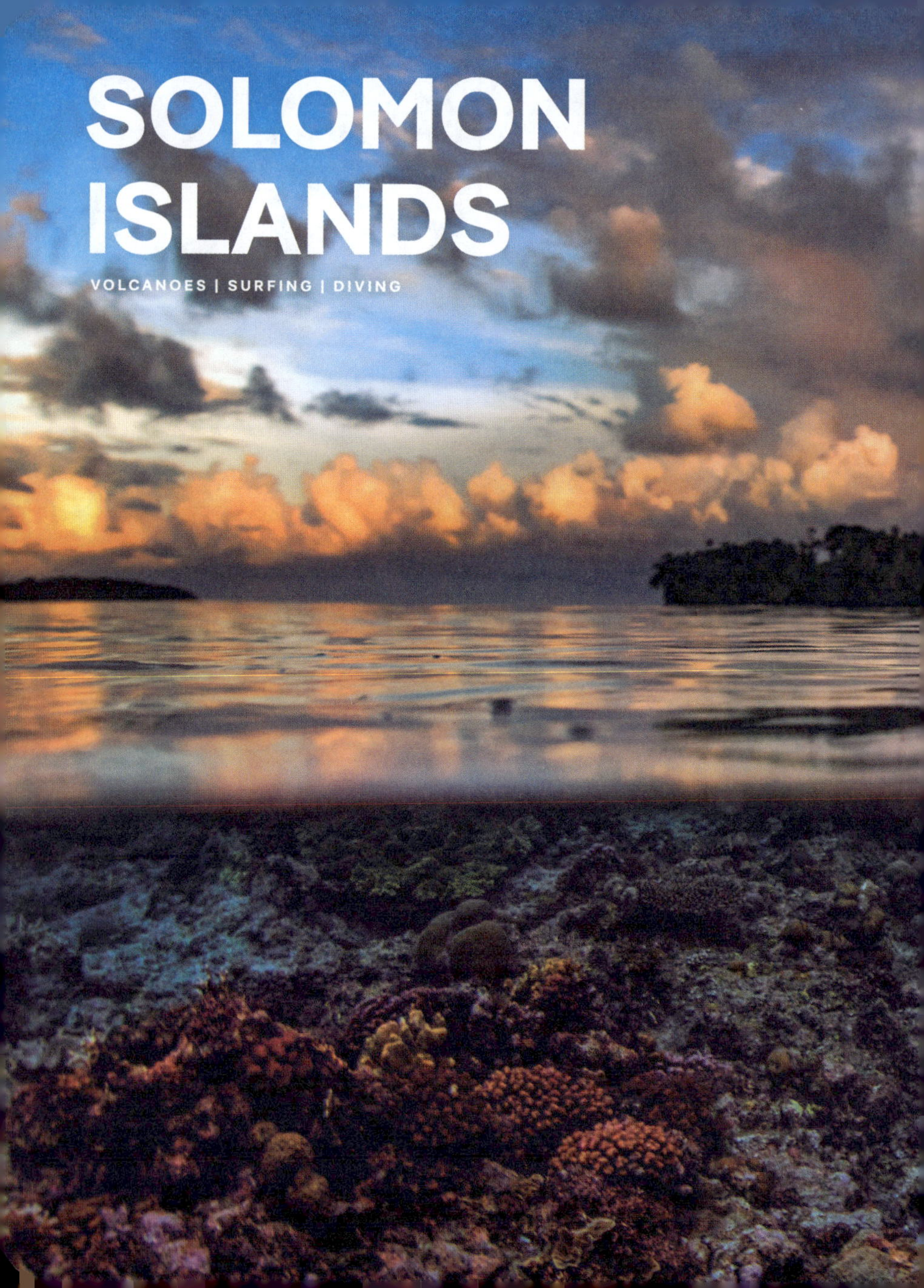
SOLOMON
ISLANDS
VOLCANOES | SURFING | DIVING

Spot sharks as you dive near the private **Njari Island** (p185).

30mins from Gizo Town

Scope out a secret surf spot off the coast of **Gizo** (pictured, p185).

1hr from Honiara

Swim in twin waterfalls hidden on **Kolombangara Island** (pictured, p188).

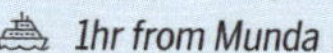

1hr from Munda

SOLOMON ISLANDS

Trip Builder

An archipelago of more than 900 mountainous islands and coral atolls harbouring incredible biodiversity, the 'Hapi Isles' is carving out its reputation as an adventure destination, with a burgeoning surf scene. Yet only 26,000 tourists – mostly birders and WWII history buffs – visit the tropical paradise every year.

CLOCKWISE FROM TOP LEFT: JAN BUTCHOFSKY/ALAMY, JULIA PETERLE/SHUTTERSTOCK, SAM LAWRENCE PHOTOGRAPHY/SHUTTERSTOCK, JESSICA LOCKHART/LONELY PLANET. PREVIOUS SPREAD: MAXIMILIAN MILZ/GETTY IMAGES

Practicalities

MTCURADO/GETTY IMAGES

ARRIVING

Honiara International Airport (pictured) Direct flights from Australia, Vanuatu and Fiji land 12km outside the city's centre. The drive into the city can take 30 minutes. Many hotels offer airport pickup, while taxis into the city cost around SI$120. Private transfers can also be booked from SI$280.

Honiara Port Cruise ships anchor a short walking distance from Honiara's Central Market.

HOW MUCH FOR A

Wood carving SI$300

Two-metre strand of shell money SI$1000

Intro PADI Dive SI$1200

WHEN TO GO

NOV–JAN
The wet season runs November until April.

FEB–APR
Humid days and bursts of rain. Cyclones are rare.

MAY–AUG
The dry season lasts until October. Good visibility for divers.

SEP–OCT
Large, clean surfing swells and favourable sailing winds.

GETTING AROUND

Solomon Airlines Services over 20 destinations, including Munda, Gizo and Auki. Luggage is limited to 16kg and airports may lack toilets. It's the quickest way to get around, but plan buffer days, as flights can be unreliable.

Banana boat Open-air vessels that are a pleasurable way to travel shorter distances on fair-weather days – less so in rough water or heavy rain. Line your luggage with a garbage bag and request a life jacket. About SI$1500 per day for a charter (not including fuel).

Inter-island ferries and cargo ships Run between Honiara and Auki and Honiara and Gizo with room for passengers. Contact Pelican Shipping, Frantji Shipping or Fair West Shipping for departure times.

TOP: HOLIDAY.PHOTO.TOP/SHUTTERSTOCK
BOTTOM: SAM LAMBENCE PHOTOGRAPHY/SHUTTERSTOCK

EATING & DRINKING

The Solomon Islands don't stray far from the winning South Pacific formula of fresh fish and seafood served with variations of coconut and root vegetables, including taro and cassava. Case in point? The national dish is *poi*, a savoury side made from taro-root paste. Cassava pudding – made by wrapping the paste of coconut, sweet potato and cassava in banana leaves and cooking it in hot stones – is also popular. Fresh fruit, including papaya (pictured) – even eaten green in curries – rounds out the offerings.

Best seafood platter
Coral Sea Resort (p188)

Must try *Ngali* nuts (pictured) at **Honiara's Central Market** (p186)

CONNECT & FIND YOUR WAY

Wi-fi Pick up a SIM card at Our Telekom's Honiara Airport kiosk or in the city centre. Mobile service is patchy, even in urban areas. Fortunately, many major hotels and resorts – even on outer-lying islands – have wi-fi, thanks to Starlink.

Navigation There are limited road networks. Most travel is done by boat.

WHERE TO STAY

Outside of Honiara – home to flashy hotels – accommodation errs on the side of basic. Think: homestays, wilderness lodges and a handful of resort-like (but still relatively rustic) overwater bungalows.

Area	Pro/Con
Honiara, Guadalcanal	The capital is the biggest and busiest city, offering everything from budget motels to glossy hotels.
Munda, New Georgia	A jumping-off spot for divers and day trippers; seaside villages offer basic accommodation and eating.
Gizo	A hotspot for surfers and divers; laid-back resorts a banana boat away from Tonga's third-largest town.
Kolombangara Island	Impressive birdwatching and off-grid hiking; accommodation includes off-grid lodges and small resorts.
Auki, Malaita	Village stays and serviceable self-contained guesthouses, some offering air-conditioning.

SAFETY & RESPECT

Beachwear is fine for resorts, otherwise cover knees and shoulders. The Solomons are relatively safe, but avoid walking or travelling alone at night.

MONEY

The currency is Solomon Islands dollars (SI$). Only major hotels will accept cards, but ATMs are limited. Make sure you have enough cash for your journey and multiple ways to access it.

26 Honiara by DAY

MUSEUMS | WWII HISTORY | FOOD

On the island of Guadalcanal, Honiara is the country's busiest city, with a population of about 92,000. It only takes a half day to explore its bustling markets, museums and monuments. Allow a full day to add WWII sites further afield, including a snorkel-friendly shipwreck.

THE ASAHI SHIMBUN VIA GETTY IMAGES

How To

Getting around: Honiara's central attractions can be accessed by foot. For Mbonege Beach (pictured) and the Vilu War Museum, you'll need wheels – and time. Road conditions are poor, with massive potholes slowing travel. The 24km drive between Honiara and the Vilu War Museum can take well over an hour.

When to go: Some attractions close on weekends, but open by appointment.

Organised tours: For tailored tours, contact Travel Solomons, Hapi Isles Tours, Guadalcanal Travel Solomons, or Iumi Tours.

Snorkel a Shipwreck

WWII wrecks make the Solomons a great diving destination, but snorkellers can also get in on the action. At **Bonegi** – 12km from the centre – you can snorkel above **Bonegi II** *(Kinugawa Maru)*, a Japanese freighter in shallow waters. Bring snorkel gear and roughly SI$100 for the entrance fee.

FROM LEFT: DENNIS COX/ALAMY, WIRESTOCK/GETTY IMAGES

27 Highland HIKING

WATERFALLS | HOT SPRINGS | VOLCANOES

Before missionaries arrived, locals lived in the highlands, where it was easier to defend themselves from head-hunting enemies. Today, most communities are scattered along the coast – but you can still hike into the interior to explore archeological evidence and sacred sites hidden in Kolombangara's mountainous rainforests and Savo Island's volcanic landscapes.

IMAGEBROKER.COM/ALAMY

How to

Getting here: Savo Island is 40 minutes by boat from Vila Village outside Honiara. For Kolombangara, fly to Munda or Gizo, then catch a banana boat. The 60-minute journey from Munda is more sheltered.

When to go: Hit the trails during the dry season (May to October) when downpours are less frequent and river crossings are easier.

Safety first: Many areas still have unexploded ordnance from WWII. This, combined with overgrown tracks, makes hiring a local guide for treks advisable.

JESSICA LOCKHART/LONELY PLANET

Volcanoes & Waterfalls

A city-adjacent wilderness escape It's just across the water from Honiara, but the volcanic **Savo Island** feels a world away. A 30-minute guided hike upwards through the dense rainforest truncates at a steaming **waterfall and hot spring** – a sacred spot said to heal ailments. It's also possible to climb into volcano's crater, where geysers gurgle and fumarole fields steam. The journey takes around four hours and involves climbing rudimentary ladders in intense heat. Your reward? Boiling an egg in a geothermally heated hot spring. Before departing, ask the staff at **Savo Sunset Lodge** if it's possible to watch a cultural performance at nearby **Kuila Village**.

An immersive off-grid adventure In the Western Province, **Kolombangara** is a birding favourite for its six endemic species. What it should be known for, however, is its hiking. Upon arrival at Ringgi Cove, travel by 4WD through a forestry plantation to an altitude of 400m. There, you'll find **Imbu Rano Lodge.** Situated in untouched cloud forest, it has stunning views of **Mt Rano** (1698m) and **Mt Tepalamenggutu** (1708m), and is a base for outdoor adventures. The most popular bushwalk is to **Myles Falls**, a set of twin falls that involves dozens of river crossings and takes four hours. Along the way, you'll pass remains of ancient gardens. It's also possible to summit **Mt Veve** (1768m) – the island's highest point – or the crater of Mt Tepalamenggutu. Both take around four days, with camps along the way. Book through booking@kolombangara.com.

Far left Savo Island **Bottom left** Cultural performance, Kuila Village

Of Languages & Lava

The official language of the Solomon Islands is English, although you'll hear most people speaking Pijin. Islanders also typically know a third language: their Indigenous tongue, with more than 70 Melanesian and Polynesian languages spoken across the 147 inhabited islands. But Savo Island's Savosavo language – overheard in Kuila Village – is unique in that it's a Papuan language, spoken by fewer than 2500 people. With no close relatives, the language is endangered and risks disappearing. It's not the only threat facing Savo – in 2021, the island's volcano became active again, with evidence mounting that it's due to erupt soon.

28 Gizo Above & BELOW

SURFING | DIVING | SNORKELLING

The Aussie surfers we met while researching this book begged us not to let you in on the secret. But Gizo Island in the Western Province can't escape its destiny. Its uncrowded clean breaks make it one of the South Pacific's best surf spots. Already, Gizo's waters are beloved by divers, thanks to good visibility, immaculate coral gardens and WWII shipwrecks.

SAM LAWRENCE PHOTOGRAPHY/SHUTTERSTOCK

How to

Getting here: One-hour direct flights from Honiara land at Nustupe Airport, a five-minute banana boat ride from **Gizo Town**.

When to go: Surfing is best from mid-October to April, with the biggest swells in January and February. Mantas can be seen from November and April, but both diving and surfing are possible year-round.

Accommodation: It's possible to find a room in Gizo Town's hotels or guesthouses. For the ultimate vacay vibes, choose an overwater bungalow on a smaller island nearby.

LEA MCQUILLAN/SHUTTERSTOCK

Surf's up The uncrowded nature of **Gizo Island's** surf breaks is what makes them so special – but it also means you'll be hard-pressed to find rentals or lessons. Some of the resorts around Gizo cater well to surfers – including **Fatboys Resort** and **Sanbis Resort** – offering boat transfer and loaner surfboards for use. But they're often worse for wear, so it's best to arrive with your own board. Reef breaks near Gizo Town include **Paelongge** (a fast and hollow right-hand break), **Titiana** (a long and shallow left) and **Outside Naru** (another right-hand break). Bring a medical kit for coral scraps – you'll be lucky to walk away without a few.

Divers get down All it takes is one banana boat ride across the warm waters surrounding the island of Gizo to understand why this is one of the world's best diving destinations. The sheltered turquoise waters boast incredible visibility – you don't even have to jump in to see what lies below. You'll be glad you did, though. Large marine wildlife – including sharks, dugongs and manta rays – frequent spots such as **Grand Central Station** off the coast of **Njari Island**, a merging point for oceanic currents. This is also a great spot for snorkellers. WWII dive sights include a shallow **American Hellcat Fighter Plane** and **Toa Maru**, an intact 140m Japanese transport ship. **Dive Gizo** is the area's leading outfitter, offering rentals, courses and tours.

Far left Fatboys Resort **Bottom left** Anemone fish, off Njari Island

Gidgets Get Waves

The Solomons' surf scene may still feel like a secret to international visitors – but it's well established locally, with regular lessons offered to residents on weekends. On Gizo, this includes free lessons offered to women by the Western Solomons Surfing Association. In 2024, the locally run organisation received funding to launch its Women Make Waves program. In addition to improving gender equity in the surf community through training and workshops, it also provides surfing-based therapy to survivors of domestic violence. Gizo also isn't the only swell surfing spot in the country. At Santa Isabel Island's **Papatura** surf retreat, you'll find more than 10 breaks with a max of 14 surfers.

Shelling Out

SHOULD SHELL CURRENCY BE LEFT IN THE PAST?

In Honiara's **Central Market**, walk past the mounds of watermelons and piles of peanuts, and you'll arrive at a small row of tables where women sell handicrafts. But the thick strands of white, black and red shells aren't ornamental jewellery – this is shell money, the traditional currency of the Solomon Islands.

Left Dolphin teeth shell money, Solomon Islands **Centre** Making shell money, Malaita **Right** Melanesian shell money, Langalanga Lagoon

Originating from the Langalanga Lagoon, the cultural tradition dates back hundreds of years, with the currency still actively in use today in the provinces of Malaita, Makira and Guadalcanal. Those fortunate enough to attend a bride-buying ceremony will see *tafuli'ae* – 10 long strands of predominantly red shells – traded alongside live pigs, root crops and mats woven from pandanus leaves. A single *tafuli'ae* can be worth as much as SI$3000.

While shell money can be used to purchase household goods or food, it remains the currency of choice for rituals like funerals and settling disputes – so much so, that it isn't unusual for families to keep a box of the currency hidden in their homes. It can also be worn on special occasions as a display of wealth and social status, not unlike a Rolex. And much like Hollywood celebrities are known to borrow diamond necklaces for major events, there are even shell money rental services in Honiara.

Shell Money Minting

Gold, coins, paper money and digital currencies all have one thing in common: they don't have any true value. It's what they *represent* that holds the value – and in the case of shell money, that value comes in part from its labour-intensive production.

At the **Shell Money Festival** – a two-day event held annually in August in Langalanga – visitors can watch the shell discs taking shape, as women break, flatten, shape, heat, drill and smooth the shells, before threading them. A single strand of shell money can take anywhere from a couple of days to a few months to make. Scarcity also contributes to the currency's value. In Malaita – the mint of the Solomon Islands – four

BENEDEK/GETTY IMAGES

PHILIP GAME/ALAMY

types of shells have traditionally been used to make shell money, including the sought-after red-lipped oyster shells. But increased production has resulted in limited supplies of shells. Locals now report sourcing materials from as far away as the Western Province.

The Effects of Supply & Demand

There are also concerns that shell money production can have detrimental effects on other native species. The Santa Cruz Islands once used feathers from the small scarlet honeyeater to make feathered coils of currency – with one coil requiring up to 600 birds. The currency is now rarely used and is no longer in production.

> Dolphin teeth are also frequently strung on shell money strands, with somewhere between 600 and 1500 dolphins killed every year off the coast of Fanalei Island

Dolphin teeth are also frequently strung on shell money strands, with somewhere between 600 and 1500 dolphins killed every year off the coast of Fanalei Island. None of the dolphin species are yet vulnerable or endangered, but environmentalists are calling for an end to the practice, with concerns about over-exploitation.

It could be easy enough to chalk it up to 'mo' money, mo' problems'. But the powerful positive role shell money plays in the Solomon Islands can't be discredited. In places like Malaita – where there's little room to grow food or raise crops for cash – making shell money is a means of survival. It provides an avenue through which local people, particularly women, can support their families, while sustaining their culture.

She Sells Seashells

Here is where you can see shell money on display – and maybe even take home a bit of your own Hapi Isles' bling.

Shaenkola Shell Money Shop Situated in Honiara's Chinatown. Expect to pay SI$1000 and up for a solid strand. Alternatively, visit the Honiara Craft Market (p181).

Laulasi An artificial island in the Langalanga Lagoon that's open to tourists, the community is the main source of shell money.

Skull Island Most tourists head here to see skulls from the head-hunting past. Amongst the graves, there are also fine examples of shell money, including discs made from giant clams and large enough to be worn as armbands.

Listings

BEST OF THE REST

 Waterfalls Near Honiara

Mataniko Falls, Lelei

A roughly four-hour return guided walk with a difficult descent from Lelei Village, these falls thunder down a cliff and straight into a canyon below.

Tenaru Falls, Tenaru

A stunning 63m drop, this set of twin falls can be accessed via a relatively easy – but perhaps a bit tedious – two-hour walk each way starting from Tenaru. Swim behind the falls to access a small cave.

Borare Cascades, Vura

Turn left past Bonegi Beach, drive to Vura village, then walk for about an hour along an old logging road before arriving at a series of cascades, ideal for swimming. Guides can be hired from the village.

 Islands with Eco Lodges

Tetepare Island Ecolodge, Tetepare

The largest uninhabited tropical island in the southern hemisphere, Tetepare is renowned for its biodiversity and favoured by nesting turtles and endemic bat species. Accommodation is available in five traditional bungalows at the edge of the rainforest.

Imbu Rano Lodge, Kolombangara Island

Situated at an altitude of 400m, this basic lodge offers birdwatchers the chance to spot rare and endemic species – including mountain white-eye and mountain pygmy parrots.

Titiru Eco Lodge, Rendova Island

Witness massive leatherback turtles nesting, explore a cave with bats and crabs, or head to a village to meet giant flying foxes near this island's fish and bird sanctuary. Bungalows are sheltered around mangroves.

Arnarvon Islands

The four small Arnarvon Islands are home to the largest rookery of critically endangered hawksbill turtles in the South Pacific region. Primarily a research station, there are three rooms available to book.

 Waterfront Hotels & Resorts

Heritage Park Hotel, Honiara

It's not unusual to see expats doing business at Honiara's bougiest hotel. Centrally located with multiple restaurants and a seafront pool.

Coral Sea Resort, Honiara

In addition to two restaurants, this flashy hotel on the waterfront houses Honiara's casino. In addition to hotel rooms, newer waterfront villas have private waterfront patios with hot tubs.

Savo Sunset Lodge, Savo Island

Offering basic accommodation and meals on Savo Island across the waters from Honiara, the stay is worth it for access to hot springs, hikes and cultural performances at nearby Kuila Village.

Qua Roviana, Munda

Rooms are clean and basic, with air-conditioning, access to filtered water and a kitchen area to prepare meals. A good option for groups of divers who wish to self-cater.

Fatboys Resort, Mbambanga Island

A short boat ride from Gizo's diving and surfing, Fatboys has rustic bungalows, including some that are overwater. Watch the fish from its overwater restaurant.

Imagination Island, Gizo

Just four family-friendly overwater bungalows make this island feel private and secluded. Two recently sunk shipwrecks are accessible directly from the island.

 Festivals & Cultural Sites

Wagosia, East Makira

This June event marks the yam harvest and includes demonstrations of traditional spear fighting.

Shell Money Festival, Malaita

Celebrating the Solomon Islands' traditional currency (p180), this two-day festival is typically held over a weekend in August at the Langalanga Lagoon. See shell money being made and cultural songs and dances performed.

Roviana Lagoon Festival, Munda

Held annually in December, this Munda festival sees villages from the Roviana gather to parade floats both on water and land.

Skull Island

See the skulls of chiefs and their enemies collected during the head-hunting days. Follow *kastom* and hire a local guide to access this small island, a short boat ride from Munda.

 Guided Day Tours

Destination Solomons

Offers day tours focused on Honiara including Honiara city tours, excursions to key WWII battle sites and guided walks to Mataniko Falls.

Iumi Tour Solomons

Based in Honiara, this operator can help you get to Savo Island, Tenaru Falls and battlefield sites.

Guadalcanal Travel Solomons

One of the country's most established tour agencies can help book accommodation on outer-lying islands, as well as WWII and shopping tours of Honiara.

TORSTEN BLACKWOOD/AFP VIA GETTY IMAGES

Skull Island

Hapi Isle Tours

Specialising in tailored multiday tours of Honiara and its surrounds, with extensive knowledge of WWII history.

Travel Solomons

Ask this operator to assist with visits to traditional villages, where you'll have the opportunity to see cultural performances, or visit a farm to learn about cacao production (and sample the goods).

Go West Tours

Based out of the Agnes Gateway Hotel in Munda. Sign up for half-day or full-day guided tours of the nearby Roviana Lagoon, Skull Island, the 'American Dump' WWII Museum and snorkelling sites.

Dive Gizo

Although this tour operator is best known for its expertise in diving, it can also help facilitate tours to Skull Island, Kennedy Island (where US President JF Kennedy was shipwrecked), local villages and to WWII land sites.

PAPUA NEW GUINEA

REMOTE | UNDISCOVERED | DIVERSE

PAPUA NEW GUINEA

Trip Builder

Pack your sense of adventure for Papua New Guinea as you immerse yourself in its breathtaking landscapes and rich cultural tapestry, and you will find it rugged and raw. From trekking in the jungle and diving into untouched coral reefs to witnessing the spectacular tribal festivals bursting with traditional sing-sings, Papua New Guinea is a land of the undiscovered.

Meet the unique Huli Wigmen (pictured, p205) in **Tari** highlands.
1hr from Port Moresby

Explore the traditional villages of the **Sepik River** (p204).
1.5hrs from Port Moresby

Head to **Madang** (p204) to island-hop in the pristine coastal waters.
1hr from Port Moresby

Shop local handicrafts at **Hagen Market** (p204).
1hr from Port Moresby

Climb **Mt Wilhelm** (p205), PNG's highest peak.
1.5hrs from Port Moresby

Vanimo · Aitape · Wewak · Maprik · Angoram · Bogia · Karkar · Madang · Central Range · INDONESIA · Tabubil · Wabag · Tari · **Mount Hagen** · Goroka · Wau · Kerema · Gulf of Papua · Bereina · PORT MORES · CORAL SEA

Admiralty Islands
Lorengau
Bismarck Archipelago
Kavieng
SOUTH PACIFIC OCEAN
New Ireland
In **Kimbe Bay** (p205), dive among vibrant coral reefs.
1hr from Port Moresby
BISMARCK SEA
Namatanai
Rabaul
Kokopo
Explore the volcanic landscapes of **Rabaul** (pictured, p196).
1hr from Port Moresby
Talasea
Kimbe
Kandrian
Buka
Bougainville
Bismarck Archipelago
Buin
SOLOMON SEA
Morobe
Mt Albert Edward
koda
Tufi
Trek the challenging **Kokoda Track** (p201), retracing WWII history.
1hr from Port Moresby
SOLOMON ISLANDS
Kupiano
Alotau
D'Entrecasteaux Islands
Milne Bay
Louisiade Archipelago
Spot rare birds of paradise in **Varirata National Park** (pictured, p198).
30mins from Port Moresby
0 200 km
0 100 miles

Practicalities

HUGO KLEINHANS/SHUTTERSTOCK

ARRIVING

Jacksons International Airport Direct flights from Brisbane, Cairns, Sydney and Honiara fly to Port Moresby. Many hotels offer pickup services, or take the airport shuttle or taxi.

Cruise Ports Passengers typically enter through Rabaul, Madang or Port Moresby. Other ports include Alotau, Conflict Islands (pictured), Doini Island, Kiriwina Island, Kitava and Samarai Island, when day trips are bookable on your cruise ship.

HOW MUCH FOR A

Handcrafted *billum* bag: K100

Local beer: K12

Street food: K5

WHEN TO GO

JAN–MAR
Wet season with heavy rainfall. Best for exploring lush rainforests and waterfalls.

APR–JUN
Drier and cooler weather, perfect for diving and snorkelling along pristine coral reefs.

JUL–SEP
Peak season for cultural festivals like the Goroka Show in the highlands.

OCT–DEC
Transitioning into the wet season. Great for birdwatching.

GETTING AROUND

Flying Domestic flights are the fastest way to navigate Papua New Guinea's rugged terrain. Air Niugini and PNG Air connect major cities and towns, with flights lasting 45–60 minutes and costing K340–440.

PMVs Privately owned public motor vehicles (PMVs) or taxis are the main public transport option for short distances within cities or nearby towns. Fares are budget-friendly, starting at just K2, but set a rate before entering the vehicle.

Boats Ferries and small boats, known as banana boats, connect coastal areas and islands. They're a scenic way to travel. Negotiate fares before boarding and use a life jacket for added safety.

EATING & DRINKING

Papua New Guinea's cuisine is a blend of traditional flavours and fresh local ingredients. *Mumu* (pictured), a traditional dish of pork, sweet potatoes and greens cooked in an earth oven, is a must-try. Street stalls and markets offer quick bites like fried *sago* (pictured) and freshly grilled fish for around K10–20. Port Moresby has an emerging dining scene, with restaurants serving a mix of local and international dishes. High-end dining costs around K80–150 per meal.

Best beer
Lamana Gold Club (p204)

Must try cocktail
Rapopo Plantation Resort (p204)

CONNECT & FIND YOUR WAY

Wi-fi Wi-fi is limited outside major hotels and cafes in cities like Port Moresby. For reliable connectivity, buy a local SIM card with data from Digicel or Telikom at the airport or retail shops.

Navigation PNG's roads are poorly marked and can be challenging to navigate. Offline maps and GPS apps are essential, especially for remote areas.

WHERE TO STAY

Accommodation in Papua New Guinea ranges from basic guesthouses to high-end hotels. Choose a location based on your itinerary and transport needs.

Area	Pro/Con
Port Moresby	Best for business travellers and international connections. Limited budget options, but safe.
Madang	Stunning coastal views and diving. Limited high-end options; remote access can be challenging.
Goroka	Great for cultural festivals. Smaller accommodation options; book early during peak events.
Lae	Central to Highlands Hwy. Mainly midrange hotels; less tourist-focused.
Kokopo	Gateway to East New Britain with luxury resorts. Quiet and remote.

SAFETY

Papua New Guinea is often subject to travel alerts; check government advisories. Stick to organised tours, use reputable taxi services like **Ark Taxis**, and always negotiate fares upfront.

MONEY

The currency is the Papua New Guinean kina (K). ATMs are available in major towns, but cash is essential in rural areas. You can barter at craft markets by asking for a 'second price'.

29 Rabaul in A DAY

REMOTE | VOLCANOES | HISTORY

Rabaul, on Papua New Guinea's East New Britain Island, lies between dramatic volcanoes and echoes of its storied past. This destination reveals active volcanic landscapes, remnants of WWII, and a thriving local culture. In just one day, travellers can uncover the layers of history and natural wonder that define this remarkable coastal town.

DAISUKE KISHI/GETTY IMAGES

How to

Getting around: Taxis, minibuses and rental vehicles. Walking is ideal for town areas, but plan transport for distant sites like Tavurvur or WWII tunnels.

When to go: Dry season (May–October) is best, with temperatures 24–30°C. Avoid the rainy season (November to April).

Speak the lingo: Tok Pisin, an English-based creole, is widely spoken. To say hello, use 'Hello po', or 'Hi po' to be more respectful.

CORBIS VIA GETTY IMAGES

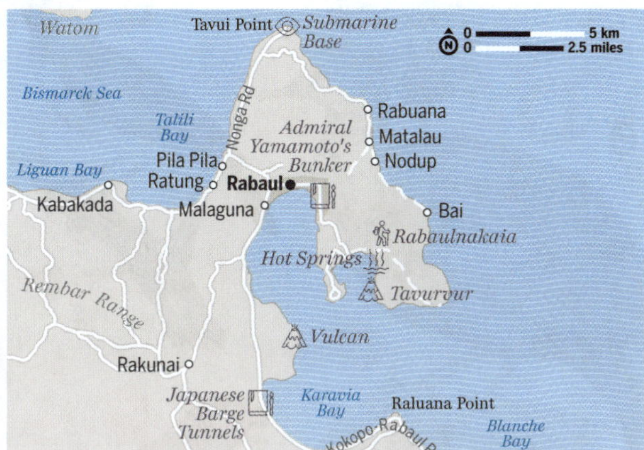

Far left Hot springs, Tavurvur **Bottom left** Japanese Barge Tunnels

Nature's Power In Rabaul, the power of nature is impossible to ignore. The volcanoes **Tavurvur**, **Vulcan**, and **Rabalanakaia** dominate the landscape, each with a story to tell. Tavurvur, still active, releases plumes of steam and ash in a rhythmic pulse. Its rocky slopes glow hauntingly in the early morning light, a poignant reminder of the 1994 eruption that reshaped the town and left it buried in layers of ash. For an up-close experience, hop into a minibus and head to Tavurvur's **hot springs**, about an hour away (K5 entry). Steam rises from the ground, creating an otherworldly atmosphere. Locals often guide visitors to the best viewpoints or demonstrate how eggs cook in seconds in the bubbling water. Nearby, Vulcan and Rabalanakaia offer quieter adventures. Trails wind through old lava flows and blackened rocks, each step echoing the town's volcanic past.

Echoes of War Rabaul's history is equally captivating. Once a Japanese stronghold during WWII, the town is scattered with wartime remnants. Guided tours with **South Sea Horizons** *(southseahorizons.com)* bring the past to life, offering access to **Japanese Barge Tunnels** and bunkers once used as supply routes and hideouts. **Admiral Yamamoto's Bunker**, named after the Japanese admiral, is a highlight. Offshore, the rusted hulls of sunken ships serve as reminders of conflict, now transformed into reefs teeming with vibrant coral and fish. Rabaul's unique blend of natural power and historical intrigue leaves a lasting impression on all who visit.

Taste the Tradition

Papua New Guinean–born Alan knows the local hotspots and insists that no visit to Rabaul is complete without trying *aigir*, the town's signature dish. *Aigir* is a traditional delicacy made by layering fresh seafood, creamy coconut milk and local greens, which are wrapped in banana leaves and slow-cooked over hot stones. The result is a fragrant and flavourful dish that captures the essence of Rabaul's culinary traditions. Alan suggests visiting the bustling local market, where vendors serve *aigir* steaming fresh. Pair it with sweet potato or sago, both staples of the region, to perfectly complement the dish's rich, coconut-infused flavours.

Insights from Alan Manning, owner of South Sea Horizons
southseahorizons.com

BIRDS of Paradise

01 Hooded Pitohui
One of the world's few toxic birds, its striking plumage warns predators to stay away. Found in **Varirata National Park**.

02 Victoria Crowned Pigeon
This elegant pigeon's striking blue crest makes it true avian royalty in the forest.

03 Lesser Bird-of-Paradise

Known for its courtship displays, it is a mesmerising sight in the island's jungles.

04 Raggiana Bird-of-Paradise
Known as Papua New Guinea's national bird, its vibrant plumage symbolises pride and tradition.

05 Black Sicklebill
Its elegant curved beak and long tail make it an unmistakable figure in the canopy.

06 Blue Jewel-Babbler
This shy bird's sapphire plumage flashes brilliantly as it darts through dense foliage.

07 Goldie's Lorikeet
A small, colourful parrot thriving in montane forests with its cheerful calls.

08 King Bird-of-Paradise
A tiny marvel of vivid reds and iridescent greens, a masterpiece of nature's design.

09 Papuan Lorikeet
A vibrant parrot with striking colours, often seen feeding on nectar in the highlands.

10 Blyth's Hornbill
A large bird with a striking casque, its echoing calls dominate the lowland rainforests.

11 Papuan Frogmouth
A nocturnal master of camouflage, it mimics tree branches with uncanny accuracy.

07 BERNARD QUARITCH (FIRM); GEORGE PHILIP & SON; KEULEMANS, J. G.; MIVART, ST. GEORGE JACKSON, PUBLIC DOMAIN, VIA WIKIMEDIA COMMONS. **08** PAUL LOUIS OUDART, PUBLIC DOMAIN, VIA WIKIMEDIA COMMONS. **09** BARRABAND, JACQUES; BOUQUET; LE VAILLANT, FRANÇOIS, PUBLIC DOMAIN, VIA WIKIMEDIA COMMONS. **BACKGROUND:** THOMÉ, OTTO WILHELM, 1840-; BENNETT, ALFRED WILLIAM, 1833-1902, NO RESTRICTIONS, VIA WIKIMEDIA COMMONS

30 Historical Hikes & SITES

ADVENTURE | HIKES | WAR HERITAGE

PNG's rich landscape is a testament to the resilience of its people and the weight of its history. From the Kokoda Track's gruelling terrain, where battles once raged, to the tranquil Bita Paka War Cemetery, every step uncovers stories of courage and sacrifice. These hikes and sites blend physical challenge, historical insight and moments of deep reflection.

HEMIS/ALAMY

How To

Getting here: Start at **Kokoda Village** or **Owers' Corner** via Port Moresby. Book with certified guides for safety and historical insight.

When to go: May to October is ideal, with optimal dry-season trail conditions for this challenging 96km hike.

Plan ahead: Remote hikes mean limited connectivity and amenities. Pack essentials like a power bank, cash and a first aid kit to ensure a smooth journey into these areas.

ANDREW PEACOCK/GETTY IMAGES

The Legendary Kokoda Track Papua New Guinea offers a profound connection to history, blending natural beauty with stories of resilience and remembrance. The Kokoda Track is a 96km trail of rugged terrain and deep historical significance. Following the footsteps of WWII battles between Australian and Japanese forces, it serves as a tribute to courage and endurance. Trekking with a certified company, such as South Sea Horizons (p197), ensures safety while promoting sustainable practices. It guides trekkers to key battle sites like **Brigade Hill** and **Imita Ridge**, through lush rainforests, and to villages where locals share wartime stories passed down through generations. Allow 6–10 days for the trek, with costs ranging from $2,500–$4,000, covering logistics, permits and meals.

Bita Paka War Cemetery For a quieter yet moving experience, visit the Bita Paka War Cemetery near Rabaul. This serene site, surrounded by lush greenery, honours soldiers from WWI and WWII. Accessible by taxi or rental car, entry is free, making it an easy yet impactful stop to reflect on history. Complement your journey with a visit to the **Kokopo War Museum**, where displays of weapons, uniforms and photographs shed light on Papua New Guinea's pivotal role in WWII. Pair this with a tour of Rabaul's **Japanese tunnels** for a comprehensive exploration of the country's wartime legacy.

Far left Bita Paka War Cemetery
Bottom left Hiking, Kokoda Track

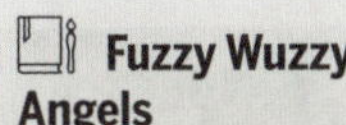

Fuzzy Wuzzy Angels

Saii is the son of Faole Bokoi, the last Fuzzy Wuzzy Angel to pass away. The Fuzzy Wuzzy Angels were Papua New Guinean locals who supported Australian soldiers during WWII, carrying supplies, evacuating the wounded and guiding troops through the rugged Kokoda Track. Saii emphasises that the Kokoda Track is more than a challenging hike – it's a journey through history and culture. He encourages visitors to connect with locals, whose stories keep alive the legacy of the Fuzzy Wuzzy Angels and the events of the Kokoda campaign.

Insights from Saii Faole, Brigade Hill Mission Tours & Kokoda Track Partner
southseahorizons.com

31 Colours of CULTURE

FESTIVALS | CULTURE | TRADITION

Papua New Guinea is a cultural mosaic, home to over 800 languages and countless vibrant traditions. Its festivals, from the fiery spectacle of the Baining Fire Dance to the striking displays of the Goroka Mask Festival, offer a vivid window into the nation's diverse heritage. Each celebration is a sensory journey of music, dance and deeply rooted customs.

PABLO BONFIGLIO/GETTY IMAGES

How To

Getting there: Fly to **Tokua Airport** for the Baining Firedance or **Goroka Airport** for the Mask Festival. There are domestic flights with Air Niugini or PNG Air.

When to go: The Baining Firedance Festival takes place in East New Britain in August, while the Goroka Mask Festival lights up the highlands in September.

Book a festival experience: Book in advance through local tour operators to avoid disappointment, including accommodation, as it fills up quickly.

CINDY HOPKINS/ALAMY

MARC DOZIER/GETTY IMAGES

Far left Goroka Mask Festival **Bottom left** Baining Fire Dance Festival **Left** Mask performers, Goroka

Dancers of the Flame & Masks of Many

Baining Fire Dance Festival This festival in East New Britain is an enthralling nighttime ritual performed by the Baining people. Dancers wearing intricate bark-cloth masks leap barefoot through roaring flames, accompanied by the hypnotic beat of traditional drumming. This ancient ceremony, celebrating life, is often held during harvests or to mark significant milestones. To attend, travel to East New Britain from Rabaul, which is accessible by road. Local guides or tour operators can arrange your visit, typically costing K100–200 for a guided experience. Confirm dates with local tourism offices, as the schedule can vary. Arrive early to soak in the atmosphere, witness preparations, and connect with the community for a richer experience.

Goroka Mask Festival Held every September in the Eastern Highlands town of Goroka, this festival celebrates Papua New Guinea's independence with a vibrant display of cultural pride. Tribes from across the region gather to perform sing-sings, traditional dances featuring elaborate masks that represent ancestral spirits. This sensory explosion of colour, sound and storytelling highlights the highlands' cultural diversity. Tickets for the festival are typically available through travel agencies or tour operators, with prices depending on the chosen package. Accommodation fills quickly, so early booking is essential. Arriving a day before the festival allows you to explore Goroka, observe performers rehearsing and gain a deeper appreciation for the event.

Dance, Masks & Performance

Dance, performance and masks are central to Papua New Guinean culture, reflecting identity, spirituality and community. These traditions, passed down through generations, hold unique meanings across the country's diverse regions. Masks, often intricately crafted, symbolise ancestral spirits or mythical beings, connecting performers to their heritage. Dances, like the Baining Fire Dance and Goroka Mask Festival, are sacred rituals that convey history, morals and communal values through storytelling. With over 800 languages and countless tribes, these art forms celebrate the diversity of Papua New Guinea's rich heritage while reinforcing cultural continuity and unity.

Listings

BEST OF THE REST

Special Stays

Walindi Plantation Resort, Kimbe Bay

A tranquil retreat surrounded by lush gardens and offering world-class diving opportunities in the heart of the Coral Triangle.

Rondon Ridge Lodge, Mt Hagen

Nestled in the highlands, this eco-lodge provides stunning valley views and easy access to cultural festivals and birdwatching.

Tufi Dive Resort, Oro Province

Stay in a traditional-style bungalow overlooking the breathtaking fjords, with activities like snorkelling, kayaking and cultural village visits.

Kokopo Beach Bungalow Resort, East New Britain

Located on a picturesque beachfront, this resort combines modern comfort with views of Simpson Harbour and nearby volcanoes.

Markets

Gordons Market, Port Moresby

One of Papua New Guinea's largest markets, offering fresh produce, handmade crafts and vibrant *billum* bags woven by local artisans.

Kokopo Market, East New Britain

Browse stalls for tropical fruits, shell jewellery and traditional Tolai masks.

Wewak Market, Sepik Region

Find beautifully carved wooden artifacts, including traditional storyboards and ceremonial masks that reflect Sepik River culture.

Hagen Market, Mt Hagen

Shop for highland specialities like organic coffee beans, colourful handwoven textiles and spices.

Spots to Sip Sundowners

Rapopo Plantation Resort, East New Britain

Sip on a tropical cocktail while watching the sunset over the Bismarck Sea from this serene beachfront location.

Madang Resort, Madang

Enjoy a refreshing drink with panoramic views of the lagoon and nearby islands, the perfect way to end the day.

Lamana Gold Club, Port Moresby

A vibrant spot in the capital with a rooftop bar offering city views and a lively atmosphere for evening drinks.

Tufi Dive Resort, Oro Province

Unwind with a cool beverage overlooking the stunning fjords, where the golden hour paints the water and cliffs in warm hues.

Festivals

Goroka Show

Held every September, this spectacular festival features tribes from across Papua New Guinea

DANITA DELIMONT/SHUTTERSTOCK

Hagen Market

showcasing traditional sing-sings with colourful costumes, masks and dances.

Crocodile Festival, Ambunti

Celebrate the cultural significance of crocodiles in the Sepik River region with performances, crafts and community-led conservation efforts.

Baining Fire Dance

Experience this mesmerising nighttime ritual in East New Britain, where dancers leap through flames in bark-cloth masks.

Marine Marvels

Snorkelling at the Duke of York Islands

Dive into the crystal-clear waters of this idyllic island group near East New Britain. Vibrant coral reefs, tropical fish and the chance to spot dolphins or dugongs make it a snorkeller's paradise.

Diving in Kimbe Bay

Kimbe Bay on New Britain Island is a diver's dream, home to pristine coral reefs, abundant marine life and incredible visibility. **Walindi Plantation Resort** serves as a great base for exploring these underwater treasures.

Discover Milne Bay's Coral Reefs

Snorkel or dive in Milne Bay, home to some of the most diverse marine ecosystems in the world, including rare critters and vibrant corals.

Cultural Encounters

Huli Wigmen, Tari

Discover the fascinating traditions of the Huli people, known for their wigs made from human hair and vibrant face paint. Their cultural performances are both captivating and educational.

Sepik River Villages & Crocodile Men

Explore remote stilt villages along the Sepik River and witness the scarification ceremonies of the Chambri Tribe, an ancient tradition honouring their sacred connection to crocodiles.

GLOWIMAGES/GETTY IMAGES

Coral, Milne Bay

National Museum and Art Gallery, Port Moresby

This museum showcases Papua New Guinea's rich history, culture and art, from ancient artifacts to contemporary works.

Natural Wonders

Mt Wilhelm

At 4509m, **Mt Wilhelm** is Papua New Guinea's highest peak. The trek offers stunning views of alpine lakes, valleys and distant coastlines – a rewarding challenge for adventurous hikers.

Port Moresby Nature Park

Escape the bustle at this lush sanctuary showcasing Papua New Guinea's native wildlife, including tree kangaroos and cassowaries. It's also a great spot to see birds of paradise up close.

Island Adventures

Island Hopping in Madang

Madang's coastline is dotted with hundreds of islands perfect for exploration. Visit Pig Island for turquoise waters, palm-lined beaches and serene solitude amidst nature's beauty.

Trobriand Islands Culture

Known as the 'Islands of Love', these remote islands offer insight into unique matrilineal traditions and vibrant local customs that remain largely untouched by modern influences.

OTHER ISLANDS
Trip Builder

TAKE YOUR PICK OF MUST-SEES AND HIDDEN GEMS

From stories of the seafaring Polynesian explorers who used the stars to navigate across vast oceans to European explorers who followed centuries later, the islands of the South and Western Pacific oceans are a place where mythology froths. How could they not be? Remote and far-flung, some of these tiny specs in the sea are amongst the least-visited countries in the world, with annual arrivals consisting largely of yachties and country counters. These are places where accommodation and eating options are in short supply, but culture and tradition thrive. If you've got ample time and a bold spirit, set your compass and raise your sails to your next adventure.

Palau
This Micronesian archipelago of roughly 340 coral and volcanic islands has a well-established tourism scene, welcoming around 42,000 annually. Diving is a must, with around 50 WWII wrecks to explore.

Federated States of Micronesia
Made up of four island states and serviced by regular flights, the top activities in this Western Pacific country are – you guessed it – diving, fishing and learning about its WWII history.

Marshall Islands
About 5000 visit annually, but tourism sector investment means you'll start to hear more about this spot. Serviced by regular flights, highlights include sailing abroad a Marshallese canoe, designed with an asymmetric hull.

Tuvalu
Become one of the 3000 people per year to visit before it disappears. Extremely vulnerable to sea levels, Tuvalu is the first nation to upload a digital copy of itself to the metaverse.

Nauru
At only 21 sq km, the world's smallest island nation is also one of the world's least visited. Yet, it's relatively easy to access thanks to Nauru Airlines.

Wallis and Futuna
Separated by 230km of open ocean, but linked by French governance. Try kitesurfing in Wallis or visit the more mountainous Futuna to surf its uncrowded swells.

0 — 2,000 km
0 — 1,000 miles

Hawai'i

Kiribati
Kiribati (prounounced 'kirr-i-bass', pictured) sits in all four hemispheres. Only about 8000 tourists arrive annually, but a new government department was launched in 2019 to actively promote Kiribati's fishing and birdwatching holidays.

Jarvis Island

Kiribati

Tokelau
The only way to reach Tokelau (pictured) is a 24-hour boat ride from Samoa. Contact Tokelau Apia Liaison Office to make accommodation and transport arrangements as there's no tourism industry.

Tokelau

Samoa

Bora Bora

Tahiti

Tonga

Cook Islands

French Polynesia

Niue

Pitcairn Islands

Pitcairn Islands
Pitcairn Island (pictured) is further from any continent than any other inhabited island on earth. Arrivals are by boat, such as the MV Silver Supporter freighter, departing fortnightly from French Polynesia.

FROM TOP: MAURICIO HANDLER/GETTY IMAGES, AUSAID, CC BY 2.0, VIA WIKIMEDIA COMMONS, MICHAEL DUNNING/GETTY IMAGES

Escape TO NIUE

CAVE | WHALES | DIVING

Known as the 'Rock of Polynesia', tiny Niue – population around 1700 – is the world's smallest self-governing nation. Explore a coastline punctuated by sea caves, swim with whales, and snorkel and dive in pristine South Pacific waters.

PHOTOS BRIANSCANTLEBURY/SHUTTERSTOCK

How to

Getting here & around: Fly direct from Auckland. Rental car availability is limited on Niue so book one before you arrive.

When to go: May to October is the cooler and drier season. Book flights well ahead for Christmas and New Year when NZ Niueans return home.

Sunday morning: Expect heavenly harmonies and a warm welcome at church. It's a day of rest until the Washaway opens.

Currency: The New Zealand dollar (NZ$) is the official currency of Niue.

GALAXIID/ALAMY

Spectacular Sea Caves

Near the Washaway Cafe, **Avatele's** stretch of sand is pretty much Niue's only beach, and the rest of the island's perimeter is marked by sea caves formed by millennia-spanning erosion of coral and porous limestone by weather and waves. Named after the legendary Polynesian homeland, **Avaiki Cave** features a towering cathedral-shaped cavern cradling a rock pool. Low tide is the best time to visit, and Niuean sunsets at Avaiki are also special. Just to the north, **Palaha Cave** is marked by stalactites and stalagmites. Walk through the cave to a rock window providing brilliant views of the reef and out to the expansive blue horizon of the Pacific.

Further north, the slender coastal inlet of **Matapa Chasm** is where Niuean nobility bathed in earlier centuries, and it's still a great place for a swim. From near Hikutavake village, a rocky

SMA1050/SHUTTERSTOCK

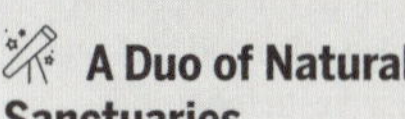

A Duo of Natural Sanctuaries

Accredited by the International Dark-Sky Association (IDA), Niue is the world's only Dark Sky nation, seen with a telescope or binoculars, after-dark highlights include the Milky Way and Magellanic Clouds. At 127,000 sq km, Niue's Moana Mahu Marine Protected Area covers 40% of the nation's EEZ (Exclusive Economic Zone).

Far left Talava Arches (p210) **Left** Coral and porous limestone **Above** Matapa Chasm

20- to 30-minute track meanders to the **Talava Arches**, a labyrinth of caves that were used as covert lookouts to warn of raiders in earlier times. Visit around low tide, pack good walking shoes, and bring a torch.

Crystal-Clear Snorkelling

Niue's raised coral atoll has no rivers, so there's no runoff to sully the waters surrounding the island, and gin-clear visibility of up to 80m is the norm. Even snorkellers can enjoy the underwater spectacle, especially at **Limu Pools**, and further north at **Hikutavake**. At Limu, walkways lead to a brace of rock pools sheltered from the Pacific, and a blurring effect is created by the mixing of cooler spring water and warmer sea water. Like giant natural aquariums, Hikutavake's bowl-shaped pools – one is 10m deep with a diameter of 25m – sit just inside the reef and host scores of fish, the occasional sea turtle, and even (benign) reef sharks. Ask at your accommodation for the best tidal conditions to experience both Limu and Hikutavake.

Niue's Best Cafes

Fana Niue's best coffee, innovative brunch dishes, and smoothies made with the island's sustainable honey and organic vanilla.

Hio Cafe On Niue's northwestern coast with fresh fish tacos enlivened with papaya salsa and cocktails infused with tennis ball-sized island passionfruit.

Kaiika Sushi, sashimi and wood-fired pizza served in an open-sided pavilion. Seared tuna carpaccio is always popular.

Vaiolama Cafe Tuna wraps, tropical fruit smoothies and great views of visiting yachts moored at Avana harbour.

Washaway Cafe Only open on Sunday afternoons with Avatele beach views, plate-covering fish burgers, and a self-service bar.

Left Hikutavake **Below** Palaha Cave (p209) **Bottom** Diving, Niue

FAR LEFT: SCSTOCK/SHUTTERSTOCK; LEFT: MOLLY BROWN NZ/SHUTTERSTOCK

DESIGN PICS INC/ALAMY

Niue's Seasonal Visitors

Humpback whales visit Niue's warm waters to give birth and nurse their calves from July to October. Interactions, including swimming with the massive cetaceans, are carefully regulated to ensure the wellbeing of the whales. Experiences with **Niue Blue** also include snorkelling on the edge of the reef and seeing Niue's resident pod of spinner dolphins. Whales are also spotted regularly from the island's coastline. Visit the **Scenic Matavai Resort** for a drink and you might get lucky from their expansive deck.

Diving & Fishing

Niue's super-clear waters and underwater caves and canyons offer some of the Pacific's best diving. Most dive sites are within a five- to 10-minute boat journey from Niue Blue's location near the Matavai. With the ocean's depth escalating to over 300m just beyond the reef, fishing for tuna, wahoo and *mahimahi* with local fishing operators is also popular.

SAMOA

CULTURE | SCENERY | ACTIVITIES

Savai'i island (p226)
Samoa's largest island is scenic and pristine.
60-90mins from 'Upolu

Falealupo-tai
Falealupo Rainforest Preserve
Tufutafoe
Papa-uta
Sataua
Asau
Lava Field
Sasina
Letui
Matavai
Fagamalo
Mauga
Samalae'ulu
Falealupo Peninsula
Falelima
Mt Elietoga
Savai'i
A'opo
A'opo Conservation Area
Mt Matavanu Crater
Mt Maugaloa
Mt Silisili
Mt Mafane
Pu'apu'a
Lano
Sa'asa'a
Faga
Tuas
Sapapali'i
Lalomalava
Salelava
Samata-i-tai
Fai'a'ai
Foailalo
Sala'ilua
Va'oto Stream
Lata River
Sili
Vailoa
Tafuauta
Salelologa
Fa'a'ala
Puleia
Gataivai
Fagaloa
Taga
Tafua
Tafua Peninsula Rainforest Preserve
South Pacific Ocean
Apolim

SAMOA
Trip Builder

Traditional and spirited Samoa considers itself the heart of Polynesia, following Fa'a Samoa (the Samoan Way), making it one of the most authentic of all the Pacific societies. Expect accessible adventures, colourful villages and some gorgeous South Pacific beaches.

FROM LEFT: MARK FITZSIMONS/GETTY IMAGES, RAMUNAS BRUZAS/SHUTTERSTOCK. PREVIOUS SPREAD: MVALIGURSKY/GETTY IMAGES

0 20 km
0 10 miles
Enjoy peaceful Manono Island (p227) with no roads, cars or dogs.
15mins from 'Upolu
Apia (pictured, p218) is the bustling capital of Samoa.
South Pacific Ocean
Skim down waterfalls at Papasee'a Sliding Rocks (p225).
15mins from Apia
Experience a touch of history at the Robert Louis Stevenson Museum (p219).
10mins from Apia
Cool off in refreshing Piula Cave Pool (p224).
40mins from Apia
Malua
Le'auva'a
Fale'ula
Leulumoega
Vaitele
Apia
Solosolo
Lauli'i
Falefa
Apolima-uta
Mt Sina'ele
Saletele
Falelatai
Mt Fito
Sauniatu
Upolu
Ta'elefaga
Lona
Matafau
Safa'atoa
Lefaga
O Le Pupu-Pu'e National Park
Le Mafa Pass
Ti'avea
Samusu
Fanuatapu
Salamumu
Sataoa
Maninoa
Si'umu
Saleilua
Malaemalu
Salani
Lepa
Lalomanu
Nu'utele
Snorkel among the molluscs at Savaia Marine Protected Area (pictured, p225).
50mins from Apia
Take a dip at enticing Togitogiga Falls (p224).
40mins from Apia
Swim in the iconic sinkhole of To Sua Ocean Trench (p223).
1hr from Apia
Stay in a beachside fale at lovely Lalomanu Beach (p231).
1½hrs from Apia

Practicalities

DAISUKE KISHI/GETTY IMAGES

ARRIVING

Faleolo International Airport Chances are you'll be arriving here, where no one needs a visa; you do however, need six months validity on your passport, onward tickets and Samoan accommodation arrangements. The airport is 35km west of Apia. Get some cash from an ATM in the arrivals hall.

Apia Harbour (pictured) Samoa is on the South Pacific cruise ship circuit; cruise ships dock here, a five-minute taxi ride or 20-minute walk from the city centre.

HOW MUCH FOR A

Cold Taula beer ST$10

Savai'i ferry ticket ST$10

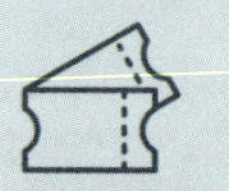
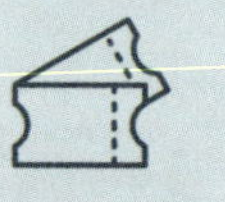

To Sua Ocean Trench entry ST$20

WHEN TO GO

MAY–OCT
The dry, cooler visitor season; lots of Kiwis and Aussies escaping their winter.

NOV–APR
The steamy summer season with more rain, fewer visitors and bargains to be had.

DEC–JAN
Peak holiday season when Samoans living abroad come home to visit.

FEB–APR
The low season for visitors; cheaper flights and accommodation.

GETTING AROUND

Car Independent types will want to rent a vehicle, best done by booking online before you go; cars can be picked up and dropped off at the airport. Rent a high-clearance vehicle as side roads to natural attractions are often unsealed with deep potholes. Do not park under a coconut tree!

Minibus Tours If you're on a packaged trip including flights and resort accommodation, your package may include airport transfers. Many resorts offer day tours that include minibus transport.

Taxis There are taxis everywhere, but none have meters, they only take cash and you'll need to negotiate a rate. They are particularly useful for short trips around Apia (ST$3–5).

EATING & DRINKING

Most resorts will have a bar and restaurant (or two) to keep everyone happy; be aware that if you're at a remote resort and have no transport, you'll likely be eating there for the duration. Apia offers a decent selection of cafes, restaurants and bars. Your resort may offer a *fiafia* night, with singing, dancing and traditional *umu* cooking. Fruit (pictured) is cheap at markets and roadside stalls.

Do not drink tap water. Taula and Vailima (pictured) are local beers, while Samoa Whiskey is the first worldwide to be produced from *taro*.

Best cafe
RiVaiv Cafe (p230)

Must-try fine dining
Ava I Toga Restaurant (p231)

CONNECT & FIND YOUR WAY

You may be able to purchase a data roaming pack in your home country that offers connectivity in Samoa. Alternatively, purchase a SIM card with one of the two local networks, Vodafone and Digicel, and use mobile data. Free wi-fi is rare in Samoa, even at accommodation and cafes.

TOP TIP

When it comes to returning your rental car full of fuel, you'll need cash at the petrol station. They won't take credit cards.

WHERE TO STAY

There are a range of hotels in Apia to suit most budgets. Resorts and *fale* (see p220) are scattered around 'Upolu; much fewer on Savai'i.

Island	Pro/Con
Apia	Hotels, cafes, restaurants, bars and shops in the bustling capital.
Airport area	A Sheraton and a transit motel, but not much going on; close to the ferry to Savai'i.
Southeast 'Upolu	Stay at a beach *fale*; consider Lalomanu and Saleapaga beaches.
'Upolu South Coast	Excellent resorts such as Sea Breeze, Saletoga Sands and Sinalei Reef Resort.
Southwest 'Upolu	A couple of nice resorts in Return to Paradise and Le Vasa Resort.
Savai'i	Hotels in Salelologa, resorts on the north coast and *fale* around the island.

MONEY

Samoa uses the Samoan tala (ST$). Make sure to carry cash because you'll need it. Save money by buying fruit at markets and roadside stalls, plus snacks at supermarkets. Tipping is not customary in Samoa.

33 Exploring APIA

CULTURE | MARKETS | HISTORY

Samoa's capital is a bustling, busy place, the commercial hub of the country. There's a lot going on, especially on weekdays, with an excellent cultural centre, a batch of buzzy markets, a historic museum, plus an eclectic collection of local eateries and shops.

PHIL WALTER/GETTY IMAGES

How to

Getting around: Downtown Apia is compact and easy to walk around; drive or take a taxi for the 5km trip south and up to Robert Louis Stevenson Museum.

When to go: Weekdays, when the Royal Samoan Police Band marches and the Samoa Cultural Village is open.

Top tip: Have lunch in central Apia at Nourish Cafe before heading up to Robert Louis Stevenson Museum.

Don't Be Late...

Be on time at 8.45am on weekdays to watch the impressive Royal Samoan Police Band (pictured) proudly march from the **Police Station** to the **Government Building** to raise the Samoan flag at 9am. This show-stopper also halts traffic, with around 40 police and 30 band members marching daily.

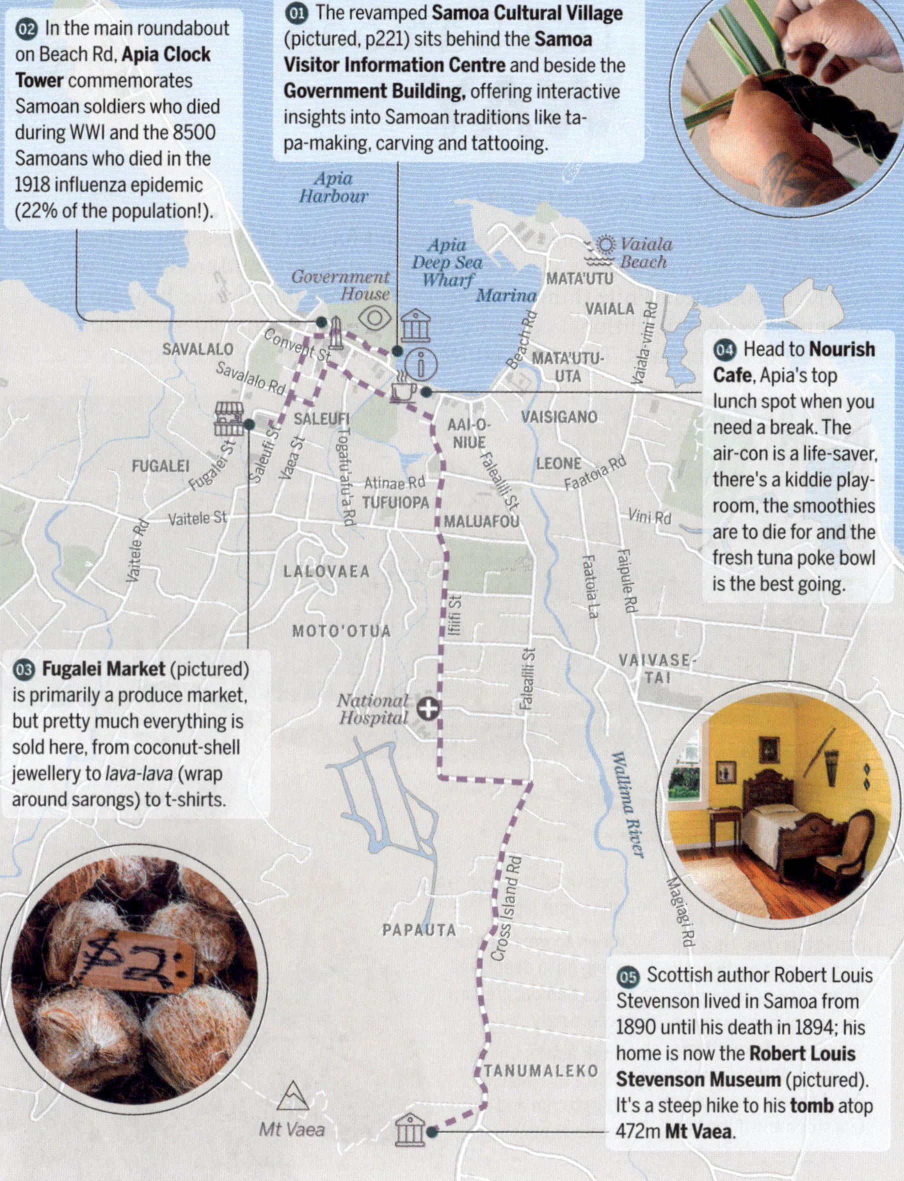

01 The revamped **Samoa Cultural Village** (pictured, p221) sits behind the **Samoa Visitor Information Centre** and beside the **Government Building,** offering interactive insights into Samoan traditions like tapa-making, carving and tattooing.

02 In the main roundabout on Beach Rd, **Apia Clock Tower** commemorates Samoan soldiers who died during WWI and the 8500 Samoans who died in the 1918 influenza epidemic (22% of the population!).

03 **Fugalei Market** (pictured) is primarily a produce market, but pretty much everything is sold here, from coconut-shell jewellery to *lava-lava* (wrap around sarongs) to t-shirts.

04 Head to **Nourish Cafe**, Apia's top lunch spot when you need a break. The air-con is a life-saver, there's a kiddie playroom, the smoothies are to die for and the fresh tuna poke bowl is the best going.

05 Scottish author Robert Louis Stevenson lived in Samoa from 1890 until his death in 1894; his home is now the **Robert Louis Stevenson Museum** (pictured). It's a steep hike to his **tomb** atop 472m **Mt Vaea**.

FROM TOP: PEACEFOO/SHUTTERSTOCK, GREG BALFOUR EVANS/ALAMY, CORNERS74/SHUTTERSTOCK

34 The Samoan WAY

TRADITIONS | CULTURE | AUTHENTICITY

Despite intervention by missionaries and foreign powers, Samoa has clung to Fa'a Samoa, making it one of the most authentic and traditional of all Pacific societies. While things may seem casual on the surface, beneath lies a complex code of traditional etiquette that is rigorously upheld and means everything to Samoans. This rich culture is a joy to discover as a visitor.

MARTIN VALIGURSKY/SHUTTERSTOCK

PEACEFOO/SHUTTERSTOCK

How to

Getting around: Riding a public bus *(pasi)* is a cultural experience in itself; drivers are as eccentric as their brightly painted vehicles and everything operates at their whim. Don't expect schedules or bus stops and if the bus is crowded, someone may sit on your lap.

When to go: Not much going on in deeply religious Samoa; prepare accordingly.

Book a *fale*: Check what's available on *trivago.com* and *samoa.travel*.

Far left *Fales* on Lalomanu beach
Below left Samoa Cultural Village
Left Fiafia Night

Samoa Cultural Village

This central **spot** in Apia offers interactive sessions with extremely affable and knowledgeable hosts, taking visitors through all aspects of Samoan cultural and traditional life, with workshops on weaving, woodworking, *siapo* cloth making, traditional *tatau* (tattoo), dance, music and more. Visitors are also treated to an *'ava* (kava) ceremony and lunch from an *umu* (hot-stone oven). The revamped village is tucked away behind the **Samoa Tourism Visitor Information Office**.

Fiafia Night

A *fiafia* (happy get-together) night involves traditional dancing, singing, music and cooking – many hotels and resorts hold their own *fiafia* nights for guests, usually on Thursdays, Fridays or Saturdays. The food will usually be cooked in a traditional *umu* and entertainment is performed enthusiastically by local villagers who enjoy the show just as much as those watching.

Staying in a Fale

At their most traditional, *fale* are wooden platforms with poles supporting a thatched roof, surrounded by woven blinds for privacy. Woven mats are laid on the floor, topped by a mattress with sheets and a mosquito net. From this, various degrees of luxury can be added, such as electric lights, ceiling fans, beds, wooden walls, doors and decks. Bathroom facilities are usually shared and the price often includes dinner and breakfast. A great spot to overnight in a *fale* is along gorgeous **Lalomanu Beach** and **Saleapaga Beach** in southeast 'Upolu.

Samoan Pride

We Samoans were so proud to host the Commonwealth Heads of Government Meeting here in Samoa in 2024. King Charles and Queen Camilla even stayed here in our resort. CHOGM was a great chance for Samoans to tell the world about Fa'a Samoa – the Samoan way. Each country in the Commonwealth was adopted by a village on 'Upolu and that village was beautified in that country's national colours. The national leader from that country then visited their adoptive village and there was so much excitement. CHOGM was a great success for Samoa.

■ Insights from Sio Alataua, Sinalei Reef Resort
@sinaleireefresort

35 Snorkelling & SWIMMING

ADVENTURE | SCENERY| THRILLS

Samoa is blessed with a number of stunning natural attractions, both on land and in the water, that will have you craving more. Most involve either freshwater or saltwater, and the locals enjoy nothing more than cooling off and enjoying life.

WIRESTOCK/GETTY IMAGES

How to

Getting around: Rent some wheels and drive around 'Upolu island; many guided tours include visiting these natural attractions.

When to go: Many of the attractions are closed on Sundays.

What to take: Go prepared with reef shoes, skin guard tops, and your own snorkelling gear, if you've brought it to Samoa.

STEFAN MOGEL/GETTY IMAGES

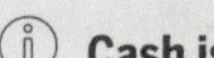

MARTIN VALIGURSKY/SHUTTERSTOCK

To Sua Ocean Trench

This outrageously photogenic spot is a Samoan icon; skip it to your everlasting regret. **To Sua** is more akin to a giant sinkhole than a trench, with sheer, green-draped rock walls plummetting 20-odd metres to the almost hallucinatory-blue waters of the pool below. Swimming access is via a precipitous but sturdy wooden ladder; it's well worth the clamber, though you'll want to take utmost care going both down and up. An underwater passage feeds the swimming hole from the nearby sea; some visitors take snorkelling gear down to check out the fish. Views of the rugged southern coastline are stunning from observation points around the grounds. Entry is ST$20 per person.

Cash is King

Cash is the most accepted way to pay and in many instances, it's the only accepted payment method – for entry fees to natural attractions, beaches, beach *fale*, buses, taxis, markets and petrol stations. Withdraw cash from ATMs. Resorts, restaurants, shops and car rental companies accept credit cards.

Far left To Sua **Left** Togitogiga Falls (p224)
Above Piula Cave Pool (p224)

Piula Cave Pool

Secreted beneath the campus of Piula Methodist Theological College in eastern 'Upolu, **Piula Cave Pool** is a beautiful, crystal-clear freshwater spring pool only metres from the sea, that originated from an old lava tube. The pool has concrete surrounds, so it's not completely *au naturel*, but it's easy to swim into the depths of the dark cave. Surprisingly, the pool teems with fish. This is a wonderfully refreshing spot and the college grounds above are beautiful. Entry is ST$10 per vehicle, ST$5 per person.

Togitogiga Falls

A glorious spot for a splash, this series of gentle **waterfalls** in **O Le Pupu-Pu'e National Park** on the southern coast is separated by blessedly cool waterholes that are far too enticing to pass up. They are a short walk up from the car park, have changing rooms and entry is free, as they are in the national park.

Good for Everyone

Creating the Giant Clam Sanctuary has been very good for Savaia village. Many tourists come to see the clams and turtles in the bay. They pay ST$20 each and the village uses that money to do good things for all the villagers, like money for our school and making the village beautiful. A few years ago, Savaia was voted the most beautiful village in Samoa. We believe the giant clams grow well here as we have five freshwater springs. The freshwater mixes with the seawater in the bay and grows very healthy clams.

Insights from Silipa Silipa, Savaia giant clam caretaker

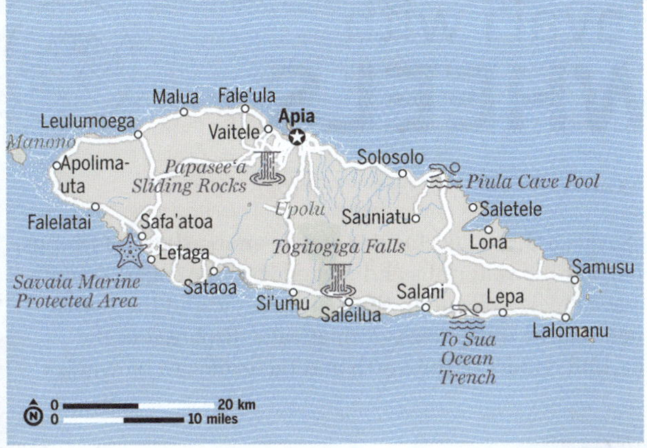

Left Giant clam **Below** Papasee'a Sliding Rocks

Savaia Giant Clams & Turtles

Savaia Marine Protected Area (Giant Clam Sanctuary) is a spot not to be missed, although you'll need to take snorkelling gear and swim 70–80m (within the reef) out to see the giant clams. The colourful, gargantuan molluscs are best viewed around high tide; you'll also see hundreds of smaller clams, and, if luck is with you, a turtle or two. Keep fingers and toes well away from the feisty clams and cool off after in the fresh water pool that connects to the bay, next to the car parking area. Leave keys with the caretaker while you're out there. Entry is ST$20 per person.

Papasee'a Sliding Rocks

Not far from Apia, local kids and adults have a brilliant time skimming down these **natural slides** – actually, small waterfalls – into refreshingly cool waterholes; you'll likely hear happy hoots even before you descend the long, precarious stairway to the pools. Check water depths before taking on the slides and if you think it smarter not to slide, it's still a top spot for a dip. Entry is ST$5 per person.

36 Savai'i with WHEELS

REMOTE | DRAMATIC | VOLCANIC

Samoa's 'Big Island', Savai'i offers a spectacular scenic smorgasbord of riotous rainforest, sea-smashed cliffs, pristine waterfalls and ragged volcanic cones. Despite its snoozy ambiance, the largest shield volcano in the South Pacific and the fourth largest island in Polynesia has volatile tendencies, dramatically displayed in the eerie lava fields, village ruins, and craters of the north and the explosive blowholes of the south coast.

How to

Getting here: Take the ferry from **Mulifanua Wharf** near 'Upolu's western tip to **Salelologa** near Savai'i's eastern tip.

When to go: Good year-round. The bottleneck in getting to Savai'i is the ferry; avoid weekends if you can.

Getting around: Rent a vehicle at Salelologa or bring one with you on the ferry; book well ahead for either option, especially in the busy season.

Top tips: Stay at least a couple of nights on Savai'i; don't miss the ferry, which can get very crowded on Friday afternoons and weekends.

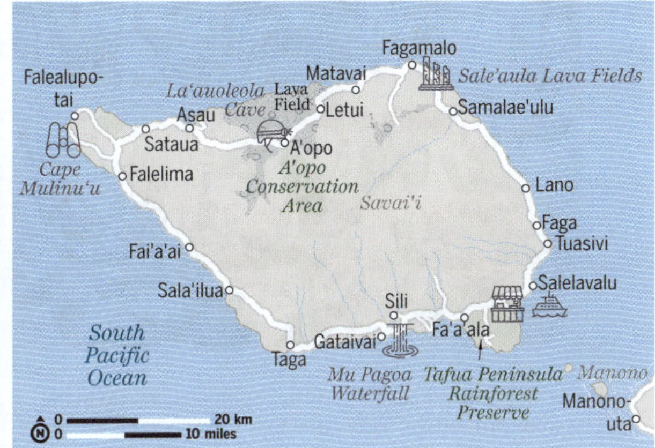

Hitting the Road

This is a real adventure. To put things in context, the 176km sealed road that runs around Savai'i can be driven in less than four hours, but that would be a shame as there are so many interesting things to see along the way. Speed limits are slow – 40km/h within villages and 55km/h on the open road – and you'll need to watch out for unexpected obstacles such as dogs, pigs, chickens and kids. It's best to rent a high-clearance vehicle, rather than a regular car, as access roads to attractions can be unsealed, with plenty of potholes. Navigation should be a breeze, there won't be much traffic, but you'll still need to keep your wits about you.

Don't Miss...

Start your trip at the **Salelologa Market**, then head anti-clockwise around the island. Don't miss the **Sale'aula Lava Fields**, featuring the ruins of a church engulfed by a lava flow, then there are resorts where you can stay in **Fagamalo** and **Manase**; make sure to book ahead. At **La'auoleola Cave** you can take a guided trip through a large lava tube. **Cape Mulinu'u**, the westernmost point of Samoa, is home to historic sites and magnificent sunsets. Turning back along the south coast, the **Alofaaga Blowholes** are a must-see, best around high tide, while **Mu Pagoa Waterfall** spectacularly tumbles 5m directly into the Pacific Ocean.

Far left Alofaaga Blowholes **Below left** Sale'aula Lava Fields

Manono Island

Only 4km off the western tip of 'Upolu, Manono is Samoa's third-largest island. With 800 people scattered among four villages, Manono is a famously peaceful place as there are no roads, cars or dogs! The thing to do here is walk the trail right around the island, taking around two hours; the locals are shy, though friendly. Take a taxi boat from the boat landing at **Manono-uta** on 'Upolu; take snacks and drinks with you. While there are two primary schools, Manono high school kids rejoice on big wave days as they can't get to the mainland for school.

Big Changes for Samoa

NOW ON THE WESTERN SIDE OF THE INTERNATIONAL DATE LINE

While Polynesians are thought to have turned up in the Samoan Islands 3000 years ago – and Europeans have been around for the last 300 – the country now known as Samoa has been making the biggest decisions for its future in the last 30 years.

Left Solomon Island workers making copra
Centre A map of the dateline
Right Samoa's Prime Minister Afioga Fiame Naomi Mata'afa at CHOGM, Somoa

Lapita pottery shards show that Samoans arrived in the islands around the same time that Tonga and Fiji were settled, and there have long been strong cultural ties. Warrior queen Nafanua set out the *fa'amatai* political system based on family, villages and chiefs. Europeans began to arrive in 1722, bringing not only unknown technology such as guns, but a number of nasty diseases to which the islanders had no immunity. While the missionaries conducted a competition for souls, the British, Americans and Germans squabbled over Samoan territory. After several attempted compromises, the Tripartite Treaty of 1899 – signed on the other side of the world in Berlin – gave control of western Samoa to the Germans, eastern Samoa to the Americans and the Brits got what they wanted elsewhere in the Pacific.

From German Samoa to Western Samoa

The Germans took over, importing over 2000 Chinese labourers to work on their large plantations, producing copra, cocoa beans and rubber. By 1908 there was widespread discontent among Samoans, but protests were quashed mercilessly and Samoan leaders were deported to Saipan in the German Mariana Islands. In 1914, at the outbreak of WWI, Britain persuaded New Zealand to seize German Samoa and finally, after a lengthy, troubled period under New Zealand governance, Western Samoa achieved independence in 1962.

A Modern Samoa

Samoa dropped the 'Western' in 1997 to become simply Samoa – though you'll still see the local currency, the

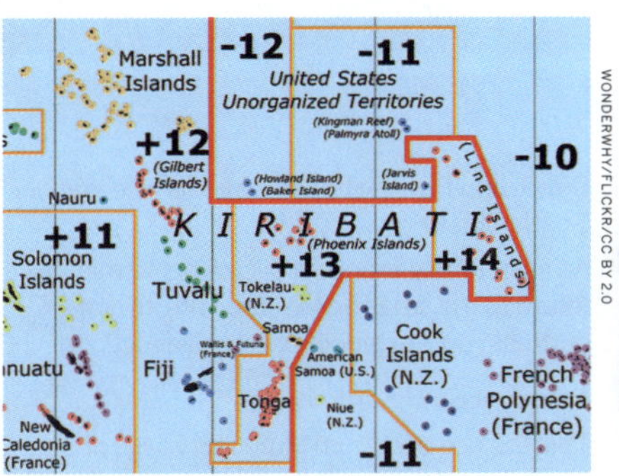

Samoan tala, occasionally listed as WSD and '.ws' in internet addresses.

In the 21st century there have been some intriguing moves to bring Samoa into closer alignment with New Zealand and Australia, where there are large expat Samoan populations. In 2009, Samoa switched from driving on the right to driving on the left, ostensibly to make things easier for Kiwi and Aussie tourists and to be able to import cheaper secondhand cars from New Zealand – they'd imported mainly right-hand drive vehicles from the US up to then.

Samoa managed to get the International Date Line moved from west of Samoa to down the middle, between Samoa and American Samoa

Then in 2011, Samoa managed to get the International Date Line moved from west of Samoa to down the middle, between Samoa and American Samoa. This effectively put Samoa in the same day as New Zealand and Australia, its biggest trading partners. Before the move, Samoa only had four days of the working week the same as the two Pacific heavyweights; now it has five. Then, in 2021, Samoa scrapped Daylight Savings Time and now stays on the same time year-round.

For Samoans, 2024 was a year of great joy. Samoa was host for the Commonwealth Heads of Government Meeting (CHOGM) in October, attended by King Charles III and Queen Camilla. Amid much fanfare, infrastructure upgrades and beautification projects, the meeting was deemed a huge success for Samoa.

What Day Is It?

The International Date Line basically runs up and down the earth at longitude 180°, but affected countries can apply for small diversions. In 2011, Samoa got the Date Line moved to between Samoa and American Samoa – there's only 70km and a 30-minute flight between the two, but there's a 24-hour time difference! It's the same time in both places but a different day. Fly from Samoa to American Samoa and you'll have the same day twice; fly back the other way and you'll lose a day altogether. Whatever you do, don't mess up dates on your hotel bookings.

Listings

BEST OF THE REST

Samoa's Top Festivals

Teuila Festival

A celebration of all things Samoan in September; dance competitions, traditional arts and crafts, tattooing, the Miss Samoa pageant and lots and lots of food!

Independence Day

On 1 June, Samoans celebrate independence from New Zealand with flag-raising, much fanfare and a party-like atmosphere.

Apia Arts and Crafts Festival

Held in March, this bustling event focuses on local artists and traditional handicrafts from all across the islands of Samoa.

Samoana Jazz & Arts Festival

The two Samoas join together on 1 May for a day of easy-listening entertainment coinciding with UNESCO International Jazz Day.

Palolo Festival

The date of this festival celebrating the annual rising of reef worms *(palolo)* changes by the year; it's either in October or November. A time to catch a rare seafood delicacy!

Walking the Trails

O Le Pupu Pu'e National Park Coastal Walk, South 'Upolu

This one-hour return walk winds its way through lush pandanus forest before emerging on rocky lava cliffs, with the waves crashing below.

Robert Louis Stevenson Tomb Trail, near Apia

There are two options to the top of Mt Vaea, near Apia; the 30-minute rough and steep route or the 50-minute easier way that zigzags its way.

O Le Pupu Pu'e National Park Ma Tree Walk, South 'Upolu

An easy, family-friendly walk taking 40 minutes return to the amazing Ma Tree, with its huge buttress roots extending out in all directions.

Namu'a Island Summit

Take the taxi boat from Mutiatele village at 'Upolu's eastern end to Namu'a Island; allow one hour to climb to the summit and back.

Apia's Best Cafes

RiVaiv Cafe $$

Famous for its turmeric juices, RiVaiv, out in Apia's western suburbs, is also the place to try a *koko* Samoa milkshake (local cocoa beans).

Coffee Roaster $$

Apia's trendiest cafe features coffee cups dangling from every spot available; the roasted coffee is superb and there are sandwiches..

Cornwall Cafe $$

Rooftop cafe and bar with free wi-fi. Breakfast and lunch with refreshingly creative fruit smoothies, all made with coconut cream.

Milani Cafe & Cakes $

An Italian-inspired cafe with a Samoan twist, right in the heart of the action, Milani serves up cakes, loaves, biscuits and pastries.

Where to Snorkel

Palolo Deep Marine Reserve, near Apia

Excellent snorkelling within cooee of the capital; hire gear from the kiosk and swim to a trench brimming with tropical fish and coral.

Manase, northern coast of Savai'i

Savai'i's top accommodation options line this

2km stretch of sandy beaches, with exciting snorkelling and a good chance of a turtle or two.

Namu'a Island

At the eastern end of 'Upolu, take a taxi boat over to the island, rent a beach *fale* and play around in the water to your heart's content.

Lalomanu Beach, Southeast 'Upolu

Lalomanu may be famous for its pristine sands and traditional *fale*, but it's also a good spot to don your snorkelling gear; rental gear available.

Top Souvenir Shopping

Eveni Carruthers, Apia

Block-printed island clothing with designs for men, women and children in air-conditioned comfort in the heart of Apia; also at the airport.

Janet's, Apia

Selling Samoan and Pacific clothing, jewellery, arts, crafts and body-care products, made in partnership with Samoan and Pacific artists.

Pacific Jewell, near Apia

With its own Garden Cafe on the outskirts of Apia, this treasure trove specialises in quality handicrafts of the highest standards produced by local families.

Best Beach Fale Accommodation

Faofao Beach Fales, Southeast 'Upolu

At Saleapaga, one of the best beaches on 'Upolu, stay in a traditional *fale* on the sand, with woven blinds for privacy and a simple mattress and mosquito net set-up.

Taufua Beach Fales, Southeast 'Upolu

On legendary Lalomanu Beach, these guys offer a variety of options, including open beach *fale*, enclosed *fale* for full privacy and even ensuite.

Vaiula Beach Fales, South 'Upolu

On 'Upolu's southern coast, over 20 attractive beach *fale* are absolute beachfront of Tafatafa

MARK KOLBE/GETTY IMAGES

Teuila Festival

Beach; bathrooms are shared and dinner and breakfast are included.

Manusina Beach Fales, Southeast 'Upolu

This boutique *fale* operation on Saleapaga Beach has both open and closed *fale* that have all the *fale* amenities plus a power outlet.

Tanu Beach Fales, North Savai'i

Lagoon-edge *fale* in the spectacular snorkelling, turtle and beach hotspot of Manase on the northern coast on Savai'i; it's easy to chill out for a few days here.

Fine Dining in Samoa

Ava I Toga Restaurant, South 'Upolu $$$

At Sinalei Reef Resort & Spa, which hosted King Charles & Queen Camilla during CHOGM, this lagoon-edge restaurant is the top fine-dining option in Samoa.

Bistro Tatau, Apia $$$

As good as it gets in Apia; try the *oka*, raw fish marinated in coconut cream and spices for a starter, then pan-fried swordfish for your main.

Waterfront Restaurant and Bar, Southeast 'Upolu $$$

At adults-only Seabreeze Resort, this elegant restaurant nestled into the coastal cliffs has it all in terms of international cuisine and wine.

37 American SAMOA

SCENERY | NATURE | REMOTE

There's a very different feel here when compared to Samoa (p212), only 70km west. There's less tourism infrastructure and enthusiasm for attracting international visitors, with the main industry being the canning of tuna for export. That said, expect a photogenic feast of green, jagged peaks, electric blue depths and idyllic beaches, along with an off-the-beaten-track vibe – well worth the effort.

How to

Getting there: Fly or ferry from Samoa; Hawaiian Airlines has direct flights from Honolulu.

When to go: May to October. Dry, cooler season with minimal risk of cyclones.

Money: US$

Visas: US passport holders travel freely; Entry Permit Waiver Program (EPWP) for most countries – details at *americansamoa.travel*.

Far left Pago Pago **Bottom left** Tropical flower, National Park of American Samoa

Tutuila & Pago Pago

The main island of Tutuila is a dramatic mess of sharp edges and pointy peaks, softened by a heavy padding of rainforest. Its craggy green silhouettes loom over the island's blindingly white sands, turquoise shallows, inviting islets and stunning Pago Pago Harbour, one of the best-protected natural harbours in the world. You'll arrive either at **Pago Pago International Airport** or by ferry into Pago Pago's harbour. While the urban environs of the capital are as gritty as they get (think tuna canneries and a working seaport), the natural harbour and backdrop of jagged peaks give the city a unique and explore-worthy charm.

National Park of American Samoa

The majority of tourists arrive to visit the territory's national park, created in 1988. It protects large swathes of pristine landscapes and marine environments on Tutuila and the Manu'a Islands, about 100km to the east. The **National Park Visitor Center** in Pago Pago is an invaluable source of information and maps; there are scores of excellent hikes to choose from. The **Manu'a Islands** are among the most ravishing and remote of all the Pacific isles – enormous cliffs sheltering seabird colonies, expired volcanic cones, pristine lagoons with a brilliant array of coral and a soul-soothing sense of quiet. **Ofu Beach** is often ranked as one of the most splendid stretches of sand in the world.

Samoa & American Samoa

The USA's only inhabited territory in the southern hemisphere, American Samoa is much smaller than its neighbour. While Samoa has a population of 205,000 and a land area of 2831 sq km, American Samoa's population of 43,000 lives on islands with a land area of only 200 sq km. While the Indigenous people of both are Samoan, the differences lie in historic foreign affiliations – Samoa drives on the left, uses the Samoan tala, Type 1 electrical plugs and looks west towards New Zealand; American Samoa looks east towards the US, drives on the right, uses the US$ and US electrical plugs.

Practicalities

Right Traditional music, Solomon Islands (p174)

EASY STEPS FROM THE AIRPORT TO THE CITY CENTRE

Unless you're hoisting the spinnaker on a yacht or kicking back on a cruise ship, getting to the South Pacific will mean a long-haul flight, usually via a gateway city such as Auckland, Brisbane, Sydney, Los Angeles, Honolulu or Tokyo. Due to the vast expanses of open ocean and the relatively small number of travellers, just getting to the South Pacific can be expensive.

AT THE AIRPORT

SIM CARDS All countries in the South Pacific have local providers; pick up a SIM card at the airport or purchase a data roaming pack in your home country that covers your destination. Alternatively, purchase a prepaid eSIM data plan.

GET SOME CASH Pick up some local currency from an ATM at the airport; chances are you will need some straight away just to get to where you're going. Local taxis or buses will likely require you to pay in cash.

SYLVAIN LEFEVRE/GETTY IMAGES

WI-FI Most international airports in the South Pacific have free wi-fi; make the most of it while you're there.

ATMS The local banks know you'll need cash; there are ATMs at the international gateway airports.

CHARGING STATIONS Don't expect ready access to charging stations; charge your devices on the aircraft on the way and arrive charged up.

THE RIGHT GEAR

If you've flown from a cold winter into a hot, humid South Pacific where the international airport may not be air-conditioned and you find yourself standing in line for 20 minutes at immigration, chances are you won't be happy if you're still wearing heavy winter gear. Think ahead and wear layers that you can shed on arrival, if necessary.

FLIGHT ARRIVALS

LOCAL OPERATORS WILL HAVE A SYSTEM On some South Pacific island countries, there may be only one or two international flight arrivals each day. Pass through immigration & customs, then head out through the arrival doors to find what may look like semi-organised mayhem. Keep in mind that local operators have seen it all before and there will be a system for getting everybody where they are going.

DO YOUR HOMEWORK BEFORE YOU GO Knowing how to get where you're going before you arrive is a good move; none of these South Pacific countries have trains or subways. Public buses may meet flights, but don't expect efficient schedules; on some islands, if the public bus is full, someone may sit on your lap! Think of it as part of the adventure.

PLAN AHEAD For some destinations, don't expect to be able to book everything online; making a booking may require back-and-forth emails or messaging.

TAKING A TAXI TO TOWN Usually, you need to pay cash in local currency and negotiate a rate before you get in; taxis may not have meters.

LIKE IT EFFICIENT? Book yourself a packaged tour that includes airport transfers, or arrange a shuttle pickup with your accommodation.

GG-FOTO/SHUTTERSTOCK

GETTING TO WHERE YOU'RE GOING

Packaged tour If you've purchased a tour that includes flights and accommodation at a resort, it likely also includes airport transfers. Once you're through immigration & customs, head out and look for someone holding a sign, either with your name or the name of the resort where you are staying.

Independent travel If you've purchased your flights and accommodation by yourself online, before you leave home, make sure to ascertain the best way to get to where you're staying. Your accommodation may have an airport shuttle or be able to arrange a pickup at the airport for you.

Rental car pickup If you hire a rental car for the duration of your visit, book it online beforehand and arrange to pick it up and drop it off at the airport. Larger rental car companies will likely have an office in the airport, while smaller companies will meet you with signage when you exit immigration & customs.

Going into the main city? There will be some form of public transport linking the airport with the city, be that public bus and/or taxi. You'll need cash. Ride-share services are yet to hit the islands.

TRANSPORT TIPS TO HELP YOU GET AROUND

Once you're on the island, you'll have a number of options for exploring, whether that's under your own steam with some rental wheels or by using public transport – or as part of an organised tour, usually with a guide, run by a local operator or the resort where you are staying.

DOMESTIC AIRLINES

If getting away from it all is your goal, taking to the air is your fastest (and often the only) way to get there. Some inter-island flights operate only once or twice a week and can be heavily booked; secure seats well in advance.

DOMESTIC FERRIES

Some South Pacific islands have an established domestic ferry system, especially if distances between islands aren't great. Some ferries will be big, fast and efficient, some. not so much. For smaller, nearby outer islands, the ferry might better be described as a 'taxi boat'.

SOUTH PACIFIC TOUR OPERATORS

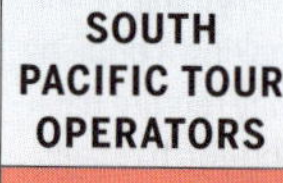

Coral Expeditions $

Intrepid $$

Oceania Cruises $$$

RENTING SOME WHEELS Larger South Pacific islands and tourist destinations will usually have some car hire companies – either big international branches (Avis, Hertz, etc) or smaller locally run outfits. If you rent for your entire stay, you can usually pick up and drop off at the airport. Shorter rentals can usually be arranged at your resort. Make sure to get insurance rules and conditions explained to you before you drive away.

BICYCLE On flatter South Pacific islands, renting a bicycle can be an excellent way to get around. Most rental bikes won't come with a helmet or lock unless you ask for them – be aware that maintenance isn't often a high priority. Hydrate well.

SCOOTERS Some countries, such as the Cook Islands, are hotbeds for scooter usage. You'll need to check whether if your driving licence covers scooters and if your insurance will cover you for any injuries.

DRIVING ESSENTIALS

Most countries drive on the left; those with US or French affiliations drive on the right – New Caledonia, French Polynesia, American Samoa.

Speed limits are slow, especially in villages; keep an eye out for roaming animals and kids.

Potholes can be cavernous, especially on side roads.

In some countries, make sure to have cash when fuelling up at petrol stations.

Don't park under coconut trees!

BUS

Large and populous islands usually have some kind of bus service. However, public transport could hardly be described as ruthlessly efficient. Buses are often privately (sometimes family) owned, and many owner-drivers set their own schedules. Formal bus stops may or may not exist – just wave your arms around if not. If there aren't many people travelling on a particular day, buses may stop altogether.

TAXIS

Fare meters aren't always present; discuss the price before you get in. Know the address where you want to go – so you don't end up at the driver's sister's guesthouse instead of the one you've booked.

NEARBY ISLANDS

'Taxi boats' often run out to nearby small islands on a by-request basis; you may have to negotiate the rate on the spot. If you wait around until more passengers turn up, you're likely to get a better rate.

KNOW YOUR CARBON FOOTPRINT

The carbon footprint for a passenger on a ferry is estimated at 20g per kilometre of travel; for flying, it's 250g per kilometre for a short flight. While ferries are the more environmentally friendly choice in terms of carbon output, in the South Pacific, your options may well be limited.

DISTANCE CHART (KMS)

	Port Vila	Port Morseby	Honiara	Noumea	Apia	Rarotonga	Tonga	Papeete	Nadi
Port Vila									
Port Morseby	2461								
Honiara	1280	1410							
Noumea	530	2499	1586						
Apia	2172	4492	3114	2482					
Rarotonga	3359	5808	4495	3482	1512				
Tonga	1768	4226	2960	1898	894	1597			
Papeete	4450	6868	1150	4611	2049	1150	2714		
Nadi	970	3392	2100	1270	1235	2416	870	3500	

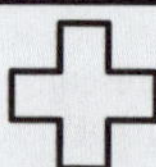

SAFE TRAVEL

The South Pacific islands are safer travel destinations than most places in the world and the locals are some of the friendliest you'll ever meet. But as when travelling anywhere on the planet, it pays to use a little common sense.

NATURAL DISASTERS It's not called the Pacific Ring of Fire for nothing – earthquakes, tsunamis, and erupting volcanoes are not as unusual as many people think. Most islands have signage about where to go in the event of a tsunami. If a cyclone is in the forecast to come close, get out if you can.

SWIMMING SAFETY Many Pacific islands have sheltered lagoons inside protective reefs that offer safe swimming and snorkelling. But currents can be strong around passages and channels that drain the lagoon into the open sea on a falling tide. If there are no other swimmers around, ask a local before plunging in. Avoid swimming alone.

OPPORTUNISTIC THEFT Many Pacific cultures have relaxed attitudes to property – it's best not to leave expensive gear lying around. Petty thefts from hire cars, beach bags and hotel rooms do occasionally occur. Look after your valuables, keep them out of sight and use the room safe if you have one.

Mosquitoes Malaria exists in western regions of the South Pacific, but even where mosquitoes don't carry malaria, their bites can cause discomfort and, in rare cases, dengue fever. Use insect repellant and cover up, especially in the evenings.

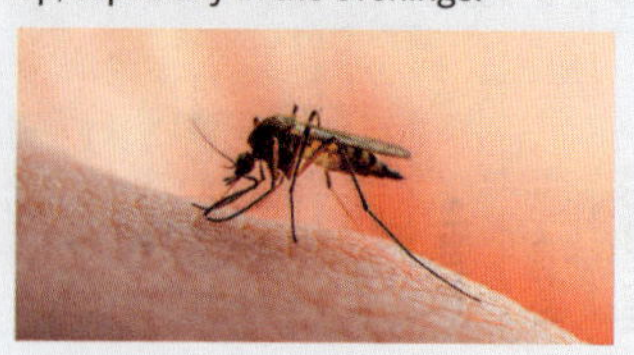

NECHAEVKON/SHUTTERSTOCK

DANA NEIBERT/GETTY IMAGES

Dangerous Wildlife Shark attacks are rare but occasionally occur, less so within lagoons. Saltwater crocodiles are found in northern Melanesian countries; avoid contact at all costs. Watch out for venomous sea life such as lionfish, rockfish and jellyfish.

KNOW THE ISSUES
Check travel advisories before you go as some countries in the region experience civil unrest, such as New Caledonia and Papua New Guinea. Travel insurance may become invalid if you travel against advice.

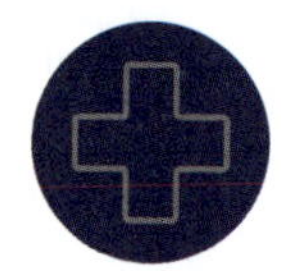

SMALL MEDICAL PROBLEMS
Grazes, coral cuts and even insect bites can become infected quickly in tropical climates; take all incidents seriously and slather any lesions with antiseptic.

QUICK TIPS TO HELP YOU MANAGE YOUR MONEY

If all the South Pacific countries used the same currency, visiting multiple countries would be a breeze. As it is, before you go, know the local currency where you are going and its current value compared to your home currency – or you could be in for a nasty shock. Knowing what you're dealing with before you go is a smart move.

TIPPING
Not expected in Pacific countries, but as everywhere, is appreciated for exceptional service; rounding up to the nearest complete number is appreciated too.

BARGAINING
In many countries, bargaining for handcrafts and souvenirs at markets is expected, but not for everyday goods like fruit and vegetables.

CURRENCY

Variable

HOW MUCH FOR

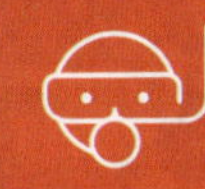

Diving in Fiji **FJ$450**

Whale Watching in Tonga **T$400**

Kite-boarding lesson in Cook Islands **NZ$250**

CASH IN HAND
Unless you're on a packaged tour at a resort and can put everything on your room and pay by credit card at checkout, you're going to need some cash – especially if you head out exploring, use local public transport or visit local markets and roadside stalls.

RESORTS The word 'resort' can mean different things; if you've chosen a resort that seems remarkably reasonable, don't expect too much. Do some homework before you decide.

ATMS
Getting some cash at the airport as soon as you arrive is a smart move; there may not be an ATM at your chosen resort or anywhere close once you get there.

TAXIS
In some countries, local taxis will be an excellent way to get around – though don't get in until you've checked out if there is a meter, and if there isn't, negotiate a rate.

VALUE FOR MONEY
Keep in mind that if you travel to the South Pacific on a packaged tour that includes flights, accommodation at a resort and airport transfers, the attractive price of the package may well be offset by the cost of meals at your resort – and if the place where you stay is remote, you won't have many choices. And if you don't actually like the place where you are staying, you're stuck there for the duration. Choose carefully.

RESPONSIBLE TRAVEL

Positive, sustainable and feel-good experiences

GIVE BACK

Before you go, study the history of where you are going. The locals lived in a Pacific paradise until Europeans turned up. The *palagi* (foreigners) brought nasty diseases to which the islanders had no immunity, colonial powers introduced waves of immigrants to work their plantations, some colonial powers never left (New Caledonia and French Polynesia) – and now, the rich nations are polluting the planet, and South Pacific islands are sinking, literally. The Tongans have a saying 'for every beach in Tonga, a *palagi*'s dreams lie buried in the sand'. Many islanders think when it comes to climate change, they are paying the price for the dreams of the rich nations.

KEVIN HELLON/SHUTTERSTOCK

ON THE ROAD

Get out and meet the locals Go for a walk, meet and talk to locals in their neighbourhood; many may actually work where you are staying.

Public bins These are scarce, so leave some room in your bag to stash your rubbish until you find somewhere to dispose of it.

Support local culture by visiting the local market, attending a cultural night or visiting a culture centre.

Support initiatives such as sanctuaries and protected reserves; in many cases, contributions you make in the form of entry fees will go directly to the local village.

Bring a water bottle with a built-in filtration system. Try not to use single-use plastic bottles, a major issue in the Pacific.

Don't use too much water Some islands, especially low-lying atolls, have limited freshwater; don't take too long in the shower.

DOS & DON'TS

Do learn a few phrases in the local language; using them will make locals smile.

Do experience a local perspective by seeking out locally owned tours and cultural experiences.

Don't expect South Pacific nations to all be alike; they all have their own unique way of doing things.

LEAVE A SMALL FOOTPRINT

Go for a walk There's no better way to leave a small footprint than with your own feet; walk around and meet the locals.

Two-wheeled adventures Explore the area where you are staying under your own power, on a bicycle; many resorts have bicycles for guests to use.

On & in the water Kayak out to nearby islets where you can leave your own small footprint in the sand; snorkel in the lagoon.

MARC DOZIER/GETTY IMAGES

SUPPORT LOCAL

Eat local Purchase fruit from roadside stalls and if there are local eating places nearby, give them a try.

Buy local Consciously contribute by purchasing locally made handcrafts and souvenirs from local markets.

Learn local Many resorts offer classes in local arts and crafts, such as making flower garlands, weaving or dancing.

CLIMATE CHANGE & TRAVEL

Lonely Planet urges all travellers to engage with their travel carbon footprint, which will mainly come from air travel. While there often isn't an alternative, travellers can look to minimise the number of flights they take, opt for newer aircrafts, and use cleaner ground transport, such as trains.

One proposed solution – purchasing carbon offsets – unfortunately does not cancel out the impact of individual flights. While most destinations will depend on air travel for the foreseeable future, for now, pursuing ground-based travel where possible is the best course of action.

The UN carbon footprint calculator shows how flying impacts a household's emissions.

The ICAO's carbon emissions calculator allows visitors to analyse the CO2 generated by point-to-point journeys.

RESOURCES

southpacificislands.travel

pireport.org

forumsec.org

sustainabletravel.org

mmel.pacificclimatechange.net

UNIQUE & LOCAL WAYS TO STAY

Where you stay in the remarkably diverse South Pacific comes down to your goals. If you want to escape your winter, head to a warm island, laze by the pool and read a book, there are plenty of packaged resort experiences available; if you want to travel independently and experience the culture at ground level, go local for a fascinating adventure.

JON RUIZ ORTIZ/SHUTTERSTOCK

THE LOCAL EXPERIENCE

The local experience need not be budget; small boutique hotels and guesthouses are increasingly popular and allow you to explore remote and fascinating islands. Some small lodgings may have air-con, while many will be fan-cooled and provide mosquito nets and coils; few have pools. All but the most rudimentary include towels and linen. While places on main islands will have a decent level of comfort, those on remote islands may have faulty plumbing, cold showers, unreliable electricity and a rustic set-up. Check in advance if you require wi-fi.

THE RESORT EXPERIENCE

Despite the stereotype, luxe resorts take up only a fraction of the South Pacific's accommodation. International chains may have moved into tourist hotspots like Fiji and French Polynesia, but you'll also find an array of charming boutique resorts that blend local style and warmth with comfort and opulence.

SAMOAN FALE

The traditional *fale*, at its most basic level, is an elongated, octagonal hut on stilts, with no walls, but coconut-thatched louvres that can be let down and drawn up depending on how much privacy or ventilation you want. Woven mats are laid on the floor, topped by a mattress with sheets and a mosquito net.

CORNERS74/SHUTTERSTOCK

MARIDAV/SHUTTERSTOCK

STAYING AT A BOUTIQUE RESORT

Expect a restaurant, bar and swimming pool, plus a shop and an activities desk. While there are a number of accommodation block-style resorts, many feature individual bungalows (*fale*, *fare*, *bure* etc – depending on the local lingo) and super swanky places may have overwater bungalows (such as in French Polynesia). You'll be met at the local airport and transferred to your resort by van, speedboat or aeroplane. From registration onwards, you'll have the choice to participate in organised activities or chill out and explore on your own. All resorts have at least one restaurant, serving a mix of Western, Polynesian or Melanesian, Asian and fusion specialities, plus a well-stocked bar with cold beer and in some countries, a decent wine selection. Some bigger places may put on a traditional dance performance and buffet once or twice a week. Breakfast is often a buffet and other meals á la carte, with simple options like burgers and sandwiches for lunch.

Resorts usually have activities available for guests or work with independent local operators they know and trust. While balmy tropical waters, pristine lagoons and empty beaches are the most obvious attractions, there's more to the Pacific than just watery pursuits. Opportunities abound for hiking, cycling, horse riding, birdwatching, caving, plus the chance to visit archaeological sites and WWII relics.

BOOKING

If you're looking for a packaged trip that includes flights, accommodation and airport transfers, keep an eye out on what is on offer from travel agencies in your home country. The price of a packaged trip can look very appealing, especially outside of the high season, when airlines are looking to put bums on seats and resorts are trying to fill empty rooms.

Outside of high season (June through August) and New Zealand and Australian school holiday periods, you can arrive just about anywhere in the South Pacific without any idea of where you are staying or what you are doing tomorrow. But during the seasonal rush, the better places will be booked out – plan in advance and make bookings.

Search engines such as Trivago, Expedia and Booking.com work with accommodation providers throughout the South Pacific and are well worth viewing if you are travelling and booking your trip yourself.

Holiday rentals are also easily booked on websites such as Airbnb, VRBO and Bookabach.

OVERWATER BUNGALOWS

On your honeymoon or a special occasion? Head to Bora Bora in French Polynesia for super-swish resorts with wow-factor bungalows hanging out over dreamlike turquoise waters. An unforgettable experience.

ESSENTIAL NUTS & BOLTS

SLOW SUNDAYS
Sunday is a day of rest in many Pacific countries; while there won't be much going on, resort restaurants will be open for guests.

CHRISTMAS CLOSE-DOWN
Despite Christmas being a busy period with many islanders living overseas coming home, many businesses will close down for a week.

TAKING PHOTOS
A little politeness goes a long way; always ask before taking images of people, especially children.

CHAMELEONSEYE/SHUTTERSTOCK

GOOD TO KNOW

Visas Most countries do not require a visa, but requirements vary by destination; check before you go.

Civil Unrest Check government safe travel advice, especially for New Caledonia and Papua New Guinea.

Language English is spoken widely across the South Pacific. French is also spoken in New Caledonia and French Polynesia.

Travel Insurance Medical evacuations may head to New Zealand or Australia.

Public Holidays Major Western holidays are observed, plus local public holidays.

ACCESSIBLE TRAVEL

South Pacific countries generally have poor facilities for travellers with disabilities. Wheelchair users will find getting around a problem. Footpaths can be patchy or non-existent, domestic aircraft tend to be small, with steps and narrow doors, ferries may not have ramp access and toilets for the disabled are few and far between. Some large, international resorts may have rooms with disabled access, but it's not common, and facilities such as beach wheelchairs are not here yet.

That said, South Pacific cultures look after their elderly, disabled and infirm as integrated members of the community – there are no special schools or aged-care facilities. Islanders won't simply look away if you need help to get into a taxi or up some stairs – they'll rally up some helpers and pitch in.

Get in touch with your national support organisation before you travel to enquire about the countries you are planning to visit. Travel Without Limits (travelwithoutlimits.com.au) is a good source of information.

COVER UP
Bare chests and itsy bitsy bikini bottoms are fine around the resort pool, but not in town.

WEAR YOUR BEST
Respectfully smarten up for the occasion if attending a local church service or formal local ceremony.

ACT APPROPRIATELY
Public displays of affection are inappropriate and flirting with locals may not be appreciated.

A GOOD CONVERSATION STARTER is often sports such as rugby or netball. Given that many islanders travel around the world, they may want to talk about where you're from and they're almost guaranteed to have a relative who moved to Auckland, Sydney or Utah.

FAMILY TRAVEL

Few regions of the world are as family-friendly as the Pacific. With endless sunshine, beaches and swimming and snorkelling on tap, there's plenty to keep kids engaged.

Children are cherished in island cultures; your kids can expect plenty of cheek-tweaking attention.

Kids will happily munch on South Pacific fruit, fish, chicken and coconut, while resorts often offer organised kids' activities.

Bring your own kid-size snorkelling gear.

WHEN VISITING A LOCAL VILLAGE

Remove your shoes when entering a home.

Sit cross-legged on the floor, rather than with your feet pointing out.

Avoid entering a house during prayers.

Avoid walking between two people in conversation.

Try to remain on a lower level than a chief to show respect.

JUAN MOYANO/GETTY IMAGES

LGBTIQ+ TRAVELLERS

Being gay or lesbian is considered sinful due to conservative Christian influences, yet in Polynesia there are long traditions of male cross-dressing and transgenderism. Melanesian countries tend to be less tolerant.

While same-sex marriage is legal in New Caledonia and French Polynesia, and same-sex relationships are legal in countries like Fiji and the Cook Islands, homosexuality is still criminalised in Papua New Guinea and the Solomon Islands.

Excessive displays of affection in public, of any sexuality, are frowned on in most Pacific societies.

Index

000 Map pages

W

'Fiji is equal parts chill and thrill – take your pick from countless beachside resorts and dive centres, or get off the beaten path and embrace village life on an off-grid adventure in the highlands.'

CHANTAE REDEN

'Pack your sense of adventure for Papua New Guinea as you immerse yourself in its breathtaking landscapes and rich cultural tapestry, and you will find it rugged and raw.'

KATE WEBSTER

'New Caledonia, with the world's largest lagoon and continuous coral reef, offers stunning beaches and vibrant reefs. It's a haven for nature lovers.'

REBECCA STIRNEMANN

'An archipelago of more than 900 mountainous islands and coral atolls harbouring incredible biodiversity, the 'Hapi Isles' is carving out its reputation as an adventure destination, with a burgeoning surf scene.'

JESSICA LOCKHART

'Vanuatu is arguably one of the most remarkable enclaves of Indigenous tradition in the world.'

NEEMA GITHERE

MIKE WORKMAN/SHUTTERSTOCK, CHRISTOPHE ROBERT HERVOUET/500PX

THIS BOOK

Destination editor
Jessica Lockhart

Production editor
Graham O'Neill

Cartographer
Mark Griffiths

Book designer
Ania Lenihan

Assisting editors
Monique Choy, Sasha Drew, Maja Vatrić

Cover researcher
Giada di Agostinis

Thanks
Sofie Andersen, Alice Barnes-Brown, Fergal Condon, Alex Conroy, Alison Killilea